How and Why Children Fail

Companion volume:

How and Why Children Hate
A Study of Conscious and Unconscious Sources
Edited by Ved Varma
ISBN 1 85302 116 4
ISBN 1 85302 185 7 pb

of related interest

Grief in Children
A Handbook for Adults
Atle Dyregrov
ISBN 1 85302 113 X

Six Theories of Child Development
Revised Formulations and Current Issues
Edited by Ross Vasta
ISBN 1 85302 137 7

Group Work with Children and Adolescents
Edited by Kedar Nath Dwivedi
ISBN 1 85302 157 1

Play Therapy with Abused Children
Ann Cattanach
ISBN 1 85302 120 2
ISBN 1 85302 193 8 pb

How and Why Children Fail

Edited by Ved Varma

Foreword by Dr James Hemming

Jessica Kingsley Publishers
London and Philadelphia

First published in the United Kingdom in 1993 by
Jessica Kingsley Publishers Ltd
116 Pentonville Road
London N1 9JB

Copyright © 1993 the contributors and the publisher
Foreword copyright © 1993 Dr James Hemming

British Library Cataloguing in Publication Data

How and Why Children Fail
I. Varma, Ved P.
155.4

ISBN 1-85302-108-3
ISBN 1-85302-186-5 pb

Printed and Bound in Great Britain by
Biddles Ltd, Guildford and King's Lynn

Contents

Foreword

Failure – persistent failure – is the most debilitating fate that can befall anyone, particularly a child. Healthy children are full of exuberant curiosity and vitality which provide them with the energy and application to actualise their powers and personalities. But that happens only to the extent that they are encouraged by people and circumstances which ensure that their self-esteem is carefully nourished throughout the crucial growing-up years.

Should the impetus to become their full selves, within the context of home, school and society, be blocked or distorted by rejection and failure, the result is a collapse of confidence and withdrawal from the struggle towards worthwhile achievement. Even worse, rejection and failure may generate within their victims vicious hatred and revolt against a society that seems to exist to frustrate them. It is all too clear today that such thwarted, rejected and angry young people are on the increase, to the great detriment of society and themselves. The truancy and school-avoidance figures alone show this children and adolescents who are happy and successful at school do not play truant. The headteacher of a very successful school in a difficult area was asked how he maintained his high attendance. His answer was 'We organize success for everyone here, especially the less able'.

The relationship between person success, self-esteem, mutual respect and social quality is gradually coming to be generally understood. Yet the bases for attaining these essentials are, even now, not reliably incorporated within the educational system. Instead we find confusion. The National Curriculum stimulates thinking about appropriate goals, but formalised group testing, rather than the assessment of personal progress, can only lead to the brutal rejection of those who fall short of the supposed norms. The true role of education is not to spotlight individual weaknesses but to maximize opportunity and stimulation for every child, while opening up a road to success for those suffering handicap or disability.

It is, then, extremely important, at the present time, to rethink the sources of success and failure within the lives of children so that we can make sure that no child is subjected to undeserved failure. That is precisely what *How and Why Children Fail* sets out to do. Dr. Ved Varma has brought together, within a single volume, the contributions of twelve authors who are highly qualified as analysts of those areas of experience that all too easily impose failure on the young. What the book has to offer will bring new insights, as

well as the confirmation of good practice, to those engaged in the hugely
important tasks of making sure that no child suffers unnecessary diminution
of effectiveness and self-esteem at home or at school.

Dr. James Hemming FRSA, FBPsS

This book is dedicated by the editor, with affection and esteem, to Ambrose Rigby, Maurice Langdell, Gwen Tabel and John Waltraud Blair.

Introduction

All of us fail at one time or another; in our health, at home, in school, at work or in all these and other areas as well. But adults are not the only people who fail. Indeed, it can be argued that failure is likely to be most prevalent during periods of rapid change and difficulty; and since childhood is the period during which we develop most rapidly, then a strong case can be made for failure being especially prevalent in children.

Afraid, bored, confused, prejudiced, abused, inappropriately taught, failing mentally, physically and socially, they fall short, and the failure is sometimes not even noticed by busy professionals.

This book by four leading and experienced child psychiatrists, four child psychologists and three educationalists, is a rare search for answers to the questions of why and how children fail and indeed how they can be helped. It is therefore an essential collection of readings for students and practioners in psychiatry, psychology and education.

Ved Varma
London

Other books edited by Ved P. Varma

Stresses in Children (1973) London: University of London Press.
Advances in Educational Psychology Vol. 1 (1973) (co-editor Professor W.D. Wall) London: University of London Press.
Psychotherapy Today (1974) London: Constable.
Advances in Educational Psychology Vol. 2 (1974) (co-editor Mia Kellmer Pringle) London: Hodder and Stoughton.
Piaget, Psychology and Education (1976) (co-editor Professor Phillip Williams) London: Hodder and Stoughton.
Anxiety in Children (1984) London: Croom Helm/Methuen.
Advances in Teacher Education (1989) (co-editor Professor V. Alan McClelland) London: Routledge.
The Management of Children with Emotional and Behavioural Difficulties (1990) London: Routledge.
Special Education: Past, Present and Future (1990) (co-editor Peter Evans) Lewes: Falmer Press.
The Secret Life of Vulnerable Children (1991) London: Routledge.
Truants form Life: Theory and Therapy (1991) London: David Fulton.
Prospects for People with Learning Difficulties (1991) (co-editor Professor Stanley Segal) London: David Fulton.
Vulnerability and Resilience in Human Development (1992) (co-editor Professor Barbara Tizard) London: Jessica Kingsley.
Coping with Unhappy Children (1993) London: Cassell.
Management of Behaviour in Schools (1993) Harlow: Longman.

CHAPTER 1

Creativity and Underfunctioning
Some Consequences for Society

Robin Higgins

What price creativity?

On the whole, parents are pleased if their children are, or are said to be, creative. Some schools set great store by and win accolades for encouraging creativity. From time to time, as when the US fell behind in the space race, a directive is fired down the corridors of education about the urgent need for enhancing creativity in the curriculum (Miller 1983). These waves of creativity hunting come and go. For creativity is an elusive activity, a delicate plant, despite its omnipresence.

The desirable goal of being creative is commonly associated with a sense of being released from inhibitions (blowing the lid off), finding and expressing oneself, and being a jump ahead of the herd (the followers and non-innovators). It is seen by many as a valuable and by some as a crucial component in learning. It is also seen as a quality of leadership, even if the leadership turns out to be that of the visionary starving in a garret.

Though few would question this favourable assessment of creativity, many might be more sceptical about how, as a society, we support or encourage it. On an informed assessment of our performance, a gap may be detected between our enthusiasm for creativity and what this enthusiasm actually achieves. What significance do we really attach to this elusive concept in the rearing of our children? In the debates on education, how often do we probe beneath the surface of curricula and immediate achievement (the 'fun' tests of the three Rs) to look at some of the issues motivating children to learn; in particular, at some of the patterns of creativity? And beyond education, in industry and those generating points on which our society depends, how far can creativity be tolerated, even if it were to be developed in our homes and schools? Do the creative among our children become leaders, at school or anywhere else? Are the innovators tolerated and encouraged? Do children retain an inherent creativity? And if they do, what are the consequences for them and for the society of which they are a part?

In this chapter we will consider the basic features of creativity; the light these features throw on why children suffer a lapse in their native creativity; the effect such lapses have on other areas of achievement and development;

and some ways in which society may collude with, influence, or pay for these lapses.

Creativity, innovation and omnipotence

A central idea in creativity is that of originating: 'making, forming, producing, or bringing into existence' says the *Oxford English Dictionary*. The god-like overtones in this idea constantly crop up in the creative experience. In our dreams, an unconscious source of creativity, we omnipotently repair the gaps in our world, meet our shadows and fulfil our wishes. Dreams are the adult equivalent of the hungry infant who seeks to satisfy itself by sucking its thumb and creatively hallucinating the breast. Poets claim to receive the dictation of their divine Muses; a mathematician like Kepler claims to think God's thoughts after Him. In myths from many sources, the creative is close to the trickster, and is often punished for his god-impersonating *hubris*. Daedalus and Prometheus are two hoary examples.

So the first of many unsettling features about exercising creativity is the way this lands child or adult in all the ambiguities of a god-complex, and society with the task of living with it.

The term 'omnipotence' merits expansion for it figures prominently in much writing about creativity. In our earliest experiences, we cannot distinguish between me and not-me, so when in later life we describe an infant's behaviour as omnipotent, or self-obsessed ('narcissistic'), we are groping to find words to describe a pre-verbal state and the words are bound to carry meanings that are in the mind of the observer and not the infant. Winnicott addresses this problem in part when he suggests a distinction between a 'brief experience of omnipotence' which the infant enjoys as a result of good-enough mothering, and omnipotence as 'a quality of feeling' (Winnicott 1965.) What seems clear, however, at this early stage of life is the vulnerability of the 'omnipotent' infant and the ease with which its creative gestures can swing from being explorative, communicative and innovative to being defensive and cut off.

Here is an example of cut-off.

Case study[1]

Miriam, at four, spent a lot of time on her own, although no one was perhaps very aware of this. Her parents, who were both caught up in the fashion world, always saw to it that she was well supplied with baby-sitters and nursery groups. The child was showered with affection by friends, relatives and anyone who came to the house. Her bedroom was awash

---

1   In this and the following case studies, to preserve confidentiality, details have been altered and in this sense fictionalised. The points exemplified, however, are all based on fact.

with toys. Yet increasingly Miriam was becoming 'difficult'. Her games took the form of constructing an elaborate world of her own which people could only enter on rigid conditions. For example, she might be Lady Queen, and the other person a servant or a dog or a robber who'd have to serve her or be killed, or both. On those rare occasions when the game might involve competition, Miriam always set the rules and changed them if she began to lose. The outcome was transparent: a battle in which the price of her survival was the loss of all companions.

Whether the creative gesture is communicative or cut off stems from how well the infant is tuned into the environment and *vice versa*. What Winnicott meant by the good-enough mother was someone who could respond adequately to the rise and fall of the infant's creative moves, meeting these when the tension climaxed, and being around when it was just rising and falling (Winnicott 1965). This rhythmic attunement between infant and responding adult has a profound effect on the later development of creativity and many other aspects of growth. Like creativity itself, the attunement needs time-space, reverie and alert inactivity on the part of parent and infant. When the attunement flourishes, it goes with joy and opening up, a sense of being one with the world. When it fails, it leads to retreat and psychic deformity. As a society, do we give this attunement sufficient attention? Here is another example where parental lifestyle under pressure of social demands put severe constraints on their child's creativity.

Case study

Hazel was launched on the path of success from the moment her umbilical cord was cut and probably before. Her parents were determined, upward-thrusting professionals, whose favourite words were 'vital', 'urgent', 'significant', and 'at the end of the day'. Not to have had a child would have been registered as a serious breach in achievement. Once formed and delivered, the infant dispelled all doubts about fertile incompetence. She was swiftly wrapped into the tight family schedule. No way was she allowed to waste a moment of valuable time, her own or her parents'. Each advance in her development was clocked assiduously and anxieties and pressures arose at any sign of delay. Feeding was a precise no-nonsense procedure, undertaken dutifully by either parent, usually in strict alternation. Fondling and dialogue between infant and parents were rationed to half-hour sessions at the most. Troubles began with Hazel when first she was slow to talk and then 'would just sit around and never play'.

Cycles in creativity

If we look in greater detail at rhythmic attunement, this base for creativity, we note a number of circular forms. For a start, creativity tends to occur in bursts with periods of apparent inactivity (lying fallow) coming in between the bursts. This rhythmic pattern of build-up, explosion and recouping follows many similar patterns in human bio-rhythms: the systole and diastole of the heart beat; the intake and release of breath; the sexual and menstrual cycles; sudden growth spurts followed by a plateau; and the hunger–eating–digestion–elimination cycle.

This cycle of lying fallow and growth spurt, of quiet and rush may be perplexing to child and parent. There may be times when nothing seems to be happening, a dearth of ideas and development. Why isn't she coming on quicker, a mother may ask of her daughter, when all that is happening is that the child is in one of these fallow periods of silent unfolding. Equally problematic may be the times of rush and overload. Creative children often suffer from a pressure of thoughts, with a resulting log-jam that may surface as a stammer or as manic ill-sustained bursts of activity that they and those around them find acutely uncomfortable and unsatisfying. This may particularly apply to children who try to express themselves in a discursive medium such as words or sounds, where the unfolding is inherent in the medium itself and where the past cannot be grasped in the same way as it can in a picture. One of the comforting things about a visual image is the sheer presence of each bit of it as it's created, the continuous ocular proof of achievement. This continuity of image may be of particular moment to a child whose creative act is still deeply caught up with establishing an identity separate from someone else and where there is as yet little assurance that what is achieved today will necessarily be achieved again tomorrow. Such continuity of image is not so easily available to children struggling to express themselves in the slippery flow of words. So an important reason for creativity failing may lie in the emphasis we place on verbal expression in our classrooms and our culture.

Falling apart and re-forming

The cycle of hunger–eating–digestion–elimination is a pattern in which children frequently phantasise their creativity. But it is only one of several forms that creative cycles may assume. Another ebb and flow pattern is the one which Bion (1962) based on Poincaré's account of scientific creativity. This entails the recurrent loosening of links which bind elements into a system and the subsequent re-patterning of new links around a new focal point. This sequence of loosening and then re-structuring of ties applies particularly to creative thought; a more general version of this same pattern is the de-integration followed by re-integration sequence which Fordham (1978) describes as the groundswell of psychic development. For our purposes, the important aspect of both models is the initial element of 'falling apart', a necessary if frightening component of any creative gesture.

'Falling apart' is the time when the unthinkable becomes thinkable, and when paradoxes emerge. Creative children at such a time have to cope not just with the confusion of sorting out these unruly ideas in their own minds, but also the confusion and incomprehension their attempts at articulating these ideas generate in the minds of others. A fragile line separates the daring shaft of an innovative lateral-thinking solution from a piece of mumbo-jumbo, which requires long patient hours to be disentangled (if indeed it ever is).

Case study

For as long as he could remember, Trevor, now twelve, had times when the world went grey and fuzzy and pointless. At these times he'd go widershins, anti-clockwise to everyone else's clockwise. He tried to talk himself out of these times (which often went with some of his best ideas) tried to get his act together and in tune with the others. But it never worked and for a while he just gave up. When things went wrong and he fell apart and caused others to fall apart in a different way, they all just laughed: 'O there's old Trevor, at his tricks again'. Once, when he stood out against them, and against his own conscious wishes, it turned out in the end that he was right and they were wrong. But they were all puzzled by this and a bit annoyed with themselves and no one thought to acknowledge Trevor's victory. He passed his schooldays being the licensed loveable laughing-stock. He rarely admitted to himself the long bouts of depression that went with this creative rhythm, this individual unconscious swim against the tide.

Destruction and repair

Another ebb-and-flow model which runs parallel to loosening and restructuring is that of destruction and reparation. The very act of loosening and abandoning ties implies the destruction of an established position, a breaking out of the mould. Most of us have a rebellious streak and delight in a break-out. Some children will take the delight a stage further and insist on destroying what they have painstakingly built up. They make the ultimate destruction of their creation an essential part of the whole exercise. More often, the initial thrusting aside of the status quo is followed by attempts to repair the damage and it was this reparative aspect of creativity which was emphasised by Klein and her followers (Klein 1929, Segal 1991).

Or a child may be caught in a see-saw of creative impulses: destructive and reparative moves alternately counteracting each other.

Case study

Briony's life for three years now was summed up by her father as 'stop–go'. She'd start to do something and within minutes was doing the opposite. With her right hand she might be spinning a top and with her left hand stopping it from going round. She'd say something and in mid-sentence check, and deny what she'd just said or deny that she'd said anything at all. Briony was now seven and, like many seven-year-olds, she had enthusiasms and when she had these enthusiasms she'd try to draw them on paper, if only to keep them under control. One of these enthusiasms was for volcanos and for months, whenever Briony sat down to draw, out would come a volcano always the same shape and size. And always as soon as it was neatly sketched out, it had to be erased. Briony's walls were covered with these volcanic ghosts.

In passing, a link may be observed between this ebb and flow of destruction – reparation and Freud's early metaphor of 'trauma', a breaking of the surface with its subsequent repair. Trauma and all the aggressive-destructive phantasies which go with trauma, spur us into creative attempts to restore the damage. Whether or not we can rise above the effects of trauma, whether we can escape from the impasse of a so-called post-traumatic stress disorder, depends on how successfully we can mobilise our creative gestures to cope with the destructive drives released by the trauma. Since children are frequently exposed to trauma of one form or another, and since this exposure may lead to many varieties of underfunctioning, the mobilising of creativity emerges once again as a key factor in development.

Sharing creativity

This mobilising and living with creative rhythms can follow two complementary courses. For, in the first place, as with any other experience that is strictly speaking 'ours', we may from time to time be unable to contain our creativity within our self. We may feel obliged to hand it over (project it on) to someone else, someone close to us, someone, indeed, of whom we may be only dimly aware of being different from us. We may for a time deposit our creativity with them, and in due course seek to retrieve it (introject it) back into ourselves reshaped by them and so found more tolerable by us.

This handing over and retrieving creative gestures (and at times the whole burden of creativity) is a natural rhythm which may start from our earliest days, and continue throughout our life. The person with whom we share our creativity during this span may change from parent, to teacher, to colleague, to lover. The response of the other person, this segment of society, will influence the growth and nature of child and adult creative moves.

The complementary mode of creative sharing is the one described by Winnicott under the term 'transitional objects' (Winnicott 1971). Here it is not a person on to whom we deposit our creative gesture, but an object: a doll, a drum, an icon on a piece of paper. For a time we live with this object in the uncanny world between the animate and inanimate. The object assists us to bridge states such as sleeping or waking, living or dying, being with someone or being alone. It also assists in the loosening – restructuring cycle. In the creative mode, the child moves in and out of the object or a succession of objects as a novelist moves in or out of his characters, a painter in or out of his landscapes. Here other people influence the child's creativity more indirectly through the provision of objects (from gifts to cultural surrounds) and through an (unvoiced) appreciation of the role the objects are playing in the child's development.

Play, phantasy and creativity

The last creative rhythm to concern us is the ebb and flow of play. For some this is a joyful activity drawing on transitional objects and indeed itself a transitional object; for others, play is an occasion for displaying and struggling with fantasies especially of an unconscious and painful kind, retrieved and shared on a more conscious level. In either event, play and creativity go closely together, two sides of the same coin, play picking up what creativity scatters in the 'fall-out'.

We have already seen something of the pain which can be provoked by the uprush of innovative ideas. One need not go to the extreme of rivaling God to taste the heady and unsettling quality of creative fantasy. The use of imagination to arrive at novel, unpredictable, but valid solutions to problems (one definition of creativity, see Rycroft 1968) will often in itself suffice to cause deep fears amid the excitement. By definition, the novelty isolates and often alienates the creator and may disturb him or her every bit as much as it disturbs those around.

The content of 'playful' phantasies released in the loosening phase of creativity, refer to the body in its many guises. Their painfulness arises because they represent the child's attempts to come to terms with frustrating physical experiences. To give one example of particular relevance to creativity: the phantasy of having inside us the God-like presence of a combined procreating parent figure (Meltzer 1973).

It is not hard to envisage the fear that such a phantasy can evoke: the fear of the risk entailed in entertaining it; the fear of probing into the forbidden, questioning how it works, or fails to work; the fear of incorporating an other into oneself, this other being an ill-defined object of untested and untestable potency; the fear of losing this object, having it stolen, misused or turned against the creator; the fear of being engulfed by it.

This phantasy along with others can be life-enhancing if the fear it evokes can be encompassed. Beyond a certain degree, and without adequate understanding from those around, the very fear which sparked creativity can also quash it.

Case studies

Peter was playing a game which consisted of modelling his parents in bed together. His mother walked in and quizzed him about what he was doing. 'Nothing' he insisted but she was clearly shocked and wouldn't believe him. When she went away he destroyed the scene, breaking the bed and cutting up the figures. Later he had a problem with his reading. 'He just can't bring himself to look at the page', his teacher told his mother. 'It can't bite you, I keep telling him. But he won't believe me'.

Catharine spent a whole weekend drawing a detailed picture of a carnival. When it was finished she hid it away in a drawer. It was so good she was frightened to show it to anyone. But her mother found it, was deeply delighted with it, and was so proud of her daughter she insisted the child take the picture to school to show the teacher and the other children. Catharine panicked and tore the picture up. Everyone was puzzled. 'Why ever did you do that?' they asked her. 'You'd gone to such trouble with it.'

The abuse of creativity

So far we have considered some of the issues involved when children exercise their creativity. What remains to do now is to examine in greater detail those occasions when the use goes awry, when creativity fails or becomes distorted. We will look at these occasions of abuse under the same headings as those given for use.

In the case study on Miriam, we have already seen how creativity though present resulted in impaired rather than enhanced social relations. Her omnipotence, an inherent component of creativity, led Miriam into disregarding the nature and rights of others, and into behaving with a false superiority which froze them off. Reasons for this counterproductive deployment of omnipotence may be gleaned from the sketch of Miriam's background: a lonely child subject to repeated changes among those looking after her.

Miriam's creative imagination was turned towards caring for herself since caring from those around her she found to be inadequate. This sense of being insufficiently cared for prompted her to feel both angry and unworthy. The images in her games, especially the Lady Queen who demanded total subservience from others, were designed to satisfy her fury and repair her lost self-esteem.

We can observe two other features about Miriam's distorted creativity. The first is that, if pushed further, the omnipotent isolation can begin to broach images which are incomprehensible to others since they are developed in the child's own secluded world. This line leads to the autistic language of psychosis, with its neologisms and self-referential slants. Such a degree of withdrawal inevitably distorts a child's capacity to learn. There will often be a highly personalised selectivity in what is pursued and what is played back. Such children tend to be labelled 'eccentric loners', sometimes slipping through the school unnoticed, sometimes becoming the butt of teasing and scorn.

A second feature in defensive creativity sees the quality of phantasy changing in a different way. Instead of becoming more deeply entrenched in the isolate, it becomes more superficial. Instead of images drawing on the whole person, culled from unconscious depths, the images become whimsical, fay, sentimental, played with for their own sake. Phantasy becomes fantasy (Rycroft 1987); the game becomes little more than an intellectual exercise. Paradoxically, in this situation, imagination which is the playground for creativity, becomes a defence against creativity itself (see Mann 1990). Collective fantasies, put out by adults trying to rediscover their own childhood and purporting to represent the 'imaginative world of the child', often foster this coy, twee, quality. Disneyland is not immune to such encouragement of fantasy.

Another distortion of a creative gesture is the change which Winnicott (1971) describes from a transitional object into a fetish. What happens here is that destructive and persecutory fantasies overwhelm constructive and reparative ones. Instinctive drives cease to be life-enhancing and instead are experienced as compulsive demands. The child sets up sadistic rituals which have to be followed; imaginative talismans become demanding guardians of these rituals. The obsessions often accompanying a post-traumatic stress disorder reflect this same shift of an imaginative solution into a compulsion.

Once again, society may collude with this distortion of creativity this time under the guise of 'discipline': for example the beating rituals once commonplace in public schools and cadet training establishments. Certain types of conditioning may be imbued with the same collusive force.

Disowning creativity

In earlier comments on the sharing of creativity, the emphasis was on the mutual give and take-back, handover and retrieval, between child and adult. Sometimes this mutuality breaks down. There may be next to no sharing, as in the instance of an omnipotent withdrawn child such as Miriam. Or there may be no retrieving, as happened with Hazel, our second case study.

In the course of the next five years, Hazel's mother had three further children, all boys, as it happened, and all insisting on their rights. Hazel was as impressed by her mother's procreativity as she was convinced that it was not for her. The procreativity corroborated another assessment the child made about her parents' potency, this one based on their careers. Both her parents were lawyers. Her father, as Hazel put it, spent his weekdays and most of the weekends sorting out people's lives, whether they should live together and how much money they should give each other, and things like that. Her mother, too, was always busy organising people's lives for them. She spent her time, weekdays and weekends, deciding how much money people should leave each other when they die.

So, from early on, Hazel despaired of owning her creativity. It seemed much more sensible to hand it over to her parents and let them do the organising for her. 'Why don't you find something to do?' they would sometimes ask her at the weekends. 'Because you two can always do it so much better', came the invariable reply which received the invariable laugh and mutual satisfaction.

One of the more significant aspects of this story lies in its sequel. Hazel went on to a private school with a good reputation for teaching and getting results in Common Entrance. To everyone's surprise she settled well there and eventually won a scholarship. Her reports stressed that she was never happier than when tackling a set task. In keeping with the child's phantasy, the school created and distributed tasks and curriculum; Hazel did what she was told, relieved of all the responsibility and pain which went with creating for herself.

Apparently without questioning, the school colluded with Hazel's phantasy of disowning her creativity. In this respect, they were behaving no differently from many of our social institutions. Miller describes how prone such institutions (family, education, employment) are to convert their role of keeping the expression of creativity within non-destructive limits into one of containing or preventing the destructiveness and so stamping out the creativity. One line that is often followed is the bestowing of a monopoly on creativity among a few selected individuals and the offer of uncreative employment to the rest. Such a line not only restricts potential creative resources, but also sets up a spiral in which the frustrated creativity of those not included in the monopoly finds outlets in the very destructiveness the line was designed to suppress (Miller 1983).

We do not have to look very far in education for further illustration of Miller's analysis. Hazel's case only hinted at some of the ways in which a school may respond to a child's decision to disown his or her creativity. An educational take-over is more determined and pervasive than is often realised. Curricula are apt to be defined with minimal consultation from those for whom they are designed; subtle measurements maybe introduced to bring the deviants (who may include a sizeable proportion of creatives) into line, like tests at a certain age or assessments of (arbitrarily defined) psychological functions such as intelligence. Methods of modifying behaviour using rewards and punishments maybe built into educational management techniques. Such methods implicitly ignore the research findings which state that contracting to do something in order to receive a reward has an unfavourable effect on creativity (Amabile *et al.* 1986).

By these and other means, an older generation ('knowing best') imperceptibly takes over a younger's creativity. Exposing these means is not to argue for an anarchic position where everyone does their own thing regardless. But the exposure should remind us that we are dealing with one further instance where a fragile balance exists between phases in which creativity is owned quite openly and without doubts and fears, and phases in which it may for a time (because of such fears and doubts) have to be shared and even handed over. Students of all ages experience periods in which, facing a mountain of knowledge, they feel paralysed about finding their individual path. In the new paradigm of teaching and research, a growing chorus of voices is calling for a less tyrannical and sustained grasp on creativity when it is shared or handed over during these periods (Reason and Rowan 1981,

Aldridge 1991). Supporting voices in this sea-change for creative dialogue are coming from the musical world where a composer-teacher like Cardew organised the Scratch orchestra or like Nigel Osborne the East London Late Starters orchestra, to offer beginners an active role from the start in the creation of a musical offering. Or again in psychotherapy, where, for example, Casement (1985) urges the case for learning from the patient.

For children, this sea-change calls for quiet non-intrusive support for a child's curiosity, with the children being allowed to make their own discoveries at their own pace. Such rewards as are offered should come primarily from the activity itself and once again the children need to enjoy their own rewards, reaped by themselves when they feel they have earned them.

The situation is complicated by the work–play ethic engrained in adults and projected on to childhood. As adults, when we think of play, it is hard not to slip at once into the habit of distinguishing it from work and of casting work and play into separate compartments with long-established separate associations going with each. With this distinction, into work inevitably creep such connotations as employment, pay, career, industry, compliance.

And, as a result, into our attitude towards play may creep connotations tinged with envy or sentimentality. Remember the nursery rhyme:

What does the bee do?
Bring home honey.
And what does Father do?
Bring home money.
And what does Mother do?
Lay out the money.
And what does baby do?
Eat up the honey.

Children in the early years make no such distinction between work and play. Their 'playful' activity is pursued with the intensity and commitment of any professional (from sportsman to barrister). But with their unconscious awareness of adult attitudes and demands, they are quick to pick up the nuances of the adult work–play distinction and this is one way in which their creativity will be shaped. The child who is in a hurry to escape from the role of simply consuming the honey will rush to doing sums and handling money and putting books and papers in a satchel in imitation of father going to work. Learning to read becomes 'work'; kicking a football becomes 'play'. Even before the shades of the school-room loom, the child may already be engulfed in the long-cherished attitude that regarded 'artistic pursuits' as 'hobbies', relaxation from the serious business of earning a living.

Such an attitude is a travesty of the role that play in its deeper childhood sense has occupied in our evolution and development. A dip into the literature of ethology and anthropology, let alone child psychology, will swiftly confirm the significance of play for exploring and mastering our environment, relating to others, co-operating and competing, defining identity and sexuality, mobilising fantasy, myth and symbol (Bruner *et al.* 1976). Such play demands time-space; it cannot be rushed. It has to evolve in the slow appropriate rhythms we have seen characterising creativity. We all of us start with this capacity to play but it can easily be distorted and curtailed, perhaps even in the womb. The combined force of a work–play ethic and a creativity take-over are two powerful ways of bringing about such distortion and curtailment, to society's ultimate loss.

References

Aldridge, D. (1991) 'Aesthetics and the individual in the practice of medical research', *Journal of the Royal Society of Medicine.* 84: 147–50.

Amabile, T.H., Hennessey, B.A. and Grossman, B.S. (1986) 'Social influences on creativity: the effects of contracted-for reward', *Journal of Personal and Social Psychology.* 50: 14–23.

Bion, W.R. (1962) *Learning from Experience.* London: Heinemann.

Bruner, J.S., Jolly, A. and Sylva, K. (1976) *Play: its role in evolution and development.* Penguin: London.

Casement, P. (1985) *On Learning from the Patient.* London and New York: Tavistock.

Fordham, M. (1978) *Jungian Psychotherapy: a study in analytical psychology.* Chichester: John Wiley.

Klein, M. (1929) 'Infantile anxiety-situations reflected in a work of art and in the creative impulse', *The Writings of Melanie Klein.* Vol 1: 210–218. London: Hogarth.

Mann, D. (1990) 'Art as a defence mechanism against creativity', *British Journal of Psychotherapy.* 7: 5–14.

Meltzer, D. (1973) *Sexual States of Mind.* Perth: Clunie.

Miller, E.J. (1983) 'Work and creativity'. Occasional paper no. 6 from the Tavistock Institute of Human Relations: London.

Reason, P. and Rowan, J. (1981) *Human Inquiry.* Chichester: John Wiley.

Rycroft, C.F. (1968) *A Critical Dictionary of Psychoanalysis.* London: Nelson.

Rycroft, C.F. (1987) *Imagination and Reality.* London: Maresfield Library.

Segal, H. (1991) *Dream phantasy and Art.* London: Tavistock/Roultedge.

Winnicott, D.W. (1965) *Maturational Processes and the Facilitating Environment,* pp.57–8. London: Hogarth.

Winnicott, D.W. (1971) *Playing and Reality.* London: Tavistock.

CHAPTER 2

Fear and Underachievement

Herb Etkin

Introduction

One of the major social changes of Western society since World War I is the way in which leadership in general has moved from the aristocracy to those who have achieved, irrespective of their status at birth. A meritocracy based on individual striving and accomplishment has become the norm although, rather obviously, only a few individuals reach the top. On the way there is a leveling off at all stages with a classic Gaussian (normal distribution) curve placing the vast majority in the middle.

Thus, on the negative side, there are those who, for various reasons, often despite average or superior intelligence, remain timid, anxious and dependent, and constitute a large percentage of the underachievers that exist in all societies, those whose potential is unrealised and seemingly unrealisable and who regard themselves as failures. They are only too often seen as such by others; hamstrung by fear and therefore unable to give of their best as a result of the energies thus wasted.

'ANXIETY IS THE COMMON COIN OF EMOTION' (FREUD)

The subject of fear/anxiety has intrigued psychiatrists, psychologists and others, ever-increasingly in recent times and, as has been estimated (Marks, 1987), between 1967 and 1984, at least 11,000 articles with relevant titles were published, as well as 46 books. There now appear in excess of a thousand articles annually which touch on the subject of anxiety in all its forms.

This chapter will not provide reference to these but will attempt to utilise recognised, oft repeated facts in order to provide an overview of the way in which anxieties (of whatever sort) lead to under-achievement in young people. Understanding what elements of a child's life causes failure at school aids in deciding what approaches are required therapeutically to compensate for or prevent continuous decline. Therapy *per se* does not, however, fall within the scope of this chapter.

Regardless of their content, fears are products of conceptions of reality created by children from perceptual and mental processes typical of their age and developmental level (Bauer, 1980). The fears of childhood, by and large, differ from those of pre-adolescence, and even more so from the anxieties of later life.

Probably the commonest comment made by teachers in reports on their pupils is, 'could do better'. This is part and parcel of the school experience of a great many children. In particular, much is made of inability to cope with examinations, but the effects of anxiety on learning, retention and recall are 'simple common sense' and accepted by everybody, teachers, pupils and parents alike.

Educational achievement is thus an observable phenomenon and, as such, tests well in the laboratory situation. It is also extensively commented upon by psychiatrists, psychologists and educationalists from their own experience with children who simply do not produce the results expected of them.

Experimental situations with animals do not bring into play the multiplicity of factors which continuously impinge on the human organism. Most experiments deal with short-term memory and the results therefrom, not the reality of examination-oriented results relating to work studied (even though revised) many months or years previously. Nor is the pseudo-sterile calm of the test situation part of the real world.

A great deal of information can be derived from the vast library of available literature on anxiety and performance taking into account observer reports and bias, self-assessments, physiological and biochemical changes and the psychological rating scales.

What is fear/anxiety?

There remain authors who distinguish fear from anxiety, but common usage among the lay public and professionals alike equates the terms. Fear (old English 'faer'), is the emotion of alarm resulting from the response to some danger, whilst anxiety (Latin 'anxius' or 'angor' – tightness of chest) though similar, may not relate to anything readily identifiable. Fear may thus be seen as anxiety in objective form, whilst anxiety may be regarded as a fear without any basis in fact.

Realistic fear is a normal and essential adaptation ensuring survival. It leads to the characteristic responses of fight, flight or freeze. In modern man, all of these manifestations are recognisable in both normal and abnormal situations, resulting in rapid preparations for response to impending attack, real or imagined.

The changes which occur are psychological, physical and biochemical. There are profound subjective experiences associated with these, although the same stimulus does not necessarily elicit the same response in everybody.

Fear is not always an unpleasant experience. It is often actively sought out as a means of providing excitement and has an addictive quality, up to certain limits (of course), which leads to repetition of the causative stimulus. This is mediated by chemical factors such as adrenalin and noradrenalin as well as the little, as yet, understood endomorphin system which causes

pleasurable sensations. Examples of this are such diverse everyday phenomena as speeding excessively, gambling, shop-lifting. Even watching horror
movies or dangerous sports and all the common forms of risk taking in which
most individuals indulge at some-time or other, for example the roller-
coaster at the fair, are pleasurable fear-promoting stimuli.

In children this might mean taunting a known bully (probably from the
safety of a group), disagreeing with adult authority figures, participating in
contact sports and even attempting to elicit a positive social response from
a peer despite feeling apprehensive and dreading possible rejection. Vandalism and destructiveness only too often produce the same anxiety/pleasurable
feelings; the 'buzz' that so many seek out in an almost addictive fashion.

The types of anxiety which interest professionals, however, are those
which handicap the individual concerned and for which help is normally, but
not always sought. The degree of distress has to be determined by the sufferer,
or his family, the professional not always in agreement as to the extent of the
pathology involved.

Normal fear

How to define normality, a problem in psychiatry generally, is particularly
relevant. There is now a burgeoning multiplicity of tests exploring every facet
of human functioning in psychiatry and psychology, many relating to anxiety
and its manifestations. Merely listing them would take several pages and it
might, therefore, be reasonably claimed that, in psychiatry at any rate, a
normal person, by definition, is somebody who hasn't as yet been fully
investigated.

The fact is that the abnormality, however it presents, may be felt by the
individual and may or may not be noted by others including the professional
to whom referral has been made.

Wing *et al.* (1974) have described three factors as being central to the
diagnosis of a psychiatric disorder. *Suffering* (that is, the unpleasant affect of
feeling), *loss of autonomy* (the symptom dominates the individual's life) and
unreality (the behaviour feels unreal and out of proportion to the circumstances in which it occurs).

Anxiety/fear can be a healthy and positive phenomenon prompting an
adequate response to instant or impending danger. It is probably not an
elementary or uniformly negative feeling but a complex of emotions which
may include curiosity, surprise and pleasure (Hodiamont, 1991).

Hodiamont quotes several authors supporting the proposition that anxiety can enhance autonomy, that is, up to a certain level, it can increase
achievement. The claim is that fear can specifically stimulate learning.
Anxiety is needed for growth and self-realisation, the alternative being stasis
or security. *Panic* (derived from Greek god Pan – said to produce some terror)
and *phobia* (derived from Greek god Phobos who terrified enemies into

flight) are part of the anxiety spectrum as are *obsessions* (thoughts) and the *compulsions* (actions) that they produce.

The compulsive ritual temporarily allays the build-up of feelings of anxiety which have preceded it, an example being checking an already locked door and having to do so again and again as anxiety returns.

There is a distinction between *trait* anxiety (general, chronic) and *state* anxiety (temporary). The latter may be the only type which is present in relation to school and, in particular, examinations, whereas the former is all-pervasive and occurs in all settings.

There are at present three major theories concerning the pathophysiology of anxiety (Nutt, 1990). These are theories which centre on the workings of three different neurotransmitter systems; GABA/benzodiazepine, 5–Hydroxytryptamine (5–HT) or serotonin; and noradrenalin. Theories relating to other neurotransmitter systems also exist, but none of these is within the scope of this chapter.

Achievement

Failure to achieve is at its most obvious in the academic sphere. Nevertheless, there are many individuals who produce outstanding academic results at school and subsequently, but are unable to function efficiently as wage earners, marriage partners or parents.

From the social point of view, fears and phobias might preclude efficient academic performance due to non-attendance at school for example, but burying heads in books is frequently an efficient avoidance technique which may produce an academic recluse.

Using other studies, Bauer (1980) notes that fear of failure to perform in academic achievement situations (test or school anxiety) begins to develop in both boys and girls as early as age 6 and is resistant to change once developed. Between the ages of 8 and 13 girls manifest greater school anxiety than boys, whose fears have caught up by mid adolescence.

Exploring the causes

A useful schema for looking into any young person's life utilises a simple mnemonic with six headings (Figure 2.1).

	Family		School
F –	Friends	S –	Self
	Future		Sex

Figure 2.1

The problems revolve around issues relating to the family, school, peer relationships, the physical self, sexuality and fears for the future.

Although any one might predominate, all are interrelated and overlapping and, as a means of understanding how or why anxiety or indeed any other psychological abnormality develops and inhibits achievement, a full awareness of all of these is required. Routine history-taking may reveal previously unsuspected stressors which have been extremely well concealed but which are remarkably disabling for all that.

Further, it is worth noting that the focus may shift from one to another or more with time. None of these are dealt with in great detail, but more extensive information is available in other chapters.

Family

Parental (not always maternal) roles in enduring timidity in children cannot be overestimated. The fledgling not pushed from the nest never learns to fly. Thus, parenting is probably the most important element in the process of the growth of confidence, given that adequate nurturing would prepare an individual for the vicissitudes of life in general and in particular, all common eventualities.

The development of the psyche has, as it first shaping force, parent–child relationships and is subsequently moulded by intrafamilial forces, physiological processes and the social world at large.

In a psychodynamically oriented paper quoting Kohut and others, Baker (1987) notes that basic identity is formed and maintained by developmental and ongoing interpersonal interactions. Repeated significant parental failure is of primary importance in the etiology of psychopathology. The child's idiosyncratic behaviours should not, of course, be excluded, but prominence has to be given to parental inability to respond empathically to critical developmental needs, though most, somehow or other, manage to do so.

In order to maintain self-esteem, to be assertive, remain calm under stress and so on, there are three basic needs of children to which parents have to respond appropriately (Baker, 1987).

MIRRORING

This means the response of delight and pride in the child's behaviour reflecting back a positive image. Consistent indifference, competitiveness or hostility provides the opposite, the child interpreting this as a true evaluation of his or her defectiveness.

Inappropriate anger or over-reaction, for example to a poor school report, may destroy whatever confidence has developed. This is important, in that several studies have shown that children throughout development begin to see themselves as projected on a linear course through space; that is, at about secondary school age they have perceptions of their future adult lives derived from their personal historical past. Parental messages are deeply introjected from an early age and will affect future scholastic and social experiences and performance.

THE IDEALISED PARENT (CALM AND SOOTHING)

These parents provide a safe world or a belief that all problems can be solved. Consistent (and inconsistent) inappropriate responses means that stress overwhelms and self-calming, which ought to have been learned by example, is not possible.

TWINSHIP NEEDS

This is similar to identification. The child has a sense of 'connectedness' with parents who tolerate being 'helped' even if this inevitably slows down whatever process is being undertaken such as cooking or DIY work. The opposite interaction makes the child feel isolated, lonely and disconnected.

Although these three processes start early on, maintenance at all levels of development is necessary in order to allow for the growth of a healthily and secure personality. Some of the obvious disruptions within a family which might prevent such development include marital stress, the birth of a sibling and the many rivalries thus engendered, parental illness or unemployment, financial hardship and so on. Many children describe profound worries relating to persistent parental arguments, generating fears of impending divorce, insecurity and abandonment. The anxieties are frequently non-reality based, but relate to increased emotionality, noise and unmeant threats as well as comparisons with classmates from so-called 'broken homes'.

SEPARATION FEAR

Fear of separation is worst at about two when mother/child attachment patterns have been firmly established. This declines from about four onwards when children seem able to understand location of objects in space. Most children, however well prepared, experience anxiety when required to leave the safety of parents to go to kindergarten or nursery school. The range of responses is vast, from the kicking, screaming child who just will not settle, to a single, rather sad look back and a fairly easy parting of the ways. Parental handling of the new experience is as important as the manner in which the school manages it. Their ability to encourage autonomy in the child is thus a vital factor.

FEAR OF DEATH

Bauer (1980) notes that 4–6-year-olds regard most frightening ghosts, monsters and other mythical creations as representing death. There have been many studies confirming that 12-year-olds frequently worry about the health and welfare of family members. Therefore, many children who fear separation worry about something happening to parents in their absence, although younger children feel something may happen to themselves with parental supervision being unavailable.

If parental worries about a child's welfare are sufficiently profound, then this exerts a powerful influence on the child; anxiety is a transmissible phenomenon and anything which troubles parents or other members of the family will have a spill-over effect on them all.

PARENTAL NEEDS

Parental needs cannot be overlooked, in particular the not uncommon practice of *school withholding*. The child who may have been attending school normally and gaining academically, emotionally and socially therefrom, is kept at home, while parents provide the school with sick notes and other excuses for non-attendance. The reasons may be as diverse as having to look after a younger sibling or waiting for a repair man but could also include a parent's personal needs.

An example causing great anxiety for the child might be the double bind produced by the mother who says to her child 'of course I want you to go to school. Don't worry about me and the fact that my pain means I won't be able to get out of bed when I need a drink' or some such. The choice of two unacceptable alternatives creates great conflict; going to school and worrying about mother, or staying at home and worrying about school.

All absences from school cause anxiety; fear that the lessons will progress excessively and make catching up impossible, as well as worries that friends will forget them and move on to others, that is to say, a clique might re-form. It follows that the longer the absence, the greater the fear. A similar emotional process might result from a physical illness of any kind, especially if chronic.

STRANGER FEAR

Stranger fear and the killing of conspecifics is dealt with in some detail by Marks (1987). Infanticide is part of this as well, especially in modern China, and among Eskimos until fairly recently. Stranger fear occurs even in infants held in their mother's arms, so it is not a form of separation anxiety and appears to derive from primitive fears relating to strange males who would wish to use the mother to create their own progeny by first eliminating competitors. The mother who deals inadequately with this form of anxiety remains inappropriately over-protective for far too long, and creates an anxious, clingy child in whom independence drives rarely come to full fruition at the appropriate stage of development.

THE ABUSED CHILD

The abused child, whether physically, sexually or emotionally, manifests a host of features, among which anxiety and hypervigilance are predominant. This is a vast subject with an ever-increasing wealth of literature and, not surprisingly, has as a major feature poor school achievement. This is fully dealt with in Chapter 7.

UNREALISTIC EXPECTATIONS

Unrealistic expectations real or imagined, whether in the academic or, for example, the sporting field, on the part of parents or teachers, have profound effects on any child, especially if his or her perception is one of failure. Repeated striving without success leads to withdrawal from those situations which seem to be unpleasurable, unsatisfying and even threatening. It may result in taunting from peers, scorn from teachers or disgusted annoyance from parents, thus eroding positive feelings of self and causing mounting anxiety if the activity is forced.

GENETICS

The role of genetics in syndromes of anxiety is beyond dispute. Marks (1987) however, notes that genetic influences on a trait need not mean that it is immutable environmentally. Normal fear is partly genetically controlled as evidenced by twin studies and there is an undoubted familial loading in all studies in which anxiety as a disorder is present.

School

Gaudry and Spielberger (1971) note that highly anxious persons tend to be self-disparaging and lacking in self-confidence and that they have an unfavourable self-image. They also tend to be low in curiosity and adventurousness and are characterised by a high incidence of daydreaming. Further, class-mates identify them with ease and react negatively. Teachers react similarly, regarding them as less well adjusted and possessing many other undesirable characteristics. Worse still, even their own fathers see them as less than mature, less well-adjusted and more dependent. With such an all-encompassing negative environment, it is easy to understand why a highly anxious child performs poorly academically and socially.

The anxiety may be of the trait variety and exhibited in all settings, but it might equally be entirely school related, that is to say, heightened in relation to school attendance only, but containable elsewhere. It may also only relate to examinations and no other aspect of school life at all.

Schools consists of several elements; the academic work, the teaching staff and the peer group. These are the more obvious ones. Apparent causes of fear need careful history taking in order to be understood if a remedy is to be forthcoming. Note has to be taken of such diverse and seemingly innocuous factors as the journey to school, especially if by bus; the size of the school, often frighteningly overwhelming at times of change from a small nurturing junior variety, to a large busy senior one, or even an inability to find and cope with toilet facilities when first arriving at the school.

A frequent cause of fear is the need imposed by the regulations of the school to expose physiques in relation to sporting activities, especially when puberty threatens and all varieties of change are occurring in previously familiar bodies. This is dealt with more fully on pp.22–23.

THE WORK

Bloom (1973) has established that 'unsuccessful experiences in school guarantee that the individual will develop a negative academic self-concept and increase the probabilities that he will have a generally negative self-concept'. Perhaps more important is the speculation that success or failure in school will profoundly affect the individual's personality and mental health. If the first six years are positive in school generally, then there is evidence suggesting that this immunises against mental illness for an indefinite period of time.

Parents initially, and teachers subsequently, have to help individuals to savour the first tiny taste of triumph to encourage further effort and so avoid the development of an unwillingness to risk failure and scorn.

Almost all available evidence shows a negative correlation between anxiety and level of academic achievement worsening as the years pass. The entire process heightens during examinations and may even affect IQ test results, with obvious long-term repercussions. There are also specific, well-described anxieties such as *mathematics anxiety* (Sepie and Keeling, 1978). They report other significant findings such as school anxiety being more related to achievement, than is neurotic anxiety. Mathematics in particular is capable of generating anxiety in pupils who are not necessarily of an anxious disposition. Specific desensitisation programmes have been suggested as an appropriate means of overcoming this.

TEACHERS

Teachers are vital instillers of confidence and self-worth in their charges. Unfortunate learning experiences, especially early on, can blaze a trail from which the child never diverges. The anxious child needs the positive conditioning of repeated successes in order to venture forth and attempt more difficult and stressful academic work. As Gaudry and Spielberger (1971) note, an important role of the teacher, especially in the elementary school years, is to promote the development of a positive self-concept in the child. Specialised test arrangements with easy beginnings, informal and relaxed settings and memory supports are suggested as a means to help alleviate the adverse effects of anxiety on pupils.

THE PEER GROUP

The role of the peer group is dealt with later in this chapter.

Generally, change *per se* causes great emotional distress in many individuals, not just children. Transitions from play group to infant then junior schools, and so on, are unsettling experiences, as the community size increases, and unfamiliar surroundings and faces have to become known. The whole is compounded greatly for those children, especially older ones, who have to change schools without any accompanying age mates. This might be as a result of family moves (highly stressful for everyone in any event) or because of individual perceived requirements. The change could conceivably be in response to advice from professionals on academic or social grounds, or may be recommended as a means of alleviating stress and anxiety which is hindering performance. It does not always work out that way.

FEAR OF FAILURE

It is worth recording that fear of failure has a somewhat paradoxically anxiety-relieving effect. The anxiety which prevents an individual from trying, leads to persistent underachievement. Birney *et al* (1970) note that anyone who consistently sets his level of aspiration below his actual performances was doing so to avoid the failure experience. An important consideration is the secondary, punishing characteristic of non-attainment, which, in addition to a low self-estimate, may reduce an individual's social value. The vicious circle of success leading to more success and failure to more failure, cannot be overlooked.

Self

NORMAL PROCESSES

Normal processes of growth can create anxiety in both children and their parents particularly if the concept of 'range' is ill-understood. For example, the girl who develops breast buds at 10, unlike her peer group, is as normal as the one whose first period only arrives at 15, again unlike her age mates. There are thus a host of physical growth factors, delayed or advanced, which can lead to crippling anxiety, initially in one situation with a spilling over effect to many others subsequently.

A common example is the child who, at 12–14, will not undress in front of others. In boys this might be due to the presence or absence of genital hair, penile size or shape, pubertal breast swelling as hormones sort themselves out, spots and so on.

Girls have similar problems, one being asymmetrical breast development, which is not uncommon initially, and may be very disturbing indeed to both mother and child who need reassurance but may fail to seek it. Many of these problems present initially at sports or physical activities at school and lead to self isolation which will affect all other areas of development subsequently including those occurring at home.

In both sexes, acne at puberty is perceived as a blinding beacon for all to see and comment upon, as with any abnormality real or imagined.

ABNORMAL PROCESSES

A child with chronic physical illness, the undernourished child, or the child neglected in general are all subjected to teasing and bullying by merciless peers, becoming increasingly anxious about school and developing avoidance techniques, while finding it ever more difficult to concentrate on school work as a whole. Malodorousness, soiling and wetting (frequently part of a vicious circle of emotional turmoil) scruffiness, even unfashionable clothing, all serve to invite the unwelcome attention of age mates, especially in the individual more vulnerable from a personality point of view, whose weaknesses and deficiencies are so readily detectable.

The 'uniform' children are required to wear by their peers is not of the school variety – make-up, jewelry, designer-clothing and other accoutrements are of an importance not given due recognition by the adults in their world, often with reason, let it be said.

Pediatricians have not been unaware of psychologically susceptible children. In describing the features of the Vulnerable Child Syndrome, Green (1986) notes that parents are characteristically not experiencing problems with their other children. Over use of medical services on the flimsiest of pretexts keeps anxiety in the family as a whole continuously on the boil, and poor general school achievement relates to the child's fear of premature death, leading on to an inability to work effectively. Pseudo-fever of unknown origin results in the child missing school as do various common complaints such as headache, abdominal pains, sore throats and minor colds, none of which stand up to medical scrutiny (if requested at all).

Excessive investigations only reinforce parental beliefs that something is wrong and anxieties within the family are exacerbated. Munchausen Syndrome by Proxy, in which school is missed to serve mother's (usually) needs, can lead to similar problems. An example of this fairly recently described syndrome might be excessive use of laxatives causing diarrhea and weakness in a child who requires constant treatment, investigation and even hospital admission without the appropriate history being revealed.

Quoting others, Green notes several groups of children who have missed more school than their peers; poor children have more illnesses generally and some illness-prone children may have a genetically acquired vulnerability that causes them to respond to stress factors in a physiologically different way from their peers. These illnesses may derive from the reaction between biological, psychiatric, cognitive and psychosocial factors.

Anxiety and fears that children experience, whatever the cause, may lead to increased susceptibility to genuine physical illness, missing school as a result and poor overall achievement as the outcome.

INTELLIGENCE

Gaudry and Spielberger (1971) have demonstrated that anxiety and intelligence have interactive effects on performance. In those of high intelligence, anxiety will facilitate performance of simple tasks and of most of those of moderate difficulty. In contrast, high anxiety will lead to performance detriments for individuals of low ability, except for very easy tasks.

Friends

The effect of the peer group on development is beyond measure. At various stages of growth, and in early to mid-adolescence particularly, loyalty to the group supersedes all else, including family standards and expectations. Conflict between the two is a frequent occurrence and choices which do not please everyone, the young person included, have to be made repeatedly. Fashions, language and behaviours, some referred to above, may do more to alienate parents and teachers than anything else, and much apprehension can be generated by apparently simple decisions which lead to the telling of untruths or manipulation of situations. Guilt and hostility follow, and the conscience-stricken individual may find easy academic tasks impossible to concentrate on with negative results in consequence. In essence, fear of ostracism may exceed any other anxieties and lead to behaviour at variance with family standards, with consequent emotional conflict and an inability to do schoolwork wholeheartedly.

Friends form an important part of the success equation which is progressively eroded as the need for social activity grows and priorities (not always in accordance with those of parents or the school), are rearranged. Financial status, whether personal or family, plays an important role in feelings of well-being or otherwise generated by the ability to possess the material basics of the group.

The role of bullying and teasing, real or imagined, does not require much elaboration. The effect on school performance and life in general can be quite catastrophic if not adequately dealt with and may arise from something as simple as an odd surname, to marked variations from the norm such as racial characteristics or the factors alluded to on pp.22–23.

Although not given much prominence here, bullying (which may sadly originate from teaching staff) is a profound and common generator of anxiety in all its manifestations, and can elicit a host of responses from increasing twitchiness to suicide attempts. The significance of unkindness and cruelty should never be underestimated and the child's perception of it never pooh-poohed!

Future

Distinctions have to be made between the immediate and the remote or distant future, and it is the latter that is of importance here. Examining children's perceptions of adulthood, Bauer's (1980) report verifies the findings of others, that the overwhelming majority of 11- and 12-year-olds prefer their life as children. They do not feel that being an adult is a positive experience, tending to romanticise childhood experiences generally and seeing adult responsibility in a negative light.

Many adolescents of the last decade spoke disparagingly of the futility of preparing for a future in which 'the bomb' was predominant. Recent worldwide political changes have shifted this to mass unemployment and fears of personal joblessness with concomitant insecurity and hardship. Rationalisation perhaps, but frightening and occasionally disabling for all that. Future fears are not a feature in young children but grow in intensity as the possibilities of school leaving draw near and evaluation of post-academic success or failure colours self-assessment.

Sex and sexuality

The awareness of sexual feelings starts long before adolescence but it is in this period that anxieties about the future role of sexuality predominates. All boys and girls develop insecurities about their fantasies especially those of a sexual variety, and may become overwhelmed by them, unable to concentrate effectively on other aspects of living – socialising, studying, relaxing. Group pressures may predominate, expectations misinterpreted with feelings of failure and uselessness, the result.

Boys in many sub-cultural groups, if not all at some stage, have a powerful need to prove their masculinity, and what better way than to discuss sexual desires or even conquests (whether true or not). In the younger adolescent there is often considerably greater pleasure derived from boasting about a liaison than from the actual event itself.

Girls and boys are frequently disappointed with their impact on the opposite sex and may become extremely worried about their self-perceived deficiencies.

HOMOSEXUALITY

Homosexual feelings are extremely common in both sexes, although more so in boys; the setting in which emerging sexuality first arises with intensity, such as a single-sex boarding school, has a considerable role to play in the way in which sexual desire focuses initially. Overwhelming panics are well recognised and described in those who feel that they are abnormal ('queer', 'fags') and occasionally lead to dramatic action such as a suicide attempt from a superficially uncomplicated individual.

The role of problems in relation to sexuality and suicide is significant and is preceded by a build up of ever-increasing anxiety with dramatic action, whether as an impulsive act or carefully planned. Among the many difficulties described are those of identity, homosexual conflicts, inhibitions, abuse, 'buying' affection with sex, pregnancy and promiscuity.

Worries about homosexual ideation are compounded by the tendency, in boys particularly, to displace feelings of anxiety they have about themselves by projective name calling of others.

SEXUAL NORMS

Sexual norms vary considerably between all societies, countries, ethnic groups and so on and, even within the same town, different suburbs or schools have differing ideas of what is regarded as acceptable or desirable behaviour. In attempts to help troubled young people with sexual identity confusions it is important to be aware of what the individual concerned, and those with whom he or she associates, regards as normal behaviour. This, of course, applies to all areas of functioning, but is nowhere as important as the potentially embarrassing (and thus concealed) area of sexuality.

SEXUAL ABUSE

Sexual abuse and its effect is a major subject and dealt with comprehensively elsewhere.

HYPOCHONDRIASIS

Hypochondriasis is a frequent occurrence in the post-pubertal stage of development. Preoccupation with bodily functions, often related to guilts about sexual feeling (for example spots perceived as punishment for having dirty thoughts) may lead to a multiplicity of psychosomatic complaints, while fears of illness and impending doom mount.

Headaches and abdominal pains lead to absenteeism and, depending on family attitudes, to over usage of medical services or lack of understanding and sympathy, with increasing isolation and time spent alone in bedrooms.

MASTURBATION

Masturbation is probably a feature in all boys; 90 per cent admit to it nowadays, but the importance of sex education, and the stressing of the normality of it all, is essential. With less peripheral sensitivity in girls initially, clitoral stimulation appears to be less important and significant.

Ever-intrusive, uncontainable feelings which emerge at unacceptable and inconvenient times, are in conflict with the repression of sexual desires demanded by Western society; biological and social demands are at odds with one another.

The early interests that children display before pubertal changes begin in characteristics of the opposite sex, such as young boys looking at and talking about mother's breasts or girls flirting with their fathers and becoming seductive, has to be denied when adolescence emerges thus leading to a host of anxiety-based defence mechanisms.

An occasional factor in older academically successful girls is the fear they experience of alienating males should they achieve better results or excel in any sphere of potential rivalry whatsoever. They therefore hold back on their possibilities for success and may become extremely anxious and guilt ridden in consequence. The old European belief that a woman's place is in the kitchen, church or with the children is still with us, and fear of success leading to career enhancement and breaking of the gender mold, needs to be considered in girls who do not realise the expectations of those around them.

Additional considerations

There are other surprising examples of the interrelationship between anxiety and underachievement.

ROLE EXPECTATION

This has been referred to above. The usual traditional female role precludes competing with successful males, but also makes identification with high-achieving female role models something of a problem.

The family that has developed long-standing traditional modes of functioning, in business or elsewhere, might expect their progeny to be following in father's footsteps. The child, however, may have other ideas, with consequent family conflict, enforcement or failure to do so. None the less, anger and hostility and inability to function properly are the inevitable outcomes.

RACE

Unexpected emotional conflicts on racial grounds are beginning to be recognised. A highly intelligent black child, who has been doing very well academically, may suddenly begin to fail in mid-adolescence as an emotional tug of war between some local community values and society at large take hold. The 'Uncle Tom' of yester-year has now become the 'Coconut' of today (black on the outside, but white inside). This arises as scorn is heaped on attempts to introject values of the majority who are feared, seen as racist, two-faced and not really wanting their participation.

Black children may develop anxieties relating to their inability to identify wholly with either group, and school achievement, whether deliberately or as an unconscious phenomenon, declines dramatically. The pressures upon them may affect speech, dress and other elements of functioning concomitantly.

POST TRAUMATIC STRESS DISORDER

This is fully dealt with in many recent papers and gives due awareness of the importance of any past major stressful event on a child which may have long-lasting effects. These may include witnessing or being part of a major accident, an assault of whatever kind, hospital admission and so on. Appropriate psychological treatment may be required to prevent many of the manifestations of the syndrome, among which anxiety and an inability to achieve appropriately are prominent.

Summary

The factors inducing anxiety in children, leading to an inability to realise their full potential, are various, and exist in many, if not all children at some stage in their development.

Full understanding of their functioning within the family or at school, as well as knowledge of other developmental phenomena, is essential if an accurate diagnosis is to be made and an appropriate therapeutic approach is to be implemented. The fears relating to school may lead to agoraphobic and anxiety-based problems in adulthood if not adequately dealt with, and may affect the individual's mental health generally, job prospects and children with time.

There are many approaches to treatment, most of them effective, but it is early recognition and diagnosis that is required before any of these can be proceeded with.

References

Baker, H.S. (1987) 'Underachievement and Failure in College: The Interaction Between Intrapsychic and Interpersonal Factors from the Perspective of Self-Psychology', *Adolescent Psychiatry,* No. 14, pp.441–6.

Bauer, D. (1980) 'Child Fears in Developmental Perspective', in L. Hersov, and I. Berg (eds), *Out of School.* John Wiley & Sons: Sydney, pp.189–209.

Birney, R.C., Burdick, H. and Teevan, R.C. (1969) *Fear of Failure.* Van Nostrand-Reinhold Co: New York.

Bloom, B.S. (1973) 'Individual Differences in School Achievement: A Vanishing Point?', in L.J. Rubin, (ed), *Facts and Feelings in the Classroom.* Ward Lock Educational: London pp.113–46.

Gaudry, E. and Spielberger, C.D. (1971) *Facts and Feelings Educational Achievement.* John Wiley & Sons: Sydney.

Green, M. (1986) 'Vulnerable Child Syndrome and its Variants', *Pediatrics in Review,* Vol. 8, No. 3, (September), pp.75, 80.

Hodiamont, P. (1991) 'How Normal are Anxiety and Fear?' *International Journal of Social Psychiatry,* Vol. 37, No. 1, pp.43–50.

Marks, I.M. (1987) *Fears, Phobias and Rituals.* Oxford University Press: New York.

Nutt, D. (1990) 'The Aetiology of Panic', in D. Gath, and N.L.M. Goeting, *Current Approaches – Panic, Symptom or Disorder?* Duphar Medical Relations: London.

Sepie, A.C. and Keeling, B. (1978) 'The Relationship Between Types of Anxiety', *Journal of Educational Research,* Vol. 72, No. 1, pp.15–19.

Wing, J.K., Cooper, J.E. and Sartorius, N. (1974) *Measurement and Classification of Psychiatric Symptoms.* Cambridge University Press: Cambridge.

CHAPTER 3

Boredom, High Ability and Achievement

Joan Freeman

Boredom is not apathy, it is a dynamic emotion, which comes from spirits which are lowered if not depressed, and from anger which comes from frustration. People who are bored would really rather be doing something else, even though they may not know what. But boredom can also have a paradoxical positive effect, such as bringing about an improved change of direction, and sometimes producing outstanding achievement. It is possible, for example, that the outbursts of the tennis star, John McEnroe, are due to his boredom in games, such that his only way to achieve his superb performance-state is by quarrelling and arguing with officials to increase his level of excitement. Used in that way, boredom can produce high-level achievement and maintain success.

However, the very much more common negative effect of boredom is in draining energy, detracting from the ability to cope and learn, and certainly from the will to strive. Unfortunately, these negative effects are also demoralising and maladaptive to the individual's progress. Being bored is a state of mind, so that in the same situation where one individual feels bored another will find excitement. But it can also become a habit, developed in early childhood, to the extent that a child learns to expect it, and so interprets too many experiences that way – including school.

Boredom – which the pupils usually associate with lessons – is at the root of most problems of discipline in school. Most children experience it at some time at school and accept it as a part of everyday life. They do not usually complain, but take it as a fact of life to be endured, even at primary level; as a seven-year-old said: 'In lessons, I draw, write a bit, think, and day-dream a bit.' Although perhaps it is the less accepting ones, those who try to take some control over their own lives, who are the stronger; they are usually the more intelligent, and certainly the ones who might change things. But maladjusted children find free time in school most difficult to fill, and teachers often have to resort to carefully structured lessons for them. The emotionally immature child has the compulsion within himself to *do* something, rather than *choose* to do it.

Children do not like being bored; they love to be active and involved. When children play, either alone or in groups, they devise means of avoiding boredom, such as competition, the invention of rhymes and codes of behaviour. They will try anything to relieve this unpleasant experience, the easiest being to numb the senses in watching without discrimination whatever is on television. It kills time, covers up any anxiety, and results in tensions being forgotten. But it takes from them the joy of looking forward, of anticipation.

In about 90 per cent of a large selection of books on teaching and learning which I examined, it was extraordinary that there is no reference to boredom of either pupils or teachers, although it is probably one of the most frequent reasons for pupil failure in school. Although these volumes contain many thousands of words on related areas, such as motivation and attention, there is practically nothing on the syndrome of boredom, which is as prevalent in schools as the common cold virus.

It is unfortunate but true that teachers are to a large extent responsible for much of the boredom of their pupils. Poor teaching trails boredom in its wake, acting as a deterrent to good learning. Because of it, many children underachieve in their school work, and possibly keep those alienating attitudes learned in school with them for the rest of their lives. The bored child does not show what he or she is capable of, and in particular any high ability may be hidden as a result. But understanding how boredom is engendered should help to make it possible to tackle the ensuing problems and so alleviate the symptoms.

The vicious circle

Although boredom is rooted in emotion, it also depends on the nature of the learning task itself, such as whether the child has acquired the strategies to cope with it. In mathematics, for instance, a girl may have picked up parental or teacher's attitudes to expect the subject to be boring. As a result, she does not listen properly, and so fails to understand the teacher's explanation. She is then confirmed both in her feelings of incapacity in mathematics, and that the subject is indeed boring.

If children are tired and over-stressed, they lose interest and can become bored (Elkind 1981, Arnold 1990). Mental and physical exhaustion means that they must use all their energy in coping with everyday life, and have little to spare for adapting to new school-type learning. Consequently they may miss out parts of the information given at school through opting-out mentally, day-dreaming or simply not paying attention; this makes their learning task even more difficult, and so induces further boredom. Children who are always bored in school do not develop habits of enthusiasm and mental discipline, and are unlikely to acquire the ability for clear thought.

Csikszentnihalyi and Larson (1984) identify this state of consciousness with a term used in physics – entropy – meaning disorder in physical systems, resulting in loss of energy. The opposite – negative entropy – they term 'flow', the buoyancy of spirit that makes achievement appear effortless. But that flow is fragile and unstable, and can easily be blocked by boredom or anxiety. For example, if a child is forced by his piano teacher to tackle a piece that is difficult, he can do one of three things – give up altogether, play at the level he already knows or learn more complex music. Thus there is a price for avoiding boredom, which is usually more learning and more practice. But these demand psychic energy and dedication, which are not always available, particularly to children who are tired or emotionally disturbed, or those who are not familiar with delaying gratification.

Boredom reaches new heights in adolescence, when the youngster's more violent swings of mood can be difficult for anyone to live with. This may not always be obvious in the behaviour and school-work of obedient children, but it nevertheless infiltrates their social lives. An apparently stable 15-year-old, who was a hard worker and high achiever at school, expressed these feelings to me: 'I've always been easily bored, and it makes me depressed, or perhaps my boredom is because I'm lonely and therefore I'm depressed. I have a very limited social sphere, really' (Freeman 1991). Though fortunately rare, the effects of boredom can be disastrous, as a 15-year-old girl described: 'A girl I knew died from drugs, She used to be in my school. I think she was simply bored, unfulfilled. She was quite clever, but she never worked at school, she was never encouraged at all there. She just left school, went to work in a supermarket, and actually she died a few weeks ago. It was really sad.'

Gifted children and boredom

Gifted children are particularly vulnerable to boredom because of their exceptionality; this potential problem should be a matter of concern in the normal classroom, where most highly able children are educated. Like any other pupils, the gifted need the enjoyable stimulation of variety, and the excitement that can come from the juxtaposition of ideas. That is why when lessons are too easy, as can happen in a mixed-ability classroom, the gifted lose what the other pupils may be getting from it – the satisfaction of tackling and resolving problems. To compensate, they may deliberately provoke disturbance, either in their own minds or among others in the classroom, just to taste the spice of stimulation. Without stimulation, school-work becomes just a rather boring and easy matter of taking in and reproducing what the teacher says, and the flame of discovery burns low. The answer, of course, is to provide the gifted with an education appropriate to the needs they have for greater speed and depth in learning.

In America, Feldhusen and Kroll (1991) questioned primary school children about their attitudes to school and whether they were bored there; 227 children had been identified as gifted by IQ test, and a control group of 226 were not so identified. The researchers found that the gifted often began school with positive attitudes, but failed to maintain them because of the lack of appropriate challenge. However, there was no difference between the two groups in the way they felt about their level of personal boredom.

In Britain, the national Gulbenkian Research (Freeman 1991) took a much broader and longer view of both gifted and control children's development at school and home. Since 1974, most of the sample of 210 children, originally aged 5 to 14, had been followed up. For the 70 children who had been presented as gifted by their parents to the National Association for Gifted Children (NAGC), without tests, each was matched with two control children for age and sex, and being in the same class at school. But whereas the control-1 child was matched exactly for general intelligence (Ravens Matrices), the control-2 child was taken at random in that respect. The children and their families were visited in their homes, and the 60 classteachers and 60 headteachers were interviewed in their schools.

There were many statistically significant differences between the groups. Parents who had identified their children as gifted and joined the NAGC, were much more likely to describe them as not only bored at school, but friendless, difficult and more troubled by problems of sleep, poor co-ordination and asthma. Other differences in outlook between those parents and all the others probably contributed to their children's feelings about themselves and their consequent behaviour, such as the greater number of complaints about the school.

The children were then statistically removed from their original experimental groups and compared on all collected data in terms of their Stamford-Binet IQ scores, but no relationship could be found between IQ on its own and the children's behaviourial problems. Nor was there any significant relationship between IQ and personality, other than a tendency to extraversion in the music performers. Those in the top 2 per cent of the IQ range had as many friends at school as other children, but fewer at home, due to the nature of their out-of-school activities, such as music practice, hobbies and more homework. As in the American study, (above) they did not describe themselves as significantly more bored and alienated in school than the others; on the contrary, they saw themselves as rather more empathetic and aware.

The children's gifts were unlikely to be a major problem for them unless either they were unhappy because of home circumstances, such as fighting parents, divorce or frequent house moves, or the school was too rigid to accept them for themselves. These are reasons that would disturb any child. In fact, as they were growing up, the young people complained far more about boredom at home than at school – 'I'm often left in the house bored stiff, with only my Mum and Dad for company.'

The idea that gifted children were bound to be 'odd', and accordingly unhappy, was found to be rife, so that some parents and teachers looked for and found it, and at times even seemed to encourage it. Yet always, in the same class as the labelled gifted children, there would be others – of identical ability – who were not identified as gifted, and so were neither expected to be nor were emotionally disturbed or bored.

The follow-up study of this sample began in 1984, with 81 per cent of the young people, then aged 14 to 23, who were again interviewed in their homes. Many of the emotional differences between the identified children and the others were found to have diminished to the point of insignificance. This may have been either because the youngsters had grown out of their childhood problems, or they had simply left the pressures and restrictions of home and school behind them. But the least well adjusted had remained the least happy, and had done less well at school, in comparison with their IQ peers.

Looking back from the follow up, most of the young people felt that any childhood boredom at school had eased off – 'The further back I remember school, the more boredom I remember, because I was enjoying fewer subjects then.' Others expressed longing for their earlier, simpler lives – 'When I was younger, I used to be very happy sitting down with a book. Now, I haven't time to do that, so there's more potential for being bored.' But the boredom they described was well within the normal range, even for those who had it badly – 'I get bored at school, I get bored at home, and I get bored in the holidays because since we moved to the country there's nothing to do.'

Several of the high achievers, however, reported the feeling of 'let-down' which can come to everyone at the end of hard work completed, with the release of tension and the sudden vacuum of time – a well-known aspect of stress in the business world. It came to many in the sample who had worked hard for a project or after examinations, and it was sometimes seen in terms of boredom. One subject said:

> The harder I work, the more bored I get when I stop, if you know what I mean. Like after exams, I've worked like mad, and I'll go straight down to the pub, put down a couple, and think what the hell am I going to do now? I can't seem to strike a balance between working too much, then not having enough to do and getting bored.

Gifted ways of coping

A normal classroom is a fairly structured place, activities focusing on the content of the lesson, which is designed so that the pupil's performance is correctable and thus improvable by the teacher. For potential high achievers in examinations, there is often a dominant concern with information, but this is limiting for pupils who are also interested in ideas for their own sakes. They may then be faced with the connected social problem of how to adapt, while remaining intellectually alive and thus different. In fact, it is virtually impossible to show intellectually gifted behaviour without distinguishing oneself from one's school-fellows; yet to conform and keep a low profile courts boredom. Some children cope with this dilemma by behaving stupidly in class, such as shouting out silly answers, to show how 'normal' they are. Others may become overly conformist, divert attention to someone who is an even more determined scholar, or become the class clown.

There is also sometimes a 'work-restriction' norm among pupils, which is more common in poorly cultured areas, but can even operate at academically selective schools. There seems to be a strange classroom lore that it is acceptable to come top of the class – as long as you are not seen to work for it, as though achievement were predestined and that to work hard is interfering with nature. At some schools, it can mean that a child who wants to achieve highly may have to study in secret to avoid the disapproval of school-mates.

Unfortunately, although they are usually unaware of it, many teachers (even those who teach the gifted) direct the class to work at around its average level. Unifying the class in this way makes teaching easier, but can cause difficulty for a gifted child in a predominantly average-ability school. Some teachers in the research sample coped with this problem by making 'assistant' teachers of the more advanced children, using them to instruct the slower ones. Those who did not enjoy this job often felt that they were bored with what they saw as a waste of time, having to wait until the rest caught up to get on with their own learning.

THE THREE-TIMES PROBLEM

In a normal classroom, the teachers usually says the same thing three times. First as an introduction – 'this is what I am going to tell you'; again to boost it – 'now I am telling it to you'; and then to summarise and make sure – 'that is what I have just told you'. But the gifted remember it the first time round, which I have termed their 'Three-times problem'. So in order to avoid the tedium of the repetition, they often devise a special technique. They teach themselves only to listen consciously on the first occasion and switch off for the following two. This, however, demands a very high level of mental skill, which takes some practice to perfect.

A gifted girl (aged 20) described how it was for her:

> In the lectures, I listen to everything the first time, but when they start going over and over the same thing, I use my automatic switch-off button. It started at school, where lessons were more or less handed to you on a plate. You can tell by the tone of the voice when it's coming again; it becomes a knack after sitting through hours and hours of lessons and lectures, especially when you keep having the same teacher. And it's the way they say, '*Now*, then', and I think, 'Right, I've got five minutes to myself now'. It can be really boring when lecturers say the same thing four times. We had one who asked, 'Now has anybody got any questions?' and nobody said a word. So he said, 'You've taken so long with nobody saying something that obviously none of you can understand it, so I'll go through it again.

Gifted children are also bored by the unrelenting pressure of highly academic schools, where they were often expected to take in information and reproduce it on demand, leaving them feeling intellectually unexercised. Many would have liked an easing-off from examination pressure and some concern for their own values and interests. It was put succinctly by a gifted boy:

> The style of teaching is uninspirational, uninteresting. The teacher talks and you take it down; homework is essays and more writing. They don't look for new ways to interest the class. They themselves are bored and, of course, so are we. I'd like to be taught in a way that is more relevant to the actual world outside, to involve more personal experiences both on the teacher's side and on mine. I'm trying to fight boredom and frustration, just to get through my exams with good grades. I expect the teachers think I'm very lazy, but I don't actually know what they think because they don't really speak to me.

In their exceptionality and their sensitivity, the gifted sometimes construct complex, inhibiting psychological defences against expected hurt. A common variety is to hide behind academic, intellectual walls of their own making, implying that they are too clever to have normal relationships with ordinary people. Alternatively, they see themselves as being bored at school, and so never learn the routines of discipline, which can be difficult to pick up later, and so this defensive boredom becomes a downward spiral, getting worse and worse.

TEACHING THE GIFTED CREATIVELY

What the gifted in this sample wanted of their teachers was that they be good at their job – expertise in the skills of teaching was very much appreciated – but the teacher did not have to be the total source of knowledge, rather a part of a genuine two-way communication with their pupils so that they could sometimes learn together. Teachers should listen as well as talk. The quality the Gulbenkian-project children most appreciated in teachers was an inspiring enthusiasm for their subject. Some teachers in highly academic schools were described as having good qualifications, but were poor communicators.

The highly able need something more than straight teaching to keep them functioning well. Research on these matters is in some agreement that talent must have the right context in which to grow. High-level achievement does not grow from a single root, such as an IQ score. David Henry Feldman deduced a term from his biographical study of six 'genius' children which he called 'trace elements', unrecognised events which are vital for gifted development (Feldman 1986). Howard Gruber (1981), in a historical case study of outstanding individuals such as Darwin and Piaget, also saw that combination and referred to such creative achievers as people in 'networks of enterprise', i.e. they have many things going on at the same time. Without the means to try out ideas and being kept on the narrow track of straight learning, the highly able child can lose interest and turn his or her attention elsewhere.

An education for the highly able should not be, as it so often is, a matter of acquiring astounding exam successes early in life culminating in a PhD at the age of 20. As with all children, it should encourage a genuine feeling for learning and considering issues, and should stimulate curiosity – 'knowing how' rather than 'knowing that'. In the long run, the goal of education must be to equip all children with the means and motivation to continue learning after they have left home and school.

Attacking boredom in the normal school

There is an abundant amount of published information and ideas about how to increase children's motivation and keenness to learn, although parents and teachers would perhaps like to see these put more effectively into practice. The particular need, in order to prevent loss of interest and boredom, is intrinsic motivation, which comes from within and so, once started, is self-perpetuating (Ryan *et al*. 1985). Anything which helps children see themselves as able to be effective helps to promote this, but whatever makes them feel incompetent will diminish it. To feel that they are truly effective, all children need the challenge of risk and failure, and even some negative feedback; the learning task must be challenging to enhance intrinsic motivation.

A great deal depends, though, on the child's perception of what happens, because feedback can be interpreted in different ways. Too much praise implies that the child is doing the bidding of the teacher, and even rewards can undermine intrinsic motivation, because the child feels that he or she is working for the reward rather than for the task itself. Too much supervision can also work against intrinsic motivation, because autonomy then becomes a psychological impossibility. This is not to encourage permissiveness, i.e. the removal of all constraints and structure, which may result in neglect and chaos. Structure in teaching provides information and guidance, to help develop and channel a child's growing capacities and abundant energies.

One decidedly gifted boy who failed to develop intrinsic motivation explained:

> I always felt that I was one of the school's better pupils, because I was usually in the top set without trying. I never studied, but I knew I could do better than most of them. It might have been the old ego thing, you know. If I turned into a studier and a boffin, all my friends might look at me and think... maybe it was just a pride thing. It wasn't that I hated school, I just couldn't be bothered. I'd come home and try to revise, but after half an hour I was bored. I'd be sat there looking through a book, and I'd prefer to be outside, physically active. Even so, I still was one of the best in the class, but I thought... well sod it... so I left school.

Thus, circumstances that provide a feeling of autonomy and that support individual competence tend to encourage intrinsic motivation. On the other hand, circumstances that pressure and control people not only convey incompetence, but even serve to undermine whatever intrinsic motivation there may have been.

Teachers do have a great responsibility for the boredom of children in school; when the bright children in my sample were bored, it was most usually because of poor teaching and learning methods. But it is not only the gifted child who appreciates skilled teaching and genuine feedback. Children respond well to teachers who will work with them, rather than for them, and to teachers who are concerned with the structure of their learning and their ability to cope as individuals. It is possible to make children lively minded and interested in what they are expected to do, and some new pointers, which are relevant to all children have emerged from the more specifically directed studies of the highly able.

Challenging learning

Not only the highly able, but all children should be encouraged to move into the realm of intellectual thought and to practise the thinking strategies of analysis and evaluation. This would involve immersing children from the very start of school life in ideas which are complex, sophisticated and stimulating: it implies that they are sufficiently able to tackle those tasks. It requires the teacher to take a more intellectually challenging approach to children's learning than is often the case at present.

A common example of unchallenging learning is in the teaching of reading. It is not unusual for very advanced early readers to be kept at the same pace as the rest of the class. Using a more challenging approach, the teacher would first recognise the child's ability, then encourage her to aim for a text at a higher level. The teacher should also spend some time talking about it and getting the child to elaborate on it – What happened next? – relating it to other ideas she might have – Was this like the story you read before about the Prince?

Involving children in their learning

Information should not be taught as unquestionable facts, even from the earliest days, but as relatively transient material to be played with and challenged. This adversarial approach is the basis of new ideas, but it calls for a good self-concept, a feeling that it is possible to challenge authority about what seem like fixed facts. Sometimes in teaching, especially in primary schools, there may be too much emphasis placed on the way children learn at the expense of information content. There must be a balance between the two because, for children, that combination of information and its creative use is, in the end, the most satisfying.

In following their interests, children have a natural tendency to take on challenges that exercise and expand their competencies. If they are given a reward, such as money or sweets, they are far more likely to choose easy tasks that lead them more easily to the reward. If they are doing it for the love of the activity, though, they choose harder tasks, just above their level (Ryan *et al*. 1985). Using the children's own interests is an effective way to involve them in learning. They could, for example, do a meta-analysis of their interests by keeping a log, and watching how they change; this might help them to get in touch with their less obvious interests which may be masked by the more popular concerns of children of the same age. Teachers can also encourage what the psychologist William James at the start of this century called a 'romance' with a subject.

Recognising individual differences in learning styles

Teachers' understanding of the styles of learning and strategies that their pupils use can avoid boredom. However, teachers cannot adapt to the individual learning styles of a whole classroom. But it may be possible to make some headway, for example, by looking for ways to blend children's own styles to fit the task and learning situation. At school, as in the outside world, children are usually able to experience a variety of instructional styles, for example discussions, projects, lectures, independent study, simulation, peer teaching, acting out and rote learning. This helps them to discover how they learn best – part of the process of learning to learn – which will stay with them all their lives.

A flexible teaching approach is essential for children's real competence and high-level functioning. Because new learning depends so much on how prior knowledge has been stored, simply telling children what to learn is not always adequate. They need to relate the new to the old, in ways which are meaningful to them, and from their own perspectives. This can sometimes be very straightforward, such as teaching geometry in terms of football pitches and the movements of the football.

Once acquired, flexible learning and thinking strategies – on a sound knowledge base – can be transferred for use in other similar subjects with problems of increasingly greater complexity. Highly successful examinees have a positive outlook on learning, with a well-practised and flexible mind, and this same procedure allows almost any child to apply and adapt a range of intellectual skills correctly in new situations.

Both teachers and parents should also try to become aware of their own repertoires of teaching strategies. These might be, for example, a heavy reliance on instructing children to remember rather than interpret, or a limited ability to cope with redundant noise, so that they demand constant silence from pupils. The strategies which adults teach children may not, in fact, be the best ways for their recipients, which is another good reason for keeping things flexible.

Enhancing self-esteem

There is evidence that children who believe that their abilities are fixed fail to aim as high as they could, particularly if they see themselves as not very bright (Chapman *et al.* 1990). Enhancing children's sense of competence is possibly the most basic way of improving their potential for learning – especially for girls and minority children – and this should include the more practical help of improving their learning strategies (Freeman 1992). Self-rating is the first step towards self-reflection and control. It helps any child (or indeed adult) towards a positive and realistic understanding of his or her own ways of thinking and learning. A very effective technique is to guide children in rating their own performances and products, as they work through practice problems, instead of depending on a teacher's marking.

Children who are very bored may have difficulties in remembering, particularly in the short term. This is not necessarily due to lack of effort, which teachers usually assume, but to difficulties in structuring and encoding. It is possible to counter that negative effect, to some extent, by being exceptionally positive and reinforcing any learning that is accomplished (Williams *et al.* 1988).

Another way of bringing direct rewards and so improving a pupil's positive attitudes to learning is through the teacher's own positive attitudes. This does not mean false praise, but seeking out aspects of what the children are doing for constructive comment. It helps the children to develop stronger feelings of proficiency in learning, which in turn makes them more likely to invest energy in it, enjoy it and do better. Once in motion, the upward spiral raises the probability of success, since enhancing positive feelings also improves the motivation to learn and takes away the boredom.

References

Arnold, L.E. (1990) *Childhood Stress*. Wiley: Chichester.

Chapman, J.W. and Lambourne, R. (1990) Some antecedents of academic self-concept: a longitudinal study, *British Journal of Educational Psychology*, 60, 142–152.

Csikszentnihalyi, M. and Larson, R. (1984) *Being Adolescent: Conflict and Growth in the Teenage years*. New York: Basic Books.

Elkind, D. (1981) *The Hurried Child: Growing Up Too Fast Too Soon*. Reading, MA: Addison-Wesley.

Feldhusen, J.F. and Kroll, M.D. (1991) Boredom or challenge for the academically talented in school, *Gifted Education International*, 7, 80–81.

Feldman, D.H. and Goldsmith L.T. (1986) *Nature's Gambit*. New York: Basic Books.

Freeman, J. (1991) *Gifted Children Growing Up*. London: Cassell.

Freeman, J. (1992) *Quality Education: the Development of Competence*. Paris and Geneva: UNESCO.

Gruber, H. (1981) *Darwin on Man: a Psychological Study of Scientific Creativity*. Chicago: University of Chicago Press.

Ryan, R.M., Connell, J.P. and Deci, E.L. (1985) A motivational analysis of self-determination and self-regulation in education, in Ames, c. and Ames, R. (eds.), *Research on Motivation in Education. Vol II The Classroom Milieu.* New York:Academic Press.

Williams, J.M., Watts, F.M., Macleod, C. and Mathews, A. (1988) *Cognitive Psychology and Emotional Disorders.* Chichester: Wiley.

CHAPTER 4

Limited Intelligence and School Failure

Michael J.A. Howe

Few would quibble with the statement that lack of intelligence may prevent a child from doing well at school. But what exactly is the relationship between intelligence and school success? Answering that question is made difficult by the fact that there are a number of legitimate alternative meanings of the word 'intelligence'. For the sake of simplicity, in this chapter I shall consider two distinct kinds of intelligence. In each case the links between intelligence and school achievement will be examined.

The first kind of intelligence to be considered in relation to success at school learning is *psychometric* intelligence as reflected in the scores a child obtains at an intelligence test. Intelligence tests can provide useful practical tools, because the measures that are obtained when a child takes a test enable reasonably good predictions to be made about the chances of the individual being able to succeed at learning tasks and other demanding challenges that are likely to be encountered at school. However, in contrast with their effectiveness at *predicting* school success, intelligence test scores are much less efficacious for *explaining* why children differ in their achievements, or for adding to our understanding of why some individuals fail at school tasks.

Achieving that latter goal, understanding the causes of success and failure at school, can better be assisted by introducing concepts or definitions of intelligence which are different from and broader than the psychometric one. For purposes of aiding our efforts to explain and understand human abilities, it is useful to regard intelligence, as referring to the various intellectual processes and mechanisms that underlie performance at the tasks of learning, remembering, reasoning and so on, that are encountered in the classroom.

The uses of tested intelligence

We shall first consider psychometric or measured intelligence, as indicated in a child's test scores. Undeniably, a child whose test score is low will be likely to encounter difficulties at school. In other words, a pupil who does not succeed at the kinds of tasks that form part of a test battery will also find it hard to succeed at classroom tasks. Why is it that scores obtained in psychometric tests of intelligence predict school success? The reason, quite simply, is that this is precisely what intelligence tests were initially designed to do. When Alfred Binet developed the first practical tests of intelligence at the beginning of the present century, he did so specifically in order to find a way to determine whether or not particular children were capable of thriving in ordinary schools. He had been appointed, in 1904, by the French Ministry for Public Instruction, who were anxious to find a fair and effective way to identify children whose intellectual limitations made them better suited for a special classroom designed to meet their particular needs. Many of the tests that Binet worked with were taken from exercises used by teachers in the schools (McClelland 1973). What Binet did was to try out on children in the schools a large number of tests that he had collected together, some of which he had developed previously, to determine which ones were most effective for discriminating effectively between children of differing ability. Those tests that helped achieve this end were included in his test battery, and those tests that did not work in this way were discarded.

The scale of intelligence that Binet and his collaborator Simon produced in 1905 included a variety of test items, such as ones that involved defining words or demonstrating comprehension of sentences, ones that required the lengths of lines to be compared, ones that required the ability to draw patterns from memory, and ones that required words to be used in a sentence. The final choice of items was made not on the basis of any definition of intelligence, or according to a theory of the nature of intelligence, but simply on the basis of their effectiveness at discriminating between children who varied in their ability to succeed at school. The main strength and also the main limitation of tested intelligence derives from this fact. That is, because the tests were specifically designed and constructed to discriminate between children of varying ability, they do so quite effectively, and enable useful predictions to be made. On the other hand, because the tests were not constructed on the basis of any specific theory or definition of intelligence, the scores obtained on them add little to our efforts to understand or explain the actual causes of differences in ability. Of course, the items that are included in tests have changed somewhat during the years since Binet and Henri first devised their scale, but the alterations have been relatively minor, and the practical rather than theoretical basis of selection has been retained.

So it is hardly surprising that intelligence test scores do predict school success reasonably well, a finding that many studies have verified. The correlation of general mental test scores with measures of educational achievement is around .60 in younger children and around .50 in older children (Snow and Yalow 1982). Note, however, that so far as making predictions about individual children is concerned, the practical value of correlations of this magnitude is not unlimited: a .50 correlation leads to predictions that are on average only 25 per cent more accurate than simple guesses.

The fact that intelligence tests scores enable predictions to be made about performance, together with the finding that a child's scores at successive intelligence tests administered at intervals of a year or so remain fairly constant, has contributed to the widespread belief that a child's measured intelligence represents a fundamental attribute of that individual, one that underlies and constrains specific abilities but which is itself largely unchangeable. However, there now exists considerable evidence that this assumption may be wrong, and that intelligence, as assessed by intelligence tests, is far from being unchangeable.

Effects of schooling on test scores

That intelligence can be systematically altered is suggested by the finding that adults' measured intelligence is highly correlated with the number of years' schooling individuals have received. That suggests the possibility that schooling affects intelligence, as well as *vice versa,* although the existence of such a correlation does not prove that amount of schooling is the *cause* of high intelligence. The existence of such correlations could be due entirely to the effects of intelligence on the amount of schooling a child receives, and there may be other factors, such as family circumstances, which similarly affect both intelligence and duration of schooling.

However, there is some convincing evidence that schooling does indeed influence measured intelligence. For example, in a number of studies in which intelligence was assessed at different times of the year it has been found that there is a definite decrease in average IQ scores during the summer school holidays. The decrease is largest in children whose family circumstances are such that school-like home activities are comparatively rare. As the school year progresses, average scores get higher, only to drop again between the end of the summer term and the beginning of the autumn term (Ceci 1990).

Research conducted in South Africa provides further evidence of the effects of schooling on measured intelligence. One investigator (Schmidt 1967) was able to examine the relationship between years of schooling and measured intelligence in circumstances which seem to rule out the possibility of the correlation being accounted for by causes other than the amount of schooling. Schmidt tested children in an East Indian community where schooling was highly valued but in very short supply. Virtually all the families in the community tried to get their children into a school, because they perceived education as being valuable, but because of a severe shortage of school places many parents did not succeed. This resulted in a situation in which, amongst the children of parents who all valued education highly, there were large differences in the number of years' schooling the children actually received. These circumstances provided a kind of 'natural experiment' which would not normally be possible in most countries, because the number of years' schooling a child receives are usually related to other factors such as social class which, indirectly, also affect achievement.

The findings of Schmidt's investigation suggest that schooling can have a large influence on children's intelligence test scores. Even when he held age constant, and partialled out socioeconomic status, there was a substantial correlation (.68) between verbal intelligence and number of years' attendance at school, and there was also a correlation of .49 between amount of schooling and non-verbal intelligence. Similarly, those children who started school relatively early had higher scores than children who began later. Also, the correlations between years' of schooling and intelligence test scores were just as substantial as the correlation between years' of schooling and measures of specific kinds of school achievement, such as success at vocabulary and arithmetic skills. These findings clearly suggest that schooling does indeed influence measured intelligence, and they provide no support at all for the belief that measured intelligence is less influenced by education than is performance at relatively specific acquired abilities.

Further evidence that schooling can have large effects on the qualities measured in intelligence tests is found in a number of studies investigating the effects of dropping out of school early. Ceci (1990) summarises a number of Swedish investigations. For example, one study looked at the effects of dropping out on children who were of comparable intelligence at the age of 13 years. For each uncompleted high school year there was an average drop of 1.8 high school points. Hence, by the time they were 18, boys who had the same IQ at age 13 but had subsequently either stayed at school until they were around 18 years or had dropped out four years earlier, differed by an average of 8 IQ points. Similarly, studies carried out in the 1930s in the United States on black Americans who migrated to northern cities from the South found that (after controlling for selective migration) children gained over half a point for every year in which they were enrolled in northern schools (in Philadelphia) rather than in the inferior segregated schools which then existed in the South.

Other investigators have capitalised on the fact that simply because of the particular month in which they have chanced to be born, by a given age some young children will have received more formal education than others. For example, since at one time the German school system required an entering child to be aged six years by 1 April, a child who was born in March and was tested at eight years and two months would by then have received a year more schooling than a child who was born in April and was tested at the same age. Making comparisons between children thus affected, Baltes and Reinert (1969) found substantial correlations between schooling and intellectual performance in children of the same age, from equivalent social backgrounds. They also observed that the mental abilities of eight-year-olds who, because they were born in March, had received a relatively large amount of schooling, were closer to the abilities of the least schooled ten-year-olds than to those of the least schooled eight-year-olds.

Intelligence as a concept

To summarise the findings described in the most recent paragraphs, there is abundant evidence that intelligence test scores are substantially influenced by schooling. So it would be wrong to infer that a child's tested intelligence level is a measure of some fundamental underlying attribute which determines what a child is capable of achieving but is not itself affected by educational processes. This conclusion raises further questions: What exactly *is* the status of measured intelligence? And, what does a test score actually mean or imply?

An answer to the first question is that measured intelligence is essentially no more than a measure of *performance*, and it is not an indication of some underlying quality. It is really no more than a statement about how someone performed at certain tests.

In answer to the second question one can similarly state that what a test score 'means' is no more than the information it conveys about test performance. And the implications of that score are simply the predictive ones that I mentioned earlier. If that view is correct, whilst the test scores do have a definite predictive value, we should not expect them to tell us much more about the individual. In particular, the widespread assumption that intelligence test scores indicate the degree to which an individual possesses some underlying quality of intelligence which serves to constrain and help determine a child's actual achievements may be largely incorrect.

But the findings surveyed above do not make that conclusion inevitable. Perhaps these findings simply indicate that underlying intelligence is not quite so fixed or unchangeable as has sometimes been assumed, but leave intact the notion of intelligence as an underlying quality, one which can be regarded as the reason for, or the cause of, differences in ability between people. Perhaps measured intelligence does provide an indication of the magnitude of such a quality.

I think not, however, for reasons which are largely conceptual rather than simply empirical. These reasons relate to the kind of concept that is legitimately invoked when people use the term 'intelligence'. It is possible that the view that measured intelligence provides an indication of some underlying human property rests on certain incorrect assumptions, in the form of conceptual errors.

There are two such possible errors. The first is that of 'reification'. Reification (or 'reifying') involves unjustifiably assuming that a word that is a noun in our vocabulary must necessarily represent (or refer to) some concrete thing or quality. With many words, such as 'boat', 'bicycle' or 'book', for example, that clearly is the case. But with other words, especially abstract ones, we cannot take that for granted. For example, take a word like 'success'. It is a legitimate English noun, but there are limits to the ways in which we can legitimately use it. We might say, 'Her efforts met with success', but we would hesitate to state 'She did well because she has success', because the term success does not actually represent the kind of thing or quality possessed by a person that is implied by the 'phrase' because she has. The suggestion is that when we invoke intelligence as an underlying cause we are wrongly assuming that intelligence is a thing in the way that a boat or a bicycle is a thing, whereas the real conceptual status of intelligence may be more akin to that of success.

There is also a second kind of conceptual error, related to the above kind but partly distinct from it, that we may be making when we invoke measured intelligence as a cause of success at school. That is the error of wrongly assuming that a word which functions legitimately only as a *descriptive* construct must also be able to function as an *explanatory* construct, one that does not just label or describe phenomena but also provides an explanation of them. The effects of conceptual errors of this kind are demonstrated in the following sentences: 'They get good grades because they are successful students', and 'My factory makes lots of goods because it is a productive factory'. Here it is clear that statements that appear to be explanatory are not in fact genuine explanations at all. The reason is that the words appearing after 'because' are descriptive ones ('successful', 'productive') and not explanatory ones. They do not point to actual *reasons* for the phenomena which they ostensibly seem to be explaining. Had the first of the two above sentences been, 'They get good grades because they are diligent students', a genuine explanation would have been provided, because the fact that the students are diligent provides a real reason for them getting good grades.

To return to intelligence, the suggestion is that one of the problems with assuming that measured intelligence levels form a basis for understanding or explaining a child's abilities is that measured intelligence is not really an explanatory concept. In that case, despite appearances which may suggest otherwise, the statement, 'She did well at school because her level of measured intelligence is high', is conceptually more like 'They get good grades because they are successful students', than it is like 'They get good grades because they are diligent students'.

Recall also that an intelligence score is essentially no more than an indication of how someone *performs* at a test. When this is borne in mind, it is apparent that the concept of measured intelligence cannot simultaneously provide both a description of someone's performance and also an explanation of the very same performance it is describing, just as the concept 'fast' cannot be used at the same time to *describe* the movement of a runner and also *explain why* the runner is moving speedily.

The main implication of what I have been saying is simply this: we should not expect too much from measures of tested intelligence. They certainly can be useful, because they can serve as a basis for making practical predictions about the likelihood of children succeeding in the school environment. But if we expect that in addition to providing this kind of information, test scores will also provide a way of explaining *why* some children do better than others, we will be disappointed. Insofar as they can be regarded as providing any kind of explanation at all, that explanation would be something like 'Some children do well because they have what it takes to do well', a statement which adds little if anything to what was previously known.

Broader approaches to intelligence: skills and knowledge

How does intelligence actually contribute to learning at school? We cannot deal with this question unless we are prepared to accept a definition of intelligence that is somewhat broad. Otherwise, it is difficult to progress beyond the rather unhelpful answer, 'It depends on what is meant by 'intelligence'. But if we make the reasonable assumption that the term 'intelligence' refers to a person's intellectual capacities, we can rephrase the above question to read 'How do intellectual capacities contribute...', and providing we can begin to answer that question we can also begin to understand how an absence of intellectual capacities will impede learning.

Intellectual capacities take many different forms, but most of them fall into either of two main categories, first the *knowledge* possessed by a person, and second, the intellectual *skills* the person has gained. In practice, of course, that simple categorisation hides considerable complexity, and some capacities could be regarded as involving both knowledge and skills. For instance, one could equally well say that a child who has learned that two plus two makes four has acquired some knowledge, or that she has gained a skill. And skills vary enormously in their breadth and range, from the most specific ones to multi-purpose skills (or 'strategies') such as rehearsing, to the even broader meta-skills that enable a person to decide, for example, when it is appropriate to make use of a particular specific skill or strategy in order to meet the demands of a particular school task.

But despite the simplification that simply categorising intellectual capacities into knowledge and skills involves, doing so has some useful practical outcomes. Take the case of a child who is failing to learn to read, for example. Instead of having to commence our efforts to understand by simply asking 'What is wrong?', we can raise two specific questions, as follows. First, can we identify knowledge that the child lacks, but which is needed for the child's efforts at reading to be successful. Second, can we identify necessary skills which the child lacks? And if we can do either of these, it may then be possible to make progress by providing instruction aimed at helping the child to acquire the hitherto absent or deficient skill and then finding out whether progress at the broader task is thereby improved.

Here is an illustration of the use of this kind of approach in practice. One pair of psychological researchers were interested in adding to our understanding of why some children experience difficulties at learning to read. These researchers also wished to provide practical help for those children who do have difficulties. They began by looking for signs of particular skills or knowledge that are required by readers but which are lacking in people who fail to learn to read. The ability to read depends upon the reader possessing a number of different mental skills, and also having various kinds of knowledge. The researchers (Bradley and Bryant 1983) found that one skill that is necessary for successful reading but which is not present in some children who are experiencing difficulties in learning to read is the ability to perceive the smallest sound units of language, the phonemes, and to discriminate between them. For example, in order to read, a person needs to be able to discriminate between, say the *b* in *bad* and the *d* in *dad*. If someone cannot do this, reading is virtually impossible for that person.

When young children were given tasks which tested phoneme discrimination by asking the child to say which was the odd word in a list of three words, in which all but one contained a common phoneme (for instance, *dot, bun, dig*), it was found that a child's level of performance at those tasks was a good predictor of the likelihood of the child later experiencing severe difficulties with reading and spelling. It appeared that the researchers had been successful in identifying one particular skill that is necessary for a child to be able to learn to read.

The next stage was to ascertain what would happen when children identified as lacking the ability to identify phonemes and discriminate between them were carefully taught that skill. Would this help them at reading? Bradley and Bryant targeted a group of young children who did poorly at the phoneme test. Some of these children were given special training at that particular skill and the other children formed a control group. The children were tested again later, and it was then found that those children who had failed the phoneme test who had not received the special training were making considerably below average progress but that the children who had been given training were progressing well. In short, in this instance at least, the researchers' approach which involved identifying specific intellectual skills that are absent or defective, and then teaching them to a child proved a highly effective one in practice.

A further illustration of the effectiveness of this kind of approach can be seen in some research investigating the use of rehearsal skills by children at school. Rehearsing is a skill or strategy that is widely used, and it would seem likely, first, that children who do not rehearse in the classroom when it is advantageous to do so will perform badly at learning tasks, and that, second, non-rehearsers who are taught to rehearse will thereby gain a useful advantage, through being able to call upon a skill or strategy that is widely applicable in a variety of learning tasks.

In one study, it was found that when children are told to look at pictures of common objects and to try to remember them, a majority of ten-year-olds and a minority of five-year-olds spontaneously rehearsed the items. (It is easy to tell if young children are rehearsing, because they almost always move their lips when they are doing so.) It was found that, at both ages, those children who did rehearse correctly recalled a considerably larger number of the objects than those who did not rehearse (Flavell *et al.* 1966). This indicates that the absence of a skill or strategy of rehearsing constrained the children's performance at the memory task. If that is the case, then training the non-rehearsers to rehearse should elevate their performance. Accordingly, the children were carefully told how to rehearse (by whispering the names of the objects they were looking at), and found the instructions quite easy to follow. Then they were given a new form of the original task. This time, most of the children did rehearse, and their level of performance at the task improved appreciably. So once more it is clear that children's ability to deal with classroom tasks is reduced when needed intellectual skills are not present, and that when care is taken to ensure that the children do acquire the needed skills, they are considerably more successful.

Finally, consider an instance in which the lack of 'intelligence' that holds children back takes the form of lack of *knowledge*. We tend to regard knowledge as essentially just factual information, and sometimes fail to appreciate how fundamentally a child's reasoning depends upon knowledge. For example, young children's thinking about the concept of being alive often appears to be somewhat confused. A six-year-old may mistakenly think that whilst people possess biological functions such as eating, breathing and sleeping, animals do not. But by ten years of age the child has a much clearer understanding, and appreciates that functions like these are shared with all animals.

What has changed? It is sometimes assumed that there has been some kind of basic change in reasoning processes, but in fact, as Susan Carey (1985) has demonstrated, that assumption is incorrect. She has convincingly shown that the reason for the improved understanding about the concept of being alive, as it relates to animals other than humans, lies essentially in additional biological knowledge which the older children have acquired. Through gaining more information about animals, children build up a body of structured knowledge that makes it possible for them, unlike younger children, to decide whether humans, animals, plants and other objects can or cannot be included under the concept 'alive'. Carey suggests that educators and others are far too prone to assume that older children's increased understanding reflects fundamental developmental changes in the ability to think and reason. She rejects this view, and shows that increases in specific knowledge play a larger role in children's thinking and learning than is generally appreciated. And conversely, lack of knowledge is a very important cause of learning difficulties, resulting in poor performance in the classroom.

Conclusion

In this chapter I have considered some implications of two very different approaches to intelligence. The form of intelligence that is associated with psychometric measurement and intelligence tests is of practical value because useful predictions can be made on the basis of a child's score at an intelligence test. However, this approach makes little contribution towards explaining failure at school, or towards suggesting ways to help children who are experiencing difficulties. A much broader approach, whereby intelligence is seen as taking the form of intellectual skills and knowledge offers certain advantages, because it points to the practical necessity of identifying skills and knowledge which, when absent, may impede a child's progress.

References

Baltes, P. and Reinert, G. (1969) 'Cohort effects in cognitive development in children as revealed by cross-sectional sequences', *Developmental Psychology*, 1, 169–77.

Bradley, I. and Bryant, P.E. (1983) 'Categorizing sounds and learning to read in preschoolers', *Journal of Educational Psychology*, 68, 680–8.

Carey, S. (1985) 'Are children fundamentally different kinds of thinkers and learners than adults?', in S.F. Chipman and J.W. Segal (eds), *Thinking and Learning Skills, Volume 2*. Hillsdale, New Jersey: Erlbaum.

Ceci, S.J. (1990) *On intelligence…more or less: a bio-ecological theory of intellectual development*. Englewood Cliffs, New Jersey: Prentice Hall.

Flavell, J.H., Beach, D.R. and Chinsky, J.M. (1966) 'Spontaneous verbal rehearsal in a memory task as a function of age', *Child Development*, 37, 324–40.

McClelland, D.C. (1973) 'Testing for competence rather than for 'intelligence', *American Psychologist*, 28, 1–14.

Schmidt, W.H.O. (1967) 'Socio-economic status, schooling, intelligence, and scholastic progress in a community in which education is not yet compulsory', *Paedogogica Europa*, 2, 275–86.

Snow, R.E. and Yalow, E. (1982) 'Education and intelligence', pp. 493–585 in R.J. Sternberg (ed), *Handbook of Human Intelligence*. New York: Cambridge University Press.

CHAPTER 5

Confusion and Underfunctioning in Children

Kedar Nath Dwivedi

Children are expected to function, perform, accomplish and achieve at a level consistent with their abilities. If they do not perform or measure up to their expected level, aptitude or standard, they may be considered to be underfunctioning or underachieving. This can result from the influences of a variety of inner and outer factors which may be short term or long lasting. Such variables include the influences of school, neighbourhood, peer group, family and others as outer systemic forces and personality, physiological and other intra psychic inner forces. External factors such as socioeconomic status, school environment, teachers' expectations, cultural variables, family relationships and sibling variables etc. have been clearly demonstrated to impinge upon children's performance (Chopra 1967). Similarly internal factors such as illnesses, nutritional status, intelligence, cognitive style, distractibility and attention, nature and intensity of feelings and self concept as internal factors have also been found to be equally important (Dhaliwal and Saini 1975, Srivastava 1976, 1977).

Lowenstein (1976a and 1976b) emphasises the role of competitive attitude, obsessional personality and impulsive temperament on educational achievement. The importance of perseverance or the tendency to 'follow through' and the detrimental effect of inconsistent or conflicting behavioural standards are also highlighted. Confusion, therefore, is an important mediating process that can appear in and influence a variety of inner and outer interactions – impinging upon one's performance and functioning.

Confusing meaning of the word confusion

Confusion is a rather confusing term with ambiguous meanings. It may mean disorder, perplexity, bewilderment, mixing up of ideas and things, being unclear, mistaking one thing for another and so forth. It implies inappropriate interaction with the environmental stimuli. In medicine or psychiatry when this term is used in a technical sense it means disorientation, incoherent thinking and disjointed, purposeless actions. The person may not know what is going on or where he or she is. Such confusional states may arise gradually and become chronic such as in dementia or may arise suddenly due to brain injury, episodes of circulation problems, epilepsy or infections.

Though rare, the *acute confusional states* with sudden alterations of the mental status have also been found in children. There may be an impairment of cognitive functioning, alteration of consciousness, disturbance of memory functions, behavioural changes, agitation, and superimposed anxiety and frustration. The child may be found walking purposelessly with disturbed memory and awareness of the surroundings. High temperature, infections involving the brain, effect of intoxicants or other toxic drugs, circulation changes, sleep problems, head injury, migraine and epilepsy may be involved (Amit 1988).

In this chapter we need not confine ourselves to this technical (medical or psychiatric) usage of the term 'confusion'. In common usage confusion is implied when a person is not sure about what to do or what to make of something. There may be conflicting demands on such a person or he or she may be exposed to contradictory messages or explanations. There may be a feeling of 'I don't know whether I am coming or going', of ambivalence, doubt, uncertainty or a lack of conviction. Such a person need not have any structural brain dysfunction.

In psychosis or borderline states a person may exhibit extreme and intensely conflicting emotions. But, in ordinary everyday life too, we experience ambivalence and confusion. Some ambivalence may be resolved by making a decision, but not most, because a decision satisfies only one aspect of the ambivalence. Sometimes the one aspect of ambivalence gets split off and projected on to others (see pp.55–56). A proper resolution of ambivalence involves a relationship in which both aspects are fully accepted.

It is not too difficult, even for adults, to confuse the reality with fantasy. In children, it may be more easy. However, if it persists or occurs in a way that is excessive or dysfunctional, it may be seen as a sign of immaturity (Alexander 1991). Similarly, conflict and confusion can arise when the introjects are at odds with the reality (Harper 1991). Our day-to-day life is full of paradoxes, ambiguities, uncertainties and mysterious happenings. Even the most wise and understanding of people often find it difficult to make sense of many things in life. Many people feel confused about the 'circles' in corn fields. Some of the evidence reported regarding 'out of body' experiences, extra-sensory perceptions, telekinesis and UFOs are equally baffling.

Professionals working in the field of mental health often come across people who feel very confused in their relationships with significant others. They feel both being rejected and indulged, wanted and unwanted, praised and punished, hated and loved, and so on. The situations where one finds oneself stuck because of 'Catch 22', 'double bind' or 'heads I win, tails you lose' conditions are equally confusing. For example, when the drastic cuts in the health service began to create unrest, the government blamed the doctors for not working hard enough. However, when an actual study of their working patterns revealed that most doctors were working far beyond what was expected of them, mainly because of inadequate staffing, the government then turned round and blamed the doctors for spending too much health service money by working so hard!

As modern physics is managing to probe into the remotest aspects of nature, the discoveries have become very difficult to comprehend. When we read about things from the point of view of quantum physics and relativity, we learn that we are made up of unsubstantial empty phenomena, a flux of ever-changing quanta of energy creating an illusion of entity, solidity, continuity and agency as 'I' and 'you'. This is like watching a film or cartoon and clearly perceiving motion, continuity, entity and agency though we intellectually know that it is an illusion created by the rapid projection of still pictures or drawings. Our cognitive processes are really extremely fast. This is why the neurophysiologists study electro encephalographic patterns in terms of milliseconds.

These ideas of transitoriness, emptiness or selflessness derived from modern science are most fascinating. However, this knowledge contradicts with the way we behave, experience and feel. We are all conditioned to act with a deep rooted conviction of 'self' and 'others' etc. Even the physicists who find the objective evidence for these truths, think, experience, react and behave in a way that means that these truths do not really apply to them, as if confused.

In the sixth century BC in India Buddha revealed the same truths about change, transitoriness and the illusory processes involved in the creation of a sense of self and others. In Buddhism the cognitive cycle is described to take 17 'khanas' (mind moments), there being 17×10^{21} such khanas in the wink of an eye. Buddha explained that in this subtle sense of misunderstanding the reality, we are all confused until we attain Enlightenment. Thus from the Eastern point of view, all of us except the enlightened ones are in a state of illusion and therefore are confused, including the modern physicists who experience the world in their laboratories and books in one way, but in the rest of their lives in another.

Here, in this chapter, let us not stretch the meaning of the word confusion to this other extreme of *subtle confusion*. However, this does help us to comprehend the complexity of the context in which children grow up and to appreciate their vulnerability to confusion and underfunctioning. Let us now examine some of the external and internal processes in a little more detail as regards their relationship with confusion and underfunctioning.

External variables

Stress and confusion related to school and learning

Even for adults, new and strange situations can produce a great deal of anxiety. Thus joining a course, meeting a group of strangers, entering a strange building, place or culture can make us feel rather nervous. We may become too self conscious and feel rather exposed. We may feel confused about what is really expected of us. In spite of clear instructions we may get lost, going the wrong way, opening the wrong doors, doing the wrong things. It might be linked with our primitive fears of having been projected into a strange, separate existence and of being overwhelmed with the feeling of helplessness, chaos and panic.

Thus, a child in a new and strange situation like joining a school, class or a group may feel confused and bewildered. Because of this feeling of anxiety and confusion, the proceedings may become so meaningless that it is very difficult to pay much attention to the lessons. The impact of strange situations can even threaten to disintegrate the boundaries of the child's ego. Salzberger-Wittenberg et al. (1983) quote the most moving feelings of a child: 'I was terrified of the teacher and the headmaster specially. I thought I might be examined, cut open like an operation and that all the mess inside me will show'.

Some children may learn to play off home against the school. A child may tell the parents that no homework is being set and tell the teacher that there is no place at home to do the homework. Separation between the world at home and that at school can also be very confusing. Many children may be taken aback by the new and unfamiliar demands of activities centred on numeracy and literacy.

Joining late, or a class that is already formed can lead to particular difficulties. The child's day is filled by finding out trivial details like where things are kept, how to get new books, who to go to for help and so forth. The child may become so preoccupied with discerning these invisible rules that it becomes impossible to concentrate on schoolwork. Transfering from a small, friendly primary school to a large comprehensive can also arouse very similar feelings. One may feel lost, rushing up and down the staircases, not knowing which room to go to and getting breathless, anxious and confused. He or she may feel that the true friends are now lost and there are no real friends left. There is a strong craving for familiarity, continuity and a wish to be known.

In addition, there are anxieties about learning, producing work and examinations. Though children are more inclined to a love of truth than are their elders, it is natural to have doubts about one's capacity to fulfil the hope and trust put into one. Thus, beginning school, having a different teacher, moving class, joining a class that is already formed, moving or leaving the school, trigger anxieties about separation, loss, uncertainty, doubt and confusion. Separation can evoke earlier situations of being left by the parent and feeling helpless. The presence of learning difficulties, dyslexia, lower IQ, lack of confidence and poor self esteem further compound the situation. Having to produce work, meeting deadlines and doing well in examinations often trigger anxieties about what one contains inside. Is it all empty or just full of mess? (Salzberger-Wittenberg et al. 1983).

Children who have a past history of emotional deprivation or are emotionally and socially immature for their age are particularly vulnerable. So are children with a history of frequent or emotionally traumatic experiences of separation. Anxieties about attending school can lead not only to educational failures and school refusal, but also to psychosomatic illnesses. Conflicts between feelings of dependence and autonomy and doubts about one's interpersonal abilities can also become major sources of anxiety and confusion. A secure and trusting teaching relationship can 'contain' many of such anxieties and to an extent can also compensate for previous emotional deprivation.

Bollas (1987) describes the concept of *transformational object* deriving from the infant experiencing his mother magically transforming his pain and distress into pleasure and happiness. The helping professionals such as doctors, nurses, teachers and others can therefore easily become objects of such infantile hopes. They are frequently used as containers for excessive mental pain and have to be receptive to this level of emotional communication. Thus teachers can also be subjected to confusing and unreasonable demands by their pupils and find themselves over involved, idealised and denigrated through various psychological means such as projective identification (see below). When such an intolerable intensity of pain or confusion is dumped into a receptive teacher by a pupil, the teacher is then possessed by the feelings of being inadequate, helpless, stupid, frightened and confused. Some teachers are able to contain, digest and utilise these feelings for creative, empathic and helpful purposes while others discharge them in a manner that can be very damaging.

Projective identification

Projective identification is a way of influencing one another outside their conscious awareness. It involves projection into another person of some emotion or quality (for example fragility) which has first been stripped off from its complementary partner (for example strength) and denied in the self. The person into whom this stripped off part is projected can unconsciously identify with what is projected and is induced to think, feel or behave in a certain way (Ogden 1979).

The functions of projective identification can be communicative or defensive (Jureidini 1990). When a baby or a child has feelings that he or she cannot manage by himself or herself, these feelings can be projected into the parent who responds to the child's needs in a way that renders the projected feelings safe. In this way, projective identification can serve as an important communicative function. When projective identification does not succeed as communication it becomes a defensive or destructive means of evacuating one's feelings or controlling others. Adults project into children who are unable to deal constructively with the complex feelings with which they identify. They are left to express the denied parental conflicts in a way that may be damaging to themselves and their family.

Many adults because of their own pathological upbringing may have very unrealistic expectations from children. Sometimes adults who were abused, neglected or made to perform beyond their ability in their childhood end up doing the same to the children they come into contact with either at home or at work. There are others who see in some children certain characters from their own childhood, for example a sibling, parent, grandparent, and unconsciously project a kind of power into the child that is unrealistic and unhelpful. In our clinics we often meet parents who feel pestered and tyrannised by their babies or toddlers. They feel imprisoned and helpless as they see the child having severe temper tantrums or demanding everything the parents have – coffee, toast, biscuit... the lot! (Dwivedi 1984).

It can become very confusing for a child if different family members project different and conflicting aspects into the child, for example, a father might strip off his fragility and deny it within himself and see it in his wife and daughter. Similarly, the mother may strip off her aggressiveness and deny it within herself but project it into her husband and daughter. This leaves the daughter confused with the impossible task of identifying with both sets of projections (fragility and strength).

Confusing effect of dysfunctional families

Children are often parts of confusing organisational structures of family, school, neighbourhood and other institutions and thus experience confusing pressures. A way of understanding organisational structures or the social groups is to use the framework of the General Systems Theory (Beckett 1973). Systems are made up of subsystems and they make up parts of suprasystems, and all of these have their own boundaries. Properties of these boundaries influence the working of the system. A well-functioning system has clear semipermeable boundaries with effective communication and feedback mechanisms between the parts of the system.

Family as a system is made up of marital, parental, sibling and other subsystems and is a part of a suprasystem such as extended family, neighbourhood, village, tribe, church, community and so on. In any system the behaviour of any of its parts influences the entire system as much as the system influences the behaviour of its parts.

Dysfunctional systems usually have boundary problems either due to erosion or diffusion of boundaries, or due to their rigidity. For example, in a family system, when certain parts become polarised or rigid, other parts may either become 'regulators' or 'opt out' altogether (DiNicola 1989).

A family where the two parents do not mesh well together, but can't survive without each other may end up settling in a mutually restrictive relationship with no room for individual growth or development. Such a rigid complementarity can lead to a symmetrical struggle in which they only

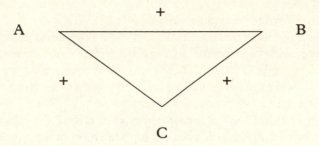

Figure 5.1 Balanced relationships

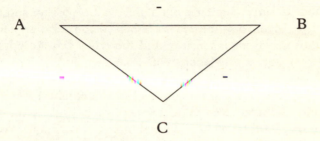

Figure 5.2 Vacuous balance

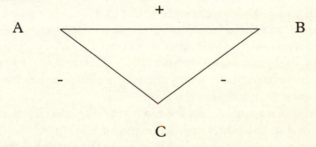

Figure 5.3 Balanced relationships

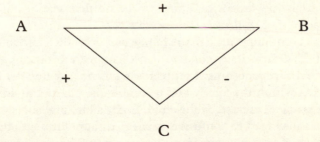

Figure 5.4 Imbalanced relationships

undermine each other. In such an atmosphere the children are needed and used to support the restrictive powers. As children also need the parents there is a subtle but extensive trade off which hinders personal growth and lacks cultivation of kindness and generosity.

As some families can be very afraid of both separation and intimacy, they experience immense conflict in regulating their interpersonal emotional distance (Bying Hall 1980). Therefore a go-between child may be triangulated-in to bring the parents together if they get too far apart or to separate them when they get too close for comfort.

Heider (1946, 1958) proposed a model of attitudinal balance. When all the three parties in a triadic relationship are either in a positive relationship with one another (Figure 5.1) or in a negative relationship with one another (Figure 5.2), they are in a kind of a balanced state, though the later situation is a vacuous balance. Similarly when one dyad is positive and the other two are negative (Figure 5.3) this too is a balanced constellation. However, when only one of the dyads is negative and the other two are positively related (Figure 5.4), the constellation is in a state of imbalance and there is a continuous pressure within the system to shift the relationships. Thus, if A likes both B and C, he expects them to like each other, and if he perceives that B and C dislike each other his perception will be imbalanced. It is therefore very hard for a child to love both parents who hate each other.

In some families the family life is a continuous paradoxical game where the players are fully convinced that as long as they keep playing, they have 'a chance of winning'. Therefore they have to go on trying and trying again. What happens in these families are merely the fragmented effects of moves that the players make. Each move in its turn solicits a counter move in the service of the game and its perpetuation. Hostility, tenderness, coldness, depression, weakness, efficiency, anguish, stolidity, confusion and requests for help are simply moves in the game.

The author of a move has the mistaken belief that he or she dominates the system and has power over it, but he or she is just another one of the slaves of the game who is ensuring its continuation with the opening of a new paradoxical escalation towards linear pseudo-power. They are all struggling to have more power in the effort to define the relationships defined as undefinable (Palazzoli et al. 1980).

Thus a continuing strife in the family can draw the child into the conflict in order to diffuse it. A child may present with educational, emotional, behavioural or psychosomatic problems in an unconscious attempt to diffuse the conflict within the family and to enable the parents to unite in dealing with the problem created by the child. Both failure and success in achieving the results may lead to confusion, anxiety, disappointment and depression, as the effect of such measures is only temporary. The child may have to keep re-doubling his or her efforts to achieve the desired results.

The rigid over-protective and enmeshed family systems where conflicts are avoided and not really resolved, predispose to psychosomatic illnesses (for example asthma, diabetes, anorexia) as a means of diffusing conflict (Minuchin *et al*. 1978).

Palazzoli *et al*. (1980) describe the fascinating case of Hugo, a 13-year-old, obese, feminine boy who presented himself as a moron, keeping his mouth constantly open. He had previously been diagnosed as psychotic and had been treated at a neurological clinic as well as by psychotherapy. After intensive work with the family the Palazzoli team presented the family with the following statement, with amazing results:

> We have been struck by the dedication of Hugo who, without having been asked by anyone, has made his duty to reassure his father. In fact, Hugo has the idea that his father is afraid that his wife will leave him. As a result, he has assumed the responsibility of pinning down his mother by playing the fool and dirtying his pants. To this conclusion, he has generously sacrificed his adolescence, friends, school and sports. In fact we can predict that seeing the apartment in Florence as a threat he will redouble his efforts to be the fool and to be even more dirty, thus pinning down his mother even more. (Palazzoli *et al*. 1980, p.123)

In some families, the child may intervene directly as a mediator repeatedly going from one parent to the other, presenting each other's points of view or by attempting to patch up their differences.

Some children may intervene on behalf of one or the other of the warring parties or behave in such a way as to draw a parent's anger towards themselves. Such mediating and peace-making tasks require a degree of emotional, intellectual and experiential maturity that is hard to come by in a child. Even a skilled family therapy practitioner may be unable to succeed. For a child, therefore, this can be most demanding, emotionally draining and intensely confusing. This increases the risk of an illness turned inward including psychosomatic illnesses such as eating disorder abdominal pain and school refusal.

Some children are unable to tolerate the emotional roller coaster and are unable to develop a personal sense of limits and ways of coping with frustration and other intense feelings. They opt out, rebel and escape the family increasing the risk of an illness turned outward, such as running away, delinquency and so forth (DiNicola 1989).

Problems due to erosion and restructuring of boundaries, in the form of new alliances and coalitions, lead to a confusing and dysfunctional family system. For example, the erosion of the boundary of the parental subsystem and formation of a strong alliance between a child and one of the parents leads to a situation where the parent–child dyad is more powerful than the parent–parent dyad. Such a dynamic of hierarchical reversal is known to lead to problems of substance abuse and conduct disorder in children. In a family with elements of violence as well the child may even feel compelled to miss school or stay up all night to protect a parent or sibling from violent abuse.

Gelinas (1983) has vividly described families in which a child (usually a girl) comes to function as a parent doing cooking, cleaning, laundry and looking after children and adults. As she grows up she is drawn to men who are dependent, insecure, emotionally immature, narcissistic and even socio-pathic, getting involved in petty crimes. Such a couple, i.e. a caring woman and a dependent man tend to get on extremely well together until the arrival of a child. As the mother has already been a surrogate mother to her own parents, siblings and to her husband, she now feels emotionally depleted and exhausted. When she feels preoccupied with the emotional needs of her child and leans on her husband, instead of caring for him, the husband feels abandoned, having to compete with his child. He there fore escalates his demands for attention and affection.

With the arrival of more children and the availability of an older child, the mother is able to give up some of her responsibilities. This older child slowly assumes various responsibilities out of her loyalty to her mother. Thus this process of 'parentification' is transmitted from generation to generation, leading to inappropriate (including sexual) relationships between father and his already parentified daughter. The psychological consequences of paren-tification on the child include an over development of the care-taking function with a heightened sense of responsibility and guilt and an under development of self-esteem, ego-strength and social skills. Such a person becomes unassertive and passive and is easily paralysed and exploited in relationships. She becomes overwhelmed by her own children and ends up parentifying them.

At times the three generational conflict leads to an alliance between the grandparents and the grandchild, thus undermining the authority of the parents. A similar situation may arise at school or a children's home where the authority of the key staff may be undermined by someone from a tier above.

In a reconstituted family, the confusion may arise as the stepfather may be seen as the head of the family and therefore very powerful but not being the natural father may render him the least powerful status. In a situation like this it becomes very difficult for a child to adjust to such a confusing nullification of structural hierarchies.

In a single-parent family the enmeshed (over-close) relationship between the parent and the child may make the child perform the role of the missing parent. A child who is over protected and infantilised by an anxious and enmeshed parent may find it very difficult to cope with the roughness of life at school, thus leading to school refusal.

Separation, divorce, custody and access disputes can further intensify the conflicts of loyalty. The child may find himself or herself confused trying to adjust to the increasingly differing roles, values, rituals, expectations and atmospheres of two different sets of families.

Confusing communications

As there are various modes of communication (e.g. play, non-play, fantasy, sacrament, metaphor), even in animals there appears to be an exchange of signals which identify certain behaviours (such as play). Thus, according to the Theory of Logical Types, there is a discontinuity between a class and its members (Whitehead and Russell 1910). However, in our day-to-day communications this discontinuity is often breached and leads to confusion and even relationship problems (Bateson *et al.* 1956).

Some people can even deliberately falsify these mode identifiers, for example artificial laughter, crocodile tears, manipulative friendliness, kidding and confidence tricks. Thus confusion can easily result if incorrect communicational modes are assigned either by the sender or the receiver.

In human communication there is supposed to be a congruity and complementarity between digital and analogic components, i.e., the message and the way it is delivered. The digital aspects are the precise and versatile verbal contents capable of abstraction and logic. The analogic aspects are the non-verbals which may be imprecise and ambiguous but are usually more effective and powerful. Confusion results from a lack of congruity between digital and analogic communication.

Much of what takes place between human beings can also be described in terms of communications and meta communications. The behavioural messages or face-to-face communications that make up the bulk of human interactions can be included under communication. Most of this is verbal in nature and embraces the actual demands and requests that people make of one another, for example 'please take out the rubbish'. The meta-communication level, on the other hand, operates non-verbally and consists of messages that are more difficult to pin down. These may be hidden, coercive threats which are implied rather than clearly spelt out, for example, someone could be asked to take out the rubbish in such a way which implies that if he didn't, his life would be made very miserable. These meta cues are hard to perceive because they are often transmitted below the threshold of perception through the feeling tones of pride, despair, blame and so on. Family life is very powerful in giving such contextual meta cues. A mismatch between the two (communication and meta communication) can be very confusing.

Though actions speak louder than words, words can be used to disqualify actions and vice versa. Some parents are very keen to emphasise that they love their children fairly equally. However, they often act lovingly towards one child and attackingly towards the other. They also confide in one about what the other one does wrong. Thus, whatever is said to the other child, the hidden meta communication is 'You are rubbish'. Being an indirect communication, it is hard for anyone to recognise and resist. Thus it stings more than the words can console and the recipient often does not know what really hit him or her.

Dysfunctional families are in an excellent position to create confusion through the incongruity between structure and the contents. They can sabotage one's conscious ways of thinking via a discrepancy between what is said (the contents) and how it is framed (the interpersonal structural context in which the content occurs). For example, the parents may preach to their children about gender equality but when the mother starts to work, the father can not stop feeling badly hurt.

In a *double bind,* for example, one is cornered from all the three sides. It is like a Zen master teaching his disciple the principle of unreality, If you say that this stick is real, I will hit you with it; and if you think that this stick is unreal I will hit you with it; if you don't say anything I will hit you with it'. Thus, double bind is a package of confusing communication that puts the receiver in a very difficult situation.

It is a bit like giving two shirts to a child and when he tries on any one of them he is told 'Don't you like the other one, son?'. One is subjected to two contradictory negative injunctions and is prohibited from escaping from either (Bateson *et al.* 1956). One of the injunctions is usually verbal and the other one non-verbal, for example a child may be told, 'If you don't do such and such I will punish you or withdraw my love'. At the same time the parent may non-verbally punish the child or withdraw love even when the child does exactly the things that the parents ask him to do. A mother might tell her child that she wouldn't like him if he didn't give her a cuddle, and when he tries to cuddle her she pushes him away.

Double binds have a very confusing effect on people. Even the development of schizophrenia has been attributed to a repeated application of double binds in many cases. It can also lead to amnesia. There is an interesting account of an experiment conducted by Erikson who arranged a seminar so as to have a young chain smoker sit next to him, but to be without cigarettes (Bateson *et al.* 1956). Members in the neighbouring seats were already briefed so that each time Erikson turned to offer the young man a cigarette, he was interrupted by a question by a neighbour and had to turn away, 'inadvertently' withdrawing the cigarette. This happened so many times that the smoker, when questioned on another day, could not even remember the incident. Thus, this double bind sequence led to amnesia and also a change of attitude from 'He doesn't give' to 'I don't want' (like the sour grapes).

A communication can be 'clear' or 'masked', 'direct' or 'indirect'. For example, a husband, who has come home and is reading his newspaper, may be feeling angry with his wife who has been on the telephone for a long time. He is reading his newspaper and his little daughter walks in with a running nose. He may react in several ways. He may shout at his daughter to wipe her nose. This would be an 'indirect' expression of his anger towards his wife. On the other hand he might express it directly to his wife but in a masked way, for example 'What the hell is going on in this house?' But, if he is direct and clear, he would communicate to his wife exactly what he feels and why.

Palazzoli *et al.* (1980) describe families in which the transactions are such that the family members are continually dealing with conflictual levels in messages they receive. They may also find that their responses are seen as 'wrong' by others, thus if one person says something there is always another who is ready to make him understand that he should have put it in a slightly different way. If he tries to be helpful he gets the message that it doesn't happen often enough or is not good enough, implying that he has been of no help at all. If he makes a decision the others doubt his motives but if he refuses to decide then the others see him as dependent. Thus there is a strong feeling that he has never quite done the right thing without its ever being said clearly as to what he should do, which will be seen as right.

One's identity is influenced by the way others react and communicate to a person. One can convey to a person a sense of who he is, in addition to what he's supposed to do. Sometimes such identity messages are contradictory. Like the double bind, *double description* may involve one message delivered clearly but the other one in the form of a meta communication. For example, a father may radiate with pride when he announces that his child looks exactly like his aunt or reminds him of his ex-wife, but the fact may be that his aunt is a prostitute and his ex-wife is in jail.

Family life is like a movie where one thing leads to another. Things that happen are usually responses to what has happened in the past. If these responses are not seen in their proper context, they could be perceived as proofs of inherent problems within the individual (e.g. sulking, temper tantrums). For example, a child may be presented as being too quiet or selectively mute. However, the fact may be that he is silenced each time he opens his mouth. Someone may ask him to speak up, to remove his hand from his mouth, to move his foot from a certain place, to look in a certain direction, or to use or refrain from using certain words. He may be quickly corrected or proved a liar or forgetful. Such interventions when repeated frequently can drive him easily into perpetual silence.

Another way of creating confusion is to *rapidly shift from subject to subject*. One can also shift from one hierarchical position to another. A teenager may be infantilised in the light of his past failures, but may also be made to feel as a rescuer in the light of parental illness or any other problem. For example, the parent may describe the son's school work, creating a context where he appears as an utter failure and then quickly jump to describe the daughter's illness, creating a context where the son appears as a strong support to the family. However the rapid shifting of contexts evoking conflicting positions can easily make him confused and drive him crazy.

Thus there are many manoeuvres to confuse communicational transactions. This may be in the order of a partial or total disqualification of the message, side-stepping of the main issue, change of subject and even amnesia. According to Palazzoli *et al.* (1980), the supreme manoeuvre as seen in schizophrenic transactions is that of disconfirmation. Such a response is neither a confirmation nor a rejection, rather it is a cryptic and incongruent response which basically states 'I don't notice you, you are not here, you don't exist'. It becomes more subtle and more deadly when the very author of the message qualifies himself as non-existent, 'I'm not really here, I don't exist in the relationship with you'.

Confusion and trance

Confusion is an important ingredient in the induction of trance (Ritterman 1983). The first ingredient is the establishment of an intense rapport to enable the individual to shut out all other external stimuli as peripheral or extraneous to the job at hand and to let the rest of the world blur and haze and disappear. The second ingredient is the shifting of attention inwards. A hypnotist may ask a subject to gaze at an object outside and then start referring to the tiring eyelids. Thus, the attention is shifted inwards. As the subject attends to internal relevancies of his own associative context, with heightened concentration, he becomes so absorbed with the inner reality that it is experienced as if it were an outer reality, complete with the emotional and psychophysiological power of a real life event.

Having established an intense rapport and secured the subject's sustained inward focus, the hypnotist in the third step de-potentiates the habitual or conscious ways the person thinks through his problems. The hypnotist may produce confusion and doubt by using the fact that the subject will close his eyes when he is tired of looking at an object. The subject is suggested to doubt his eyelid control and his ability to open his eyes once they are closed. This sense of doubt and confusion can be intensified by repeatedly challenging the subject to test things out. These manoeuvres distract and destroy the subject's ordinary sequences of thinking and introduce doubts about the way he ordinarily sees things or otherwise disorient or confuse him. At the moment of uncertainty a wish for clarity is activated and the likelihood of responsiveness to a suggestion is strongly increased. Thus, the fourth step is to initiate an unconscious search by evoking certain words or events which may have particular implications. Both pathological and healing responses can thus be induced by activating the unconscious mind to reconcile and synthesise contradictory or confusing messages into a meta message in its own unique way.

Family processes and trance

A hypnotist is not the only person capable of making suggestions affecting reactions typically considered automatic. Like a hypnotist, family members can also transmit suggestions to individuals within the family (Ritterman 1983). As family members are emotionally and financially interconnected to each other they are already in an intense relationship, and organise each other's fantasies and experiences. As children we can carry a flexible and playful boundary between the inner and the outer reality, and can enjoy the company of playmates who are invisible to others. The sounds of our parents and others experienced during childhood do deeply reverberate within us. The family members can easily share in the re-vivification of various events, complete with special smells, sights, laughters and chills.

As confusion disrupts the conscious, habitual, ordinary, sequential, linear or secondary processes of thinking and reacting, this activates unconscious, primary, lateral processes of thinking and reacting as they happen in dreaming, symptom formation or healing. Similarly, family life is full of confusing processes, as already mentioned.

Simple words like loneliness, cowardice and sacrifice, though used in an ordinary sense in family conversation, can direct a search for clarity by guiding the unconscious processes, and assume intense personal significance to reconcile multiple and incongruous messages into a meta message. For example, a decision by a teenager to stay at home and attempt suicide may reconcile the contradictory messages of being a rescuer and a 'baby'. In a state of trance, the mind is unconsciously searching for clarity in the midst of confusion and is ready for any direct or indirect suggestion leading to healing or to symptom formation.

Cross cultural confusion

Cultural values constitute an active dynamic force in most institutional functions and family processes. The values can be very different between different cultures and ethnic groups. For example, *independence* is a cherished ideal in the Western culture and is held as a goal of personal growth with an excessive emphasis on its early training. Parents may be at pains to make their children independent as quickly as possible. When they grow old they find that their children have already become so independent that they cannot really be depended upon. In contrast, the Eastern culture places more emphasis upon *dependability* than on independence and the parents are usually at pains to ensure that the children grow up in an atmosphere where parents are very dependable and are a model of dependability. There is a great deal of sensual physical closeness, common sleeping arrangements and immediate gratification of physical emotional needs prolonging their babyhood. Transitional objects (and commercial toys) assume very little importance as the mothering person should be always available to alleviate any separation anxiety (Roland 1980).

Another feature of the traditional Eastern culture is the suppression of narcissistic *individuality* by heightening the sensitivity to each other's feelings, so, as children grow up they learn to communicate in such a way that avoids direct confrontation, loss of face and hurting of feelings. Instead, there is more use of indirect means such as references to folk parables or sayings to communicate the real issues in a non-hurtful and constructive manner. In the Western culture, however, the direct, clear and *open expression* of one's feelings, opinions and views are highly valued. Thus the cultural differences in the conditioned habitual modes of communication and expression of feelings can lead to serious problems arising due to inter-cultural misunderstanding and confusion.

Even the most well-meaning professionals brought up in the Western culture are often misguided as they struggle to 'liberate' children and adolescents from families of Eastern culture from their so-called 'oppressive structures'. These attempts are usually driven by subconscious racist assumptions about the superiority of Western child-rearing methods and pathologising of non-Western lifestyles. The Asian families may therefore be seen, just as Jewish immigrant families were criticised earlier this century, as being too self contained, constricting and not being prepared to adjust to British life. Schools seldom regard Asian culture and languages as valuable enough to be taught in school (Littlewood and Lipsedge 1989).

Because of such a gulf, the entry to school for an Asian child can be a very traumatic experience. The potential for confusion and contradictory expectations can continue to be serious and even grow worse. The distress caused by such a confusing pressure is then usually explained away by popular stereotypical cultural explanations. In such a climate the young Asians may present problems to white professionals in a way in which experience has told them elicits a sympathetic response, for example fear of arranged marriages, generation gap or complaint of ill treatment (Ahmed 1986).

The nature of relationships in traditional Eastern families are well defined, preventing the need for a power struggle. However, the processes of immigration, stressful life events, power imbalances and infusion of Western cultural influences on individuals can cause confusion leading to struggles for power within the family relationships. Moreover, older members speaking their native language and younger members speaking only English may lead to a lack of a common language by which they can communicate or share emotionally significant viewpoints. This can become a breeding ground for inappropriate, invalid or paradoxical communicative exchanges and confusion (Ho 1987).

Internal variables

Developmental perspective

Children get confused when they are expected to perform roles that are too big for the resources they have. People or situations may make demands upon them which may be beyond their ability. These demands may be made unwittingly because of certain circumstances of loss, catastrophe or disaster. Sometimes the adults responsible for them are unable to appreciate the cognitive, emotional and behavioural limitations of children or the differences in the assumptive worlds of children and adults. Significance of proper school curricula and teaching methods commensurate with the developmental stage of the child is dealt with in detail elsewhere.

Children's cognitive structures take time to mature. Piaget (Sigel 1964) describes the following cognitive developmental stages.

1. Sensory motor stage (0–2 yrs) leading to the achievement of object attainment or sameness.
2. Pre-operational thought (2–7 yrs).
   a) pre-operational phase (2–4 yrs). Egocentric thinking and thinking in terms of single features.
   b) intuitive phase (4–7 yrs). Attainment of conservation.
3. Concrete operations (7–11 yrs). Logical, hierarchical and serial thinking.
4. Formal operations (11–15 yrs). Abstract thinking and use of concepts and hypotheses.

Because of the maturational limitations the thinking and understanding of children in certain circumstances and those of emotions and motives can be rather confusing (Harter 1983).

Pre-operational children are unable to acknowledge mixed feelings. It is also difficult for young children to realise that people can hide their inner or true feelings or can put their feelings out of their own awareness. It is only during adolescence that one appreciates that some feelings can also be unconscious.

Between 5 and 9 years, children are able to see people as intentional beings with motives behind their behaviours. Later (7–12 years) they begin to appreciate that the motives can be concealed from others. Between 10–15 years they realise that it is possible to have mixed motives, and only when they become adolescents are they able to integrate conflicting motives (e.g. ambivalence) and recognise unconscious motives.

Because of a magical type of thinking a young child may confuse his thoughts with reality. He may feel that things in his environment have happened because he has wished, feared or thought about them. Many children, therefore, can feel totally responsible for parental break-ups or various accidents, losses or disasters around them.

Because of egocentric thinking, young children tend to project the cause of their own emotions on to others. If a child gets upset by losing a toy or because of not being able to watch a particular television programme, he feels that the same must be true for his parents. Young children also feel responsible for others emotions. Between the ages of 4 and 11 years feelings of responsibility for parental anger is extremely common. It is only later that children realise that their parents and significant others can have an emotional life outside their own (Harter 1983).

Confusion between feelings

It is very easy to be confused about one's emotions. One may misunderstand excitement as anger or desire as fear. One reason for this kind of confusion is the familiarity with certain types of emotions due to their frequency and unfamiliarity with others due to their rarity. Some children may not have consciously experienced love and comfort to know it when they have it. Confusion can also arise due to cognitive distortions so common in states of emotional arousal. Thus, because of the physiological changes, proper thinking and judgement may be impaired, leading to misattribution.

In addition, the residues of excitation from the preceding emotional state enter into (i.e. transfer into) and intensify the subsequent emotional state. Similarly, excitation from factors other than the predominant stimulation can also transfer and intensify the emotional reaction through misattribution. This leads to an enormous potential for confusion and overlap between various feelings and emotions, such as fear, anger, violence, sex, excitement, anxiety and so forth (Zillman 1984).

Overanxious Disorder

Confusion and underfunctioning are often present in Overanxious Disorder. According to the DSM (1987), there is a constant state of tension and worry related to a need for reassurance in Overanxious Disorder. Such children have an intense need to be accepted by authority figures and try to strive for perfection, thus generating intense pressure upon themselves. They are so desperate to achieve that they agonise over homework, only to find that it is impossible to concentrate (Mandel and Marcus 1988).

The Dodson Law (Yerkes and Dodson 1908) describes the relationship between motivation (anxiety) and learning (performance) as an inverted U-shaped curve. There is an optimal level of drive for each kind of task which energises the individual and helps to improve performance. Children with high-anxiety score significantly lower in class tests than those with low anxiety, as high anxiety tends to impair their problem solving ability and to interfere with complex learning processes leading to maladaptive responses (Lokare 1984).

According to Mandel and Marcus (1988) the overanxious children may in fact feel extremely ambivalent regarding the issue of achievement. They may wish to achieve for their significant others (e.g. parents, teachers) but this may also mean 'giving in' to the demands of the powerful and feared person. Thus, in a passive-aggressive way, underachievement may become a weapon to punish the persons in authority, i.e., by withholding what they really want. However, the resentment and anger aspect of the ambivalence may be split off from consciousness and the child may not even be aware of it. He is only aware of the need for approval, thus leading to striving for perfection and unwittingly undermining the same.

Anxious reactions in the child are also more likely if the general level of anxiety in the family is very high, leading to a circular effect. Moreover, many of the children's emotional experiences are about their parents, since they are among the few people with whom young children have most contact.

Parents, like other human beings, may find it hard to see the impact of their behaviour on those they love most. Such a defence mechanism (to fail to recognise what one cannot bear to see) is very common. It is also very distressing for parents to be exposed to the suffering of their children (Elmhurst 1984).

Motivation problem

Mandel and Marcus (1988) describe the category of academic problem underachiever. These are normal, well-adjusted children with good ego strength and full control of their emotions. They rarely express strong feelings either of elation or unhappiness. They have paucity of self-concepts and avoid any meaningful introspection. They get on well at home except when the parents push them to achieve. They are easily distracted while doing their homework, and are often described as lazy, unmotivated, 'could do better, only if tried harder'. They float through life without a sense of purpose and are always making different excuses, promising to do better 'next time', which never comes. They come to believe their own excuses, e.g. 'Good grades are not everything in life'. They avoid personal responsibility and have to be continually reminded to tidy up the room, finish the homework, do the laundry or the washing up, take out the rubbish and so on.

Mandel and Marcus believe that their 'lack of motivation' is, in fact, an unconscious, highly motivated choice. Because success brings with it a lifetime burden of additional expectations and responsibilities, they are afraid of achievement and success. However, they hide this real motivation (of avoiding success) from their own awareness, thus creating a depressing and confusing puzzle both to them and to those around them.

Narcissistic disorder and confusing injunctions

Individuals with narcissistic personality disorder tend to be rather seductive, articulate, grandiose and scornful of others. They are often very enthusiastic about ideologies. However, they are covertly doubt-ridden, envious, bored, incapable of genuine love, corruptible and forgetful. They appear impressively knowledgeable, but their knowledge is often limited to trivia (headline intelligence). The details (especially names) are usually forgotten and the capacity for learning new skills is rather impaired. They are fond of short cuts to acquisition of knowledge. They also have an ego-centric perception of reality and tend to change their meanings when facing a threat to self esteem. They are rather self-opinionated, decisive and are capable of being intensely enraged (Akhtar 1989, DSM 1987).

Personality disorders are often recognisable by adolescence or even earlier and continue throughout most of adult life. The grandiose sense of self in children with narcissistic disorder is reflected at school where the child gives up putting effort in if there is no immediate success. The child gets either very good or very bad grades. Kernberg (1989) describes this strange and confusing situation as follows.

> A frequent and characteristic symptom suggesting Narcissistic Personality Disorder is the presence of *severe learning problems*. Despite their superior intelligence, these children can fail grades, their school performance can be erratic and they rarely finish their homework. This is a characteristic expression of the grandiose self in children. Moreover, teachers report how these youngsters can be arrogant and haughty. Indeed these children think nobody is entitled to tell them what to do. (Emphasis mine)

Apart from problems of functioning at school and lack of joy in their learning experiences, these children according to Kernberg (1989) also have a driven quality about their work and in certain areas they attain outstanding achievements. They work for admiration but admiration does not really touch the core of their selves. They also tell tales and have an intense envy, thus alienating their peers. They may choose friends who are 'freaks' or ugly, though they themselves may be very appealing and charismatic. They are preoccupied with self image, spend a lot of time looking at themselves in the mirror, treating their body as their double self, providing sustenance. They also have a tendency to avoid eye contact and get easily bored even with new toys. When defeated in games they can have terrible temper tantrums. When frustrated they react with intense narcissistic rage.

According to Grunberger (1975) a narcissist is like a foetus that receives everything but has to give nothing in return. But in the outside world there is an unavoidable human necessity for emotional dependence upon others. A narcissist has a chronic, intense sense of entitlement, selfishness, mistrust, exploitativeness, coercion, possessiveness, excessive demandingness, ruthlessness towards others and marked lack of empathic understanding. There is a heightened sense of vanity and 'God complex' (Jones 1964) with excessive self absorption and a driven quality, sometimes rewarded by fame and leadership.

There is very little reciprocity in a relationship with these children as they are always the receivers, while others are always givers. The parents contribute to this situation by continually giving in to the child in a covertly hostile way in order to appease his or her narcissistic rages. As the parents do not enjoy caring for such a child and behave as if manipulated, coerced and emotionally flat, this in turn leads to the child being caught in a parasitic relationship with them, devoid of warmth, gratitude or respect.

Narcissistic love itself arises as a defensive response to excessive frustrations and disappointments in early childhood, especially due to the fact that the mothering person is not available to authenticate the child's experiences. The growing child has a need for 'mirroring' by and 'merger' with the mothering person, i.e. to feel that 'I am perfect and you admire me' (mirroring) and 'you are perfect and I am a part of you' (merger) (Greenberg and Mitchell 1983). Failure of the mothering person to empathise with and respond to the growing child's needs of grandiose exhibitionism by mirroring (idealisation), and merger, leads to the hungry child turning away from the mothering person to manufacture its own narcissistic structures to meet these needs (Cohen 1990).

The mothering person's own unconscious needs and fantasies make the child become part of her self, especially those aspects that she did not dare express except vicariously through the child. By means of verbal and non-verbal behaviours, she transmits in innumerable gross and subtle ways her double-binding' message to the child, 'You may go through the motions of separating from me and appear accomplished and successful, but only if everything you achieve is ultimately in relation to me' (Rinsley 1989). This leads to a degree of individuation without adequate separation, the condition of a pathologically pseudo-mature child.

Kernberg (1989) describes the mechanisms leading to such a disorder in children of divorced, adoptive, narcissistic or abusive parents. Narcissistic parents have a tendency to de-personification, i.e. treat the child as a surrogate figure (for example sibling, spouse, infantile baby or parent). A parentified child may function as an ideal self for the parents. The anorexic children behave as appendages, usually of their mothers. Adopted children may distrust for having been rejected and may have a compensatory sense of entitlement to choose his or her parents. The child with a divorced parent may be coerced 'to be' the offspring of the rejected parent. The abused child may be expected to behave like a little adult. Thus in various ways, the double binding influences may contribute to the induction of narcissism.

Oppositional defiant disorder and conduct disorder (and confused attachment and play)

Children with *oppositional defiant disorder* can be very argumentative especially with authority figures. They tend to be actively defiant, angry, quick tempered, bitter, vindictive, spiteful, blaming, coarse and vulgar (DSM, 1987). They give others (for example parents, teachers) a great deal of trouble, as if they get immense satisfaction from making life difficult for others. In spite of negative consequences, they maintain such behaviours in a rather compulsive way. If an authority figure invites such a child, even politely, to do something, the child usually refuses to do it or starts arguing. But the child may happily do that activity another time, if suggested by a like-minded friend (Mandel and Marcus 1988).

However, these children do not violate others' rights, and in fact, may be altruistic towards the 'victims' of the system. A child with conduct disorder, on the other hand, has all the features of the above and also violates others' rights. There may also be present certain features of narcissistic disorder. There is a pervasive impulsiveness in which the needs of the moment must immediately be satisfied.

Willock (1990) highlights the hidden play element in children with conduct disorder who can be destructive, aggressive and defiant with problems of running away. This arises due to the arrested and distorted development of interactive play at various stages. The normal developmental line of certain interactive play to master the separation anxiety has been described by Kleeman (1967, 1973). Between the ages of four to six months, parents usually initiate a game like 'peek a boo' which has a sequence of optimal frustration and reward. The baby is then able to actively initiate such games between the ages of six and eleven months. As the child gains autonomy, his or her confidence grows, that despite separation the primary object is still there and reunion will occur. Such a confidence and trust is also achieved by a sequence of play proceeding from active 'peek a boo' to object tossing, being chased, early hide and seek, the bye bye gesture, verbal bye bye and other uses of language.

Playing of such developmentally important games to resolve developmental conflicts and crises requires an engagement of sustained and active interest of the care givers. When this does not happen adequately, the developmental line described above is distorted and interfered with as the child feels unable to engage a sustained and loving concern of care givers and begins to feel that no-one really cares about him or her and is driven to devise strategies to force care takers to become involved. Confusion arises due to the deep longing for such crucial playful relationships on the one hand and the fear of such wishes on the other. The child deals with this intense conflict by creating situations whereby he or she might be chased and held, but simultaneously denies any wish for such interactions.

If the child's care givers can be engaged in chasing and holding in a therapeutic manner the child's dangerous, defiant, destructive run away behaviours gradually take the form of legitimate play of 'chase me' hiding and 'hide and seek'. Unfortunately most care givers are overwhelmed by the destructive aspect of this acting out and are unable to see the hidden play element of it. Even if they do see it, they find it very difficult to put up with such a prolonged and dangerous acting out, thus the child's strategy of forcing adults to be interested often ends up backfiring. Even those who have some commitment end up giving up in a fury of frustration and despair because of the prolonged nature of these distorted behaviours. Thus such a useful device, designed to master separation anxiety, when mal-developed, leads to the child being expelled from school, home and other caring agencies and to the escalation, and graduation into delinquent behaviour where only police and jails can be counted to 'chase' and 'hold'.

Mandel and Marcus (1988) highlight the tendency of these children to explain their situation in long, involved and complex stories. Such explanations with details about who said what, when and to whom, become so *confusing* that it becomes impossible to get a clear picture of the story.

Aggression can also be seen as a variant of attachment behaviour (Mawson 1987). Attachment behaviour is aimed at maintaining proximity or contact with attachment objects. We know that babies from the very beginning are stimulation seeking. Initially it is non-specific, but gradually they begin to repeatedly approach particularly stimulating objects which leads to attachment or bonding. This helps to form and maintain a cognitive map of the sensory characteristics of the attachment object. During periods of stress, there is an intensified need to have body contact and to get in touch with such soothing objects, so when we are faced with disasters, loss or stress, our typical response is to seek the proximity of familiar persons or environments, even though that very person may be the cause of the stress. If the attachment figures are either unavailable or rejecting, the stimulation-seeking behaviour then becomes rather generic or even indiscriminate. And the desire to 'reach out and touch someone' can become so intense that it can become disguised, confused, violent, harmful and even fatal (Mawson 1987).

Identity confusion

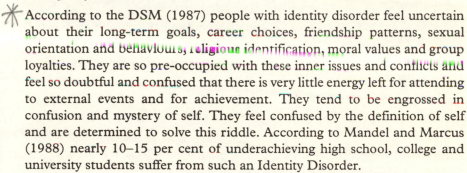

According to the DSM (1987) people with identity disorder feel uncertain about their long-term goals, career choices, friendship patterns, sexual orientation and behaviours, religious identification, moral values and group loyalties. They are so pre-occupied with these inner issues and conflicts and feel so doubtful and confused that there is very little energy left for attending to external events and for achievement. They tend to be engrossed in confusion and mystery of self. They feel confused by the definition of self and are determined to solve this riddle. According to Mandel and Marcus (1988) nearly 10–15 per cent of underachieving high school, college and university students suffer from such an Identity Disorder.

Acknowledgement

I am very grateful to Lesley Curtress for typing the manuscript again and again and to my colleagues, Peter Harper and Richard Alexander and my sons, Amitabh and Rajaneesh, for their valuable suggestions.

References

Ahmed, S. (1986) Cultural racism in work with Asian women and girls, in S. Ahmed, J. Cheetham and J. Small (eds) *Social Work with Black Children and their families*. London: B.T. Batesford.

Akhtar, S. (1989) Narcissistic personality disorder: descriptive features and differential diagnosis, *Psychiatric Clinics of North America*. 12, 3: 671–94.

Alexander, R. (1991) Personal Communication.

Amit, R. (1988) Acute Confusional State in childhood, *Child's Nervous System*. 4: 255–8.

Bateson, G., Jackson, D.D., Haley, J. and Weakland, J. (1956) *Behavioural Science*. 1: 251–64.

Beckett, J.A. (1973) General systems theory, psychiatry and psychotherapy, *International Journal of Group Psychotherapy.* 23: 292–305.

Bollas, C. (1987) *The shadow of the object: psychoanalysis of the unthought known.* London: Free Association Books.

Bying Hall, J. (1980) 'Symptom bearer as marital distance regulator: clinical implications', *Family Process.* 19: 355–65.

Chopra, S.L. (1967) A Comparative study of achieving and underachieving students of high intellectual ability, *Exceptional children.* 33, 9: 631–4.

Cohen, M. (1990) Narcissistic organisations and sexual identity – a clinical presentation, *Journal of Child Psychotherapy.* 16 1: 115–26.

Dhaliwal, A.S. and Saini, B.S. (1975) A study of the prevalence of academic underachievement among high school students, *Indian Educational Review.* 10 1: 90–109.

(DSM) Diagnostic and Statistical Manual for Mental Disorders (3rd edn – revised) (1987) Washington DC: American psychiatric association.

DiNicola, V.F. (1989) The child's predicament in families with a mood disorder, *Psychiatric Clinics in North America.* 12, 4: 933–949.

Dwivedi, K.N. (1984) Mother–baby psychotherapy, *Health Visitor.* 57, 10: 306–7.

Elmhurst, S.I. (1984) A psychoanalytic approach to anxiety in childhood, in V.P. Varma (ed.) *Anxiety in Children.* London: Croom Helm, pp.1–14.

Gelinas, D.J. (1983) 'The persisting negative effects of incest, *Psychiatry* 46: 312–32.

Greenberg, J.R. and Mitchell, S.A. (1983) *Object Relations in Psychoanalytic Theory.* Cambridge, Mass.: Harvard University Press.

Grunberger, B. (1975) *Narcissism: psychoanalytic essays.* New York: International University Press.

Harper, P. (1991) Personal Communication.

Harter, S. (1983) Cognitive developmental considerations in the conduct of play therapy, Chapter 5 in C.E. Schaffer and K.J. 0'Connor (eds) *Handbook of Play Therapy.* New York: John Wiley.

Heider, F. (1946) Attitudes and cognitive organisation, *Journal of Psychology.* 21: 107–12.

Heider, F. (1958) *The Psychology of Interpersonal Relations.* New York: John Wiley.

Ho, M.K. (1987) *Family Therapy with Ethnic Minorities.* London: Sage Press.

Jones, E. (1964) The god complex, in: E. Jones (ed.) *Essays in Applied Psychoanalysis (Vol 2).* New York: International University Press, pp.244–65.

Jureidini, J. (1990) Projective identification in general Psychiatry, *British Journal Psychiatry.* 157: 656–60.

Kernberg, P.F. (1989) Narcissistic personality disorder in childhood, *Psychiatric Clinics of North America.* 12, 3: 671–94.

Kleeman, J.A. (1967) 'The peek-a-boo game, Part I: its origins, meanings, and related phenomena in the first year', *Psychoanalytic Study Child.* 22: 239–73.

Kleeman, J.A. (1973) 'The peek-a-boo game: its evolution and associated behaviour, especially bye-bye and shame expression during the second year', *Journal American Academy of Child Psychiat.* 12: 1–23.

Littlewood, R. and Lipsedge, M. (1989) *Aliens and alienists: ethnic minorities and psychiatry.* London: Unwin Hyman.

Lokare, V.G. (1984) Anxiety in children: A cross cultural perspective, in V.P. Karma (ed.) *Anxiety in Children.* London: Croom Helm,.pp.71–88.

Lowenstein, L.F. (1976a) Helping children to achieve, *Journal of the Parents National Educational Union.* 11, 1: 20–1.

Lowenstein, L.F. (1976b) Helping children to achieve II, *Journal of the Parents' National Educational Union.* 11, 2: 59–61.

Mandel, H.P. and Marcus, S.I. (1988) *The Psychology of Underachievement: Differential Diagnosis and Differential Treatment.* New York: John Wiley.

Mawson, A.R. (1987) *Transient criminality: a model of stress induced crime.* New York: Praeger.

Minuchin, S., Rosman, B.L. and Baker, L. (1978) *Psychosomatic families: anorexia nervosa in context.* Cambridge, Mass.: Harvard University Press.

Ogden, T. (1979) On projective identification, *International Journal of Psychoanalysis.* 60: 357–73.

Palazzoli, M., Boscolo, L., Cecchin, G. and Prata G. (1978) *Paradox and counter paradox.* London: Jason Aronson.

Rinsley, D.B. (1989) 'Notes on the developmental pathologies of narcissistic personality disorder', *Psychiatric Clinics of North America.* 12, 3: 695–707.

Ritterman, M. (1983) *Using hypnosis in family therapy.* London: Jossey-Bass Publishers.

Roland, A. (1980) Psychoanalytic perspectives on personality development in India. *International Review of Psycho-Analysis.* l: 73–87.

Salzberger-Wittenberg, I., Henry, G. and Osborne, E. (1983) *The emotional experience of learning and teaching.* London: Routledge & Kegan Paul.

Sigel, I.E. (1964) The attainment of concepts, in M.L. Hoffman, and L.W. Hoffman, (eds) *Review of Child Development Research.* New York: Russell Sage Foundation. 1: 209–48.

Srivastava, A.K. (1976) Motivational variables and discrepant achievement patterns, *Psycholoia: An International Journal of Psychology in the Orient.* 19, 1: 40–6.

Srivastava, A.K. (1977) 'A study of intercorrelation between some variables found to be significantly related to underachievement', *Indian Journal of Behaviour.* 1, 3: 26–8.

Whitehead, A.N. and Russell, B. (1910) *Principia Mathematica.* Cambridge: Cambridge University Press.

Willock, B. (1990) From acting out to interactive play, *International Journal of Psycho-Analysis.* 71: 321–34.

Yerkes, R.M. and Dodson, J.D. (1908) The relation of strength of stimulus to rapidity of habit formation, *Journal of Comparative Neurology and Psychology.* 18: 459–82.

Zillman, D. (1984) *Connections between sex and aggression.* London: Lawrence Erlbaum.

CHAPTER 6

The Effects of Physical Illness

Philip Barker

Physical illnesses may have both direct and indirect effects on the developing child. The direct effects are those that the illness itself has on the child's functioning. Thus an illness that causes damage to the brain may leave the child with impaired cognitive functioning or other disabilities. These may affect adversely the child's educational and/or social functioning.

On the other hand a chronic or recurrent illness such as asthma may lead to failure because of the amount of school the child misses or because of the secondary emotional problems which some asthmatic and other chronically or recurrently ill children develop. Chronic illness in a child may also have its effects on the functioning of the family group. These may affect not only the sick child but also other family members.

The central nervous system and other bodily systems may also be affected adversely by the treatment given for a variety of illnesses. For example, children with acute lymphoblastic leukemia (ALL) are frequently treated by means of cranial radiation. This is done because the central nervous system (CNS) has been found to be the most frequent site of relapse following remission of ALL. Relapse in the CNS is often followed by bone marrow relapse. Cranial radiation can reduce greatly the rate of such recurrences. Unfortunately it may also have adverse effects on cognitive functioning (Rowland *et al.* 1984). Cranial radiation is also employed in the treatment of other malignancies.

Diseases of the nervous system

Direct effects are most often clearly evident when there is disease of the brain or other parts of the nervous system. The classic epidemiological studies in the Isle of Wight demonstrated, many years ago, that psychiatric disorders were five times more common in children with definite evidence of brain damage than they were in the general child population. They were also found to be three times more common than they were in children with chronic physical handicaps not affecting the brain (Rutter *et al.* 1970). The associations found were with psychiatric disorders generally, rather than with particular syndromes.

Many diseases may affect the brain. They include infections such as the various forms of encephalitis and cerebral abscesses; metabolic disorders such as phenylketonuria, a genetically determined abnormality of the metabolism of phenylalanine, and hepato-lenticular degeneration (Wilson's Disease), a genetically determined disease of copper metabolism; inherited degenerative diseases such as tuberous sclerosis and various disorders of sphingolipid metabolism ('lipidoses'); other degenerative disorders such as diffuse cerebral sclerosis and subacute sclerosing panencephalitis; and acquired immune deficiency syndrome (AIDS).

Epilepsy, a disorder of the brain itself, may lead to further damage to the brain when it causes severe, prolonged and/or frequently repeated seizures which lead to cyanosis and anoxic brain damage. *Status epilepticus* is a condition in which one seizure follows immediately upon another without recovery in between. If prolonged it may lead to brain damage.

Even when epileptic seizures do not themselves cause brain damage, the recurrent lapses of consciousness which the epileptic child experiences – especially when the disorder is severe – can have significant effects on the child's development. If diagnosis is delayed – as it may well be in children suffering from the less obvious forms of epilepsy, especially those which do not involve major seizures – the cumulative effect on the child's learning and development may be considerable.

'Non-convulsive status epilepticus' is a condition in which epileptic discharges in the brain continue for days, weeks or even months without typical seizures appearing. The resulting behaviour may include disorientation for time, place or person, fluctuating responsiveness, regression to earlier stages of development and aggressive behaviour (Manning and Rosenbloom 1987). This has obvious implications for the child's learning processes and development.

'Complex partial seizures' – which are usually associated with epileptic discharges in the temporal lobes of the brain – can lead to behaviour which may seem purposive and can be quite complex. It may include running about, shouting, screaming, aggressiveness and attacks of temper. 'Automatisms' – the performance of physical activities without the subject being aware of them – may also occur (Stores 1987).

Yet another form of epilepsy which may cause ongoing problems for a child is that which is characterised by 'absence seizures'. These are lapses of consciousness which usually last 5 to 15 seconds. They may occur hundreds of times a day and may be mistaken for emotionally determined inattention.

Any of these forms of epilepsy may directly affect a child's development by the interruption of consciousness they cause. It can be hard to learn when you lose consciousness, even if only briefly, many times per day.

Epilepsy may also have secondary effects. Repeatedly having major seizures in school or public places, and losing consciousness or displaying abnormal behaviour in the presence of one's peers, may lead to difficulties for the epileptic child. Such children may be shunned by other children who may be frightened, hostile or puzzled. Much depends, however, on how the situation is handled by all concerned and by the attitudes towards the child's disability of family, friends, teachers and others. In some societies these can be highly damaging – as when the epileptic child is considered to be possessed of an evil spirit.

Proper medical treatment and the regular administration of the anticonvulsant medication which is usually needed, as well as healthy family attitudes, can greatly mitigate the effects of epilepsy. These requirements are more likely to be met in healthy, stable families and in the 'developed' world. It is tragic to see the after effects of prolonged *status epilepticus* – effects which are commonplace in countries in which proper medical care is unavailable to many. The common after effects include hemiplegias and other gross neurological disorders – conditions which are largely preventable.

Epileptic children, like other children with chronic disorders requiring special continuing management and support, tend to do less well in disorganised, chaotic families. In them the epilepsy may be but one of a multitude of risk factors, the cumulative effects of which may be seriously disabling.

Many metabolic diseases may affect children's development in ways which may lead to failure in various areas of development. Among those which affect the central nervous system are phenylketonuria, hypothyroidism and, rarely in children, hyperthyroidism.

In *phenylketonuria,* a genetically caused autosomal recessive condition, the basic disorder is a lack of the enzyme phenylalanine hydroxylase. The function of this enzyme is to convert phenylalanine to tyrosine. Failure of this process causes the accumulation of phenylpyruvic acid, phenylacetic acid and phenylacetamine. Untreated, this condition usually leads to mental retardation. Some of these children also develop hyperkinetic behaviour, autistic symptoms and epilepsy. Behaviour problems may also be associated with the mental retardation. Fortunately dietary treatment instituted early in life is generally effective in preventing the symptoms developing. The diet is one containing very low levels of phenylalanine. In most developed countries newborns are routinely screened for this condition. In other parts of the world, though, the outlook for these children is less favourable.

Hypothyroidism in children is also preventable by the screening of newborns. It is usually due to a congenital abnormality of the thyroid gland, or to an inborn error of metabolism. In either case there is defective production of the thyroid hormones which, if untreated, leads to delayed mental development. If detected early this can be prevented quite simply by replacement therapy. There are nowadays programs for the early detection of this condition in most developed countries. *Hyperthyroidism,* in which there is overactivity of the thyroid gland, is very rare in childhood but is a possible cause of hyperactivity.

Diseases of other bodily systems may cause secondary damage to the brain by their effects. For example, diabetes may lead to coma which, if severe and prolonged, may cause anoxic brain damage. Severe hypoglycemia, usually due to some combination of excessive dosage of insulin, insufficient food intake and excessive exercise, may also cause coma and, if this is severe and prolonged, permanent brain damage.

Cerebral anoxia may also be the result of cyanotic congenital heart disease and severe diseases of the respiratory system which impair oxygenation of the blood. It is a possible complication of severe attacks of asthma.

Impairment of hearing may be a cause of serious difficulty for a child. It may result from a variety of causes but the commonest is chronic or repeated ear infections. These may cause damage to the ear drums, accumulation of fluid in the middle ear and other forms of damage to the organs of hearing. While early diagnosis and prompt treatment can largely prevent serious long-term hearing loss, if these are not provided the child may be left with a continuing disability which may adversely affect both school progress and social adjustment. Once again, neglect of such problems and inadequate treatment are more likely in the child from the poorly functioning family in which the care and concern of the parents is generally substandard. It is more common in poor societies and in 'third world' children who do not have access to good medical care.

Visual impairment of any degree, which may be congenital or acquired, can have seriously adverse effects on a child's development. What effects it has, and how far these lead to failure in one or more areas of life, depends largely on the quality of the care the child receives. Particularly important is the highly specialised education required by severely visually impaired children. Again, the special needs of such children are usually better met in the more developed societies and, within those societies, among those born into higher socioeconomic groups.

Various disorders may affect other parts of the nervous system. Spinal cord disorders may cause motor weakness in various parts of the body. A variety of 'peripheral neuropathies', some of them of genetic origin and many of them progressive, may lead to severe motor weakness with wasting of the muscles and ultimately death. The effects of such conditions are mainly the physical disability they cause but secondary emotional disorders may also develop.

Diabetes

We have already mentioned some of the effects that diabetes may have on the developing child but, as a relatively common and serious chronic condition, this disease merits further consideration. An excellent summary of the stresses that persons with diabetes may experience, and the effects these may have at different stages of the disease and in different age groups, has been provided by Holmes (1986). He writes:

> When a child develops diabetes, the family usually experiences extensive turmoil. The parents' distress and sense of their child's vulnerability

to sudden catastrophe is intensified by the often dramatic symptoms of onset in children – unquenchable thirst, bedwetting, vulvitis, extreme tiredness and weakness, rapid emaciation, and sometimes a lapse into a stuporose or comatose state. With its implication that a child may become disabled or die early, diabetes tends to increase any feeling that parents may already have that perhaps they did something wrong. (Holmes 1986, p.195)

Holmes goes on to discuss the special challenges facing the adolescent with diabetes:

Speaking metaphorically, adolescents without diabetes generally feel in the position of the youngest child in the fairy tale in which he sets out to slay the dragon and win love and kingdom against all odds – they feel need of stout heart, a head start, and a little magic to achieve their goals. At this critical juncture, instead of feeling confident, lucky, and indestructible, the onset of diabetes confronts an adolescent with bad luck and vulnerability to early disability and death. (Holmes 1986, p.195)

Holmes goes on to point out that the adolescent has to master not only the ordinary developmental tasks of this period of life, but also the special ones confronting a diabetic – measuring blood glucose, eating regularly and being careful about what he or she eats, injecting insulin and in a variety of ways behaving differently from his or her peer group. It is small wonder that many adolescents rebel against this and thus achieve less than optimal control of their diabetes.

In a section of his paper subtitled 'The sword of Damocles in youths and adults', Holmes (1986) describes the danger that overdependence may develop. He believes that the roots of overdependence lie in the 'dramatic onset plus a parent, usually the mother, discovering the child clammy and unresponsive at night during inevitable insulin reactions' (p.196). This may be experienced by the parent, even if only fleetingly, as the child's death. It is not too difficult to understand how this may lead to such parents becoming reluctant to leave their children alone and developing generally overprotective behaviours and attitudes.

Children, of course, are neither unaware of, nor immune to, such parental fears and feelings and may also develop fears of death or of disaster threatening, if a parent is not always near at hand and available.

While in some respects the above scenario is particularly characteristic of the situation of the young person with diabetes, in many respects it is also a model of the stresses that may face any family in which there is a child with a serious, chronic and potentially fatal illness.

Impaired cognitive functioning may occur with the fluctuations in the blood glucose level that occur in children with severe forms of this condition – that is those who are insulin dependent (Holmes *et al.* 1983). Children with early onset of diabetes tend to have an increased prevalence of learning problems, these being more severe the earlier the onset of the condition (Gath *et al.* 1980).

Physical diseases of other parts of the body

All chronic diseases have the potential of leading to serious problems for the developing child. According to Mrazek (1991), 'serious physical illness should be conceptualised as one of the most important early risk factors of emotional disturbance'. although, as Mrazek goes on to point out, 'the range of adaptation to physical illness is broad' (p.1041).

Whether serious problems actually do result from chronic physical illness depends on a variety of factors, including the care and treatment the child receives and the child's own vulnerability. Age also appears to be a relevant factor. Younger children seem to have most difficulty in dealing with painful and distressing diseases because they are unable to understand the nature of their illnesses and the need for the procedures used to treat it. Very young infants may be an exception to this because, as Mrazek (1991) points out, they 'may be spared the association that links physical traumas with the as yet incompletely differentiated significant caregivers' (p.1042).

Greater cognitive development seems to be associated with a greater capacity to deal with medical procedures (Brewster 1982). It seems, therefore, that it is the young child (though perhaps not the infant) who does not understand what is happening and why, who is likely to suffer the greatest emotional stress which may adversely affect long-term adjustment.

The prognosis of the illness is also important. We have a different situation when we are dealing with a child with asthma – a condition for which effective treatments are available and which often improves over time – than when the illness is cystic fibrosis, which is chronic and progressive, even though treatments are nowadays available which can substantially prolong life.

Illnesses of short duration usually do not cause lasting adverse effects, unless certain complications develop. Occasionally acute infections such as mumps or measles are complicated by encephalitis which may leave lasting brain damage.

On the other hand, almost any chronic or relapsing illness may adversely affect a child's development. It may interfere with the child's schooling; some chronically ill children miss so much school that they fall seriously behind in their academic attainments. In other cases the emotional repercussions in child and family may be the crucial factor in leading to difficulties for the child. Some chronically ill children are overprotected by their understandably anxious parents. Parental anxiety may be communicated to the child who comes to look upon himself or herself as vulnerable and 'different'. Some sick children are subject to teasing or even ridicule by other children. Obese children are often the butt of jokes and negative attitudes. The experience of attitudes of that sort can seriously damage a child's sense of self-esteem and confidence.

Cancer

Childhood cancer takes many forms. The treatment of some of these has become much more effective during the last decade or two than it used to be. This has resulted in the survival of children who formerly would have died. Unfortunately some are left with psychological problems, though these are probably avoidable in most cases. Such problems may result from the emotional trauma which the diagnosis of cancer and its treatment cause both to afflicted children and to their families. In addition, the treatment itself may cause impairment of cognitive functioning. Both cranial irradiation and the intrathecal administration of drugs such as methotrexate have the potential to cause such impairment (Jannoun and Chessells 1987, Moore *et al.* 1986).

Residual physical impairment following the treatment of cancer may affect adversely subsequent psychological adjustment, though some studies have found little effect. However children with severe late medical effects seem to have poorer self-concepts, lower popularity and more depressive symptomatology than those with mild or moderate late effects. They also feel that their 'locus of control' is more external. There is evidence that girls tend to be more anxious and concerned about their physical appearance than are boys (Hymovich and Roehnert 1989). It seems that in the absence of neurological damage or late effects on cognitive functioning the educational progress of most child cancer survivors is normal.

Hymovich and Roehnert (1989) have reviewed studies of the psychosocial adjustment of children who have survived cancer. They concluded that a variety of factors appear to be associated with how well survivors adjust. It seems that adjustment is better the younger the onset of the illness, the longer the time since diagnosis, and the shorter the treatment course. The outlook also appears to be better if there has not been a relapse, if communication with the affected child has been open and supportive, and if denial has been used effectively, the child's social maturity is higher and the 'self report of adjustment' is relatively good.

Parental attitudes and fears can affect the progress of cancer survivors and even that of other children in the family. Peck (1979) studied 24 families of children who had survived after treatment of Wilms tumours. All had been off treatment for at least two years. The parents continued to believe that their children would die and none was convinced that the child who had had cancer was cured.

I have mentioned elsewhere (Barker 1992, p.183–4) the long-term effects in one such case. The child concerned had had a kidney removed in infancy because of a Wilms tumour. Following this, the parents had continued to fear that their daughter would die and had indulged and overprotected her, making few demands on her as she grew up. The family came for treatment when the daughter was aged 19. She presented as a self centred, narcissistic and rebellious young person who expected everything to be done for her and was quite unprepared to take responsibility for her own life. It seemed likely that the situation was due, at least in part, to the parental attitudes which had developed as a result of the diagnosis of a cancerous tumour when the daughter was an infant.

It seems that growing up in the anxious family environment that many children with cancer experience can have seriously adverse effects on their development and later functioning. Whether, and to what extent, this happens depends on just how the family reacts to the child's illness. This would appear to be an area in which preventive intervention may be helpful.

Other chronic physical illnesses

Hamophilia, an X-linked recessive condition, and other, less common, diseases in which there is a tendency to excessive bleeding can have both physical and emotional effects. In these conditions one or more of the factors necessary for the clotting of the blood are absent. In hamophilia this is either Factor VIII or Factor IX. In mild cases the consequences may be slight but in severe ones quite minor traumata may lead to excessive bleeding, for example into the joints. This can lead to permanent disability. Hamophilia is treatable by infusion of concentrated plasma containing the missing factor. Unfortunately some children have been infused with contaminated plasma containing such pathogens as the human immunodeficiency virus (HIV) – the virus that causes AIDS, though the precautions which are nowadays taken have greatly reduced the risk of this.

As with other chronic and potentially life-threatening diseases, there is ever present the possibility that the parents will overprotect the child, adding secondary emotional problems to the basic physical one. Appropriate counselling and group support usually prevent this happening

Some general points about the effects of physical illness

Rather than list the many other, though mostly rare, diseases which may afflict children, it may be more helpful here to summarise the factors which may make failure in one or more areas of development more likely in children with serious physical illnesses of any sort. Graham (1991) has provided a good brief review of the psychiatric aspects of such pediatric disorders and, in the same volume, Schonfield (1991) discusses the importance of the child's cognitive understanding of physical illness. This has a bearing on the effects the illness has on the child's emotional state and development.

The following points require consideration in each case:

First, *The extent to which the child loses normal educational experiences.* This depends in part on the duration of the illness or the periods of sickness. Physical illnesses may lead to interruptions of the sick child's schooling. Some children spend so much time away from school that they fall seriously behind in their studies. This has obvious implications for their success in many areas of their lives. The potentially adverse educational consequences of spending prolonged periods of time in hospital or other institutions can be obviated by providing schooling in hospitals and other institutions in which children may spend long periods. This can certainly help prevent children falling behind in their studies. Nevertheless such children may suffer from the lack of a rounded school programme.

Prolonged periods spent in institutions are less of an issue nowadays than they were in the days when children were treated for illnesses such as tuberculosis or poliomyelitis by means of months or years in long-stay hospitals or sanatoria. Nevertheless repeated admissions to hospital can add up to a lot of school missed and, especially if the child is not a quick learner, this can lead to significant educational failure. The effects, though, vary from child to child. Some are bright, motivated students who manage to learn what they need despite prolonged absences from school. Others, especially those with more modest cognitive skills and those who have specific learning difficulties, may be seriously affected. Moreover school is not just a place where children learn 'classroom' subjects; it also has social learning aspects on which the chronically sick child may miss out.

Second, *The extent to which the child is deprived of normal relationship experiences*. An important childhood developmental task is that of learning to live as a member of a community of people. Children learn the skills of group living in the family setting, in school, in their peer groups, and in their interactions with people of other ages – in youth groups, boy scouts, girl guides, army cadets and so forth. All these situations provide learning experiences of which the sick child may be deprived.

Fortunately the need for these experiences is being increasingly recognised by health care providers and, in many parts of the world, by society generally. Steps are nowadays often taken to make leisure and other facilities wheelchair accessible so that sick or disabled persons can enjoy the same range of social opportunities as the general population. Such facilities, like the availability of high quality medical care, tend to be confined to more affluent communities and are usually lacking in the lesser developed parts of the world. This is yet another aspect of the generally disadvantageous situation of 'third world' children.

The recognition of the rights and also the potential of chronically sick and disabled persons is manifested in the organization of wheelchair sports – even wheelchair Olympics – and the appearance of magazines such as *Abilities*, which is devoted entirely to issues concerning people with disabilities.

Third, *The emotional consequences of physical illnesses*. Physical illnesses which do not have a neurological or other component which directly affects the child's functioning may nevertheless have serious emotional repercussions. These, in turn, may adversely affect the afflicted child in various ways.

One of the most important developmental tasks of childhood is the acquisition of self confidence, emotional stability and a balanced way of dealing with life's challenges and frustrations. In other words, we all function better in society if we have a stable personality that enables us to cope constructively with the stresses and challenges of daily life. The process by which we acquire such personality strengths is complex and is by no means fully understood. Personality and temperament are in part genetically determined but our childhood experiences also contribute powerfully.

The basic question here is whether the developing child acquires, as he or she grows up, a feeling of being a whole, competent person, able to face and cope successfully with the 'slings and arrows of outrageous fortune' – as Shakespeare put it. Many factors play their respective parts in determining how far this happens. In other chapters I discuss how abuse and growing up in a chaotic family can affect a child's feelings of competency, and chronic or recurrent physical illnesses can also have their effects.

The child who is physically ill is obviously at risk of feeling less than a completely whole person. When the illness imposes limitations on the child's activities – as for example when there is an associated physical handicap – the risk of that child feeling imperfect and 'different' is so much greater. Feelings of being imperfect and of having less potential than others can also have their effect on the child's educational progress. Not only may sick children miss a lot of schooling but they may also come to believe that they are less able to achieve success than their healthy peers. This need not happen, though, and some children are able to perceive their apparent disadvantage as a challenge to be met.

We do not fully understand what determines which of the above attitudes develop, and to what extent they develop. Much probably depends on the attitudes of parents, teachers and others. If the child feels valued and regarded as a worthwhile person by others, despite his or her physical problems, this can be a major protective factor. This leads us on to the next point.

Fourth, *The attitudes of the child's family and other important people.* In some societies, sick or disabled children are shunned and their families are blamed, or at least feel blamed, for having an imperfect child. In certain parts of the world the sick child may be seen as possessed of an evil spirit or as a manifestation of an occult or supernatural force which is negatively regarded.

Even in some of the affluent, upwardly mobile, economically successful parts of the 'developed' world we find families which experience – even if they do not acknowledge it – a sense of shame that they have a chronically sick or 'imperfect' child. Just as their houses, cars, clothing, stereo equipment and lifestyles generally have to make a good impression, so must their children. Their disappointment at having a sick child may never be voiced, or even consciously acknowledged, but the child may nevertheless become aware of it.

The range of possible parental reactions to having a sick child is wide. On the one hand there may be anxiety and guilt which may be associated with overprotection and/or rejection. On the other, there may be acceptance and encouragement. Parents and others may choose to emphasise their child's illness and limitations, or they may prefer to concentrate attention on the talents, strengths and successes the child displays. It is indeed a fact that many individuals with disabilities develop compensatory strengths in areas of their lives unaffected by their illness. Thus the hearing of a blind child may become particularly acute, or the autistic child, who has difficulty dealing appropriately with human relationships, may become extraordinarily adept at mathematics, which requires little or no relationship capacity.

Another possibility is denial of the child's illness or handicap, or at least denial of its severity. Up to a point, this may be helpful. Treating the child as 'normal' rather than as 'sick' is in general to be desired. This attitude can, however, be carried too far, if it results in the denial to the child of the special services, education or help that realistically are required. In the rearing of sick children, as in most other endeavours, a measure of balance is required.

Self-esteem issues

I have mentioned the issues of children's self-esteem and self-concept repeatedly but they merit at least a short section of their own.

It is worth stating again that, for practical purposes, we are what we believe we are. A frustrating experience for psychotherapists can be that of dealing with those who come for therapy but have a profoundly damaged sense of their personal worth – that is their self-esteem is very low. One may even be confronted with an apparently highly talented person who believes that he or she has the capacity to succeed at practically nothing. This may make no sense until we take into account the profound effects – positive or negative – that our childhood experiences have on the development of our self-concepts.

So far as is known, children are not born with any particular self-concept. Of course, we are all born with our own particular genetic endowments and temperamental traits. These may make some of us more, or less, determined, for example to overcome any disability we have. But much of how we view ourselves is derived from the responses of others. We take our cues from others, especially our families. Physical illnesses are but one category among many that may affect a child's self-concept, but how such illness are managed, and whether some relative degree of unnecessary failure results, depends on the environment, especially the family and school environments, in which the child grows up.

Summary

Physical illnesses may have both direct and indirect effects on children's development. The direct consequences are those which result from the disability which the illness causes. Cognitive functioning and emotional stability may be affected by neurological damage due to any form of brain disease or injury. Other physical disorders may cause a variety of disabilities which may affect a child's development and lead to failure in one or more areas of functioning. The treatment of physical illnesses may also have adverse effects, for example the deterioration of cognitive functioning that may follow cranial irradiation for malignant diseases – whether this is given for malignant growths of the brain or for blood diseases such as leukemia.

Repeated attacks of epilepsy can compromise a child's development in a variety of ways, leading to educational problems as well as problems of social adjustment. The fluctuations in the blood glucose level experienced by children with diabetes may be associated with variably impaired cognitive functioning.

The indirect effects of serious and particularly chronic diseases can lead to failure in a number of ways. The self-esteem of chronically ill or handicapped children may become impaired as they compare themselves and their capabilities with those of other children. Their emotional development may be retarded as a result of overprotective and anxious care by their worried parents. They may have difficulty in their peer group relationships and are sometimes teased or shunned by others. In some societies the handicapped are seen as possessed of evil spirits or as manifestations of the operation of occult forces.

Chronic illness and repeated admissions to hospital may cause a child to miss a lot of school and the consequent failure to make appropriate educational progress may lead to later academic and vocational failure.

Whether or not failure results from factors such as those we have discussed depends in large measure on the care provided for sick children, both by their families and by the wider community. This tends to be of higher quality in affluent and developed societies than among the poor and underprivileged, especially those living in the lesser developed countries of the world.

References

Barker, P. (1992) *Basic Family Therapy*, 3rd edition. Oxford: Blackwell.

Brewster, A.B. (1982) Chronically ill hospitalised children's concepts of their illness. *Pediatrics*, 69: 355–62.

Gath, A., Smith, M.A. and Baum, J.D. (1980) Emotional, behavioural, and educational disorders in diabetic children. *Archives of Disease in Childhood*, 55: 371–5.

Graham, P.J. (1991) Psychiatric aspects of pediatric disorders, in Lewis, M. (ed.), *Child and Adolescent Psychiatry: A Comprehensive Textbook*. New York: Williams and Wilkins.

Holmes, D.M. (1986) The person and diabetes in psychosocial context. *Diabetes Care*, 9: 194–203.

Holmes, C.S., Hayford, J.T., Gonzales, J.L. and Weydert, J.A. (1983) A survey of cognitive functioning at different glucose levels in diabetic persons. *Diabetes Care*, 6: 180–185.

Hymovich, D.P. and Roehnert, J.E. (1989) Psychosocial consequences of cancer. *Seminars in Oncology Nursing,* 5: 55–62.

Jannoun, L. and Chessells, J.M. (1987) Long-term psychological effects of childhood leukemia and its treatment, *Pediatric Hematology and Oncology,* 4: 293–308.

Manning, D.J. and Rosenbloom, L. (1987) Non-convulsive status epilepticus. *Archives of Disease in Childhood,* 62: 37–40.

Moore, I.M., Kramer, J. and Ablin, A. (1986) Late effects of central nervous system prophylactic leukemia therapy on cognitive functioning. *Oncology Nursing Forum,* 13: 45–51.

Mrazek, D.A. (1991) Chronic pediatric illness and hospitalizations, in Lewis, M. (ed.), *Child and Adolescent Psychiatry: A Comprehensive Textbook.* New York: Williams and Wilkins.

Peck, B. (1979) Effects of childhood cancer on long-term survivors and their families. *British Medical Journal,* 1: 1327–9.

Rowland, J.H., Glidewell, O.J., Sibley, R.F., Holland, J.C., Tull, R., Berman, A., Brecher, M.L., Harris, M., Glicksman, A.S., Forman, E., *et al.* (1984) Effects of various forms of central nervous system prophylaxis on neuropsychologic function in childhood leukemia. *Journal of Clinical Oncology,* 2: 1327–35.

Rutter, M., Graham, P. and Yule, W.A. (1970) *A Neuropsychiatric Study in Childhood.* London: Heinemann.

Schonfield, D.J. (1991) The child's cognitive understanding of illness, in Lewis, M. (ed.) *Child and Adolescent Psychiatry: A Comprehensive Textbook.* New York: Williams and Wilkins.

Stores, G. (1987) Pitfalls in the management of epilepsy. *Archives of Disease in Childhood,* 62: 88–90.

CHAPTER 7

The Effects of Child Abuse

Philip Barker

Slave Children Rescued

Malnourished children, many beaten so badly they couldn't walk, have been rescued from a Bangkok sweatshop, police said Friday.

Thirty-one children, most in their early teens or younger, were found during a police raid locked in a small squalid room used as a factory to make paper cups, an officer of the Crime Suppression Division said.

'I have never seen such a terrible scene as this before. I just can't believe how cruelly these children were treated', said Maj. General Rangsit Yanothai, the head of the CSD.

Nearly all the children were malnourished and suffered from skin diseases... One boy told police they had been forced to work 18 hours a day and given very little food. He said anyone who was too tired to work was tied up and beaten with a heavy piece of wood. (From a Reuter report published in the Calgary Herald, 2nd November 1991)

As the above report illustrates only too starkly, child abuse, even in its most horrendous forms, is still very much with us today. Indeed it is a widespread phenomenon. The gross exploitation of children may be more common in the third world, but we are far from immune to the serious abuse of children in our 'developed' Western societies.

Child abuse takes many forms. The categories most usually defined are those of physical abuse, sexual abuse and emotional abuse.

Physical abuse

The physical abuse of children is nothing new. Lynch (1985) pointed out that it is referred to in literature dating back at least as far as the second century A.D. The London Society for the Prevention of Cruelty to Children was founded in 1884 and within three years it had dealt with 762 cases, comprising 333 cases of assault, 81 of starvation, 130 of 'dangerous neglect', 30 of desertion, 70 of 'cruel exposure to excite sympathy', (which nowadays might be classified as emotional abuse), 16 of 'other wrongs' and 25 deaths.

One hundred and thirty-two cases were taken to court and there were 120 convictions (Lynch 1985).

Charles Dickens, in several of his books, described the plight of children in Victorian times, but by the mid twentieth century a certain complacency seemed to develop, at least in Western society. Dickens' days were past, many people assumed, and these things happened no longer. Then in 1946 Caffey, a radiologist, reported cases of children with multiple fractures of the long bones, associated with bleeding within the skull. He suggested that these injuries were due to inflicted trauma. We now know that such injuries are often due to physical abuse.

Almost any injury may result from physical abuse. As interest in the medical consequences of child abuse increased it became clear that brain injury was a not infrequent result and that this could cause serious problems of adaptation in later life, including mental retardation (Scott 1977). It may also cause epilepsy in any of its forms, learning problems and impaired motor function. The latter may be of any severity up to severe cerebral palsy.

Ocular injuries are sometimes caused by severe physical abuse of infants. There may be hamorrhage into the eye and detachment of the retina. The result may be visual impairment or even total blindness. Han and Wilkinson (1990) report the cases of six children who had been subject to shaking injuries early in life. All had significant retinal damage and in three the injury appeared to be responsible for profound loss of vision. Such injuries may occur without external signs of injury. Injuries to other parts of the body may also have lasting effects, such as permanent scarring and deformities due to imperfectly healed fractures.

The boundary between physical abuse and neglect is a thin one. Children who are reared in neglectful and otherwise damaging environments, who are poorly nourished, or are denied proper medical or dental care are in effect abused by default.

The role of physical punishment in child rearing – if there is one – is disputed by many. Some parents believe strongly that it is sometimes necessary, or at least desirable. Others – and I am one – believe that physical punishment is never necessary and is often harmful. In this matter, however, cultural norms vary a great deal.

Payne (1989) defined 'corporal methods of discipline and punishment in child rearing' as 'any intent to inflict some measure of physical pain, either through striking the child or in some other manner placing the child in a physically discomforting situation, such as suspending or restraining with rope, kneeling on a rough surface, or lengthy deprivation of food' (p.389).

Using this rather unusually wide definition of corporal punishment, Payne (1989) proceeded to obtain the opinions on corporal punishment of 499 Barbadian adults aged 20 to 59 years, using a questionnaire. She found that about 70 per cent of the respondents 'generally approved' of corporal punishment, and of the remaining 30 per cent, three-quarters thought it 'occasionally appropriate'. Payne comments that 'the majority considered serious disadvantages to arise only if parents resorted to punishment in an unsystematic, excessive, or self-serving manner'.

Payne (1989) points out that some contemporary writers in Western industrialised societies have considered all physical punishment as 'elements of a continuum of undesirable family violence'. Nevertheless there is, in many cultures, a continuing view that the experience of deliberately inflicted pain is 'vital to the development of strength, endurance, and/or cultural allegiance' (p.389). In the Carribean, or at least in Barbados, this would certainly seem to be the case. It is my own experience that families which have recently migrated from areas such as the West Indies to the United Kingdom or to Canada (the only countries in which I have practised) may have difficulty understanding and coming to terms with what is considered acceptable child rearing practice in the culture to which they have migrated.

It may be that the context in which physically painful punishment is administered is important in determining what its psychological effects will be. If it is the cultural norm for children to be beaten under certain circumstances, it may have a different meaning for the children – and for adults also – than it may have in societies in which it is considered abusive. Nevertheless it is hard to understand how inflicting violence on a child can fail to provide a model of the use of force to effect compliance on another person's part. Moreover there is a great inequality in the power of the two participants in this process. A relatively big and strong adult is striking a small, weak and perhaps terrified child. What does this say about the value that is attributed to the child?

Failure, of course, is the converse of success. In some cultures a 'successfully' reared child is one who has acquired a disciplined and 'tough' character. To achieve this, physical punishment may be deemed necessary. In ancient Sparta, for example, physical punishment and hardship were necessary features of the rearing of children so that they could become the brave and disciplined adults that were the norm for that Greek state.

The physical environments in which children are raised are important. Damaging and unhealthy environments take their toll. Poor hygiene increases the risk of infections. In recent years the adverse effects of second-hand smoke and atmospheric pollution have become clear. Tobacco smoke contains more than 100 substances, a considerable number of which are thought to be harmful. Moreover many of those considered harmful are present in higher concentration in 'sidestream smoke' – that is, smoke produced from the burning ends of cigarettes and released into the environment – than in the smoke inhaled by the smoker ('mainstream smoke') (Ronchetti *et al.* (1990).

Ronchetti *et al.* (1990) review the literature on the effects of environmental tobacco smoke (ETS) – a combination of mainstream smoke and sidestream smoke – on children, as well as reporting some studies of their own. The most significant effects are found in infants and these authors conclude that, 'there can be little doubt that maternal cigarette consumption is related to a significant increase in the number and severity of lower respiratory illnesses during the first year of life' (p.315).

It is probable also that the offspring of smokers are at risk of developing a number of other health problems. At any age the symptoms and physiological consequences of asthma may be worsened by exposure to ETS, especially that generated by the mother (Ronchetti *et al.* 1990).

It seems clear that cigarette smoke is bad for infants and children. Current medical advice is that, especially in households containing families with a history of chronic respiratory disease, 'efforts to create a smoke-free environment... should be stressed' (Tager 1989). Smoking in the presence of children is not yet, in most circles, considered abusive but a good case can be made for the proposition that it should be.

Even more striking are the effects on children of living in polluted cities. In Mexico City, for example, studies are said to have found that almost half the children examined have elevated blood lead levels. Add to that the effects of gross atmospheric pollution with dust and other industrial emissions and, in many cases, suboptimal nutrition, and it is not surprising that the progress of children in Mexico City's schools tends to be generally poor.

Sexual abuse

The sexual abuse of children has been the subject of increasing attention during the last decade or two. Estimates of its prevalence vary, partly because of the use of different definitions of abuse. It is also virtually certain that there are also real differences in the prevalence rates in different populations.

Sexual abuse may be anything from a single episode of the inappropriate fondling of a child or adolescent, through repeated sexual intercourse with the child by an older person to forms of extreme ritualistic abuse. It may be a brief episode in a child's life or it may continue through much of childhood. The perpetrator may be a family member or it may be someone outside the family. Various deviant sexual practices inflicted on children have also been reported. Children, even young ones, have been made to participate in the production of pornographic movies and some have been used in satanic and other destructive rituals. As one would expect, the circumstances and nature of the abuse, and the identity of the abuser affect the outcome and the extent and nature of the damage to the child.

Emotional abuse

Emotional abuse is harder to define than the two previous categories. As with physical abuse, a line, which is inevitably arbitrary, has to be drawn between what is abuse and what is acceptable child-rearing practice.

In the case of emotional abuse, drawing the line between what is acceptable and what is not is even harder than it is with physical abuse. Attempts have been made in many jurisdictions to define it in legislation. In the

Canadian Province of Alberta, for example, it is quite broadly defined. The Alberta Child Welfare Act (Government of Alberta 1984) refers to 'emotional injury' in the following terms. A child is emotionally injured if:

1. There is substantial and observable impairment of the child's mental or emotional functioning that is evidenced by a mental or behavioural disorder, including anxiety, depression, withdrawal, aggression or delayed development.

2. There are reasonable or probable grounds to believe that the emotional injury is the result of

   a) rejection,

   b) deprivation of affection or cognitive stimulation,

   c) exposure to domestic violence or severe domestic disharmony, or

   d) inappropriate criticism, threats, humiliation, accusations or expectations of or towards the child, or

   e) the mental or emotional condition of the guardian of the child or chronic alcohol or drug abuse by anyone living in the same residence as the child.

The inclusiveness of this section of the Child Welfare Act limits its practical value. On the basis of these criteria, broadly interpreted, a reasonable case could probably be made that a large proportion of the child population is subject to 'emotional injury'. What these criteria do offer us, however, is an indication of the sort of things people refer to when they talk about emotional abuse.

Children need to grow up with good feelings about themselves. They need to feel that they are worthwhile people with their own proper and valuable roles in the world. They need to see their world as a safe and secure place and to experience satisfying relationships with others, especially the adults caring for them. The latter include not only parents and other key family members but also teachers, youth leaders and other significant figures in children's worlds.

It is emotionally damaging for children to be told that they are stupid or 'dumb' or in any way 'bad'. Unfortunately many children are subject to just such abuse. Garbarino and his colleagues (1986) use the term 'psychologically battered child' and list five forms of 'psychically destructive behaviour'. I have summarised these elsewhere (Barker 1988) but they merit repetition here:

• Rejecting: in these cases the adult refuses to acknowledge the child's worth and the legitimacy of the child's needs.

• Isolating: here the child is cut off by the adult from normal social experiences, prevented from forming friendships and made to believe he or she is alone in the world.

- Terrorizing: the child is verbally assaulted by the adult who creates a climate of fear.

- Ignoring: the adult deprives the child of needed stimulation and fails to respond in suitable ways, stifling emotional growth and intellectual development.

- Corrupting: the child is 'mis-socialised', being stimulated to engage in destructive antisocial behaviour and reinforced in such deviant behaviour.

Syndromes of abuse

Definitions such as those mentioned above are useful for legal purposes and perhaps as bases for research into causes, effects and treatment, but in reality it is artificial to isolate the three forms of abuse. In practice we often find that children subject to one form of abuse are experiencing other forms of abuse and neglect. Physical and emotional abuse often go together. The emotional messages conveyed by acts of physical abuse may sometimes be the most harmful aspect of such children's beatings or other physical abuse.

The sexually abused girl is unlikely to be one who is valued as a worthwhile individual with her own rights, at least by the abuser. And we must face the fact that much sexual abuse of children occurs within the family, often by parents and others responsible for the care of the children who are abused.

But even this broader view does not provide us with the whole picture. The abused child is so often disadvantaged in many ways, not all of them always defined as abuse. Consider the children who grow up in the poor ghettos of the world's big cities. Their mothers may lack proper antenatal care and may not be properly nourished during the pregnancy; other prenatal risk factors may be operative, for example maternal drug or alcohol abuse, or smoking; the quality of the care the mothers receive during labour and delivery may be substandard; these children are often raised in unstimulating, deprived and/or unhygienic homes; the physical environment may be polluted; they may suffer from lead poisoning and pollution-induced respiratory diseases; their nutrition may be poor; they may suffer a lack of emotional nurturance and love; they may be neglected and then shouted at abusively when they seek attention; they may be physically beaten when they do not conform; the quality of the education they get in school may be poor – if indeed schooling is available for them at all; and a depressingly large number of them come to live 'on the streets' long before they reach puberty. In this situation sexual abuse is commonplace.

Allowing children to grow up in circumstances such as the above amounts to abuse by society and its institutions. The world was shocked recently to learn on television, of the plight of children in Romanian orphanages – this while the country's rulers lived in great comfort. This is severe abuse on a large scale.

Many of the above scenarios are by no means uncommon. Indeed they are the lot of many children in the cities of the 'third world' and the shanty towns surrounding them. Yet those of us who live in the more affluent 'developed' world should not be complacent. Similar problems, if less dramatic and severe, problems face many of our children too. The difference is more one of degree and frequency than an absolute one. We have our mothers who smoke and abuse drugs and alcohol; we have our slum ghettos and deprived Indian reserves; we have polluted cities and abusive alcoholic homes; we have our institutions in which children are abused physically, sexually and emotionally; and we seem to have an ever-increasing population of 'street kids'.

Finally, it is worth emphasising that abuse is not confined to the poor and disadvantaged. Children growing up in the homes of the affluent are by no means exempt from this plague. They may be beaten, emotionally denigrated, put down, or sexually abused inside or outside their seemingly 'perfect' middle- or upper-class homes.

The effects of abuse

Since in many cases we are dealing with complex syndromes of abuse, neglect, deprivation and exploitation, there is no universal picture of the abused child. We can nevertheless say that many such children do fail to achieve their potential in various areas of their lives.

Many abused children have had the cards stacked against them from before birth. They may have been born into families in which the parents – if there are two in the family group, which often there are not – have themselves been abused and neglected as children. The 'internal models' of parenthood that such parents have may be less than ideal because they themselves were reared in dysfunctional families. Thus if *their* parents always beat them when they did something 'wrong', it should not surprise us if they assume that this is the appropriate way to deal with misbehaviour in their own offspring.

While generalisations are, on the whole, to be deplored, it is legitimate to consider the effects that particular forms of abuse may have, while bearing in mind that the vulnerability of children varies greatly.

A common reaction to abuse among older children, and especially adolescents, is running away. Precisely what proportion of runaway children have been abused is unclear but of 223 runaway adolescents reported by Powers *et al.* (1990) 60 per cent had allegedly experienced physical abuse, 42 per cent emotional abuse, 48 per cent neglect and 21 per cent sexual abuse.

The consequences of runaway behaviour are liable to be grave. Running away may mean the premature end to the young person's formal education, and life 'on the streets' – the fate of many runaways – tends to involve crime, drug use, violence, prostitution and the development of health problems.

Physical abuse may lead to failure as a result of neurological damage or physical disability or deformity. The child who is brain damaged, mentally retarded or blind as a result of abuse is obviously at a disadvantage. Sometimes the learning disabilities resulting from abuse are subtle and it is not always possible to determine the extent to which academic difficulties are the result of past abuse, and how far they have other causes.

In both the assessment and the subsequent clinical management of such children a detailed consideration of all the factors operating and their relative contributions to the child's problems is necessary. It may be difficult to distinguish the effects of physical abuse from those of chronic malnutrition or exposure to toxic substances such as lead, since these may co-exist. Emotional abuse also often accompanies physical abuse; indeed in many societies physical abuse is considered emotionally harmful.

A full history should be obtained, not only from the parents or other caregivers, but also from others who have knowledge of the child and family. These may include teachers, social workers, daycare staff and extended family members. Whenever a child has been previously assessed or treated by other professionals or in other hospitals or institutions, records from those professionals or institutions should be obtained. These may shed much useful light on the case and help determine how far the child's problems are due to abuse as opposed to other medical or psychological causes.

The effects of *sexual abuse* are generally less obvious than those of physical abuse. While they may be physical – for example physical injury to the vaginal or anal areas, sexually transmitted disease or pregnancy – the psychological and emotional effects are often the main ones.

Studies of the effects of child sexual abuse have been reviewed by Beitchman *et al.* (1991). But, as these authors point out, the issues involved in research are complex: 'The high prevalence of marital breakdown and psychopathology among parents of children who are sexually abused makes it difficult to determine the specific impact of sexual abuse over and above the effects of a disturbed home environment' (Beitchman *et al.* 1991, p.537).

It seems that the psychological effects of sexual abuse vary according to the circumstances of the abuse, the age of the child, the identity of the abuser(s) and the frequency and duration of the abuse. Incestuous activity between siblings is generally considered to have fewer harmful effects than intergenerational abuse, as by parents, guardians or other adult relatives, but much depends upon circumstances. If force is used or the child is intimidated or manipulated into the activity, a conflictual situation may result.

The intrafamilial, intergenerational sexual abuse of children – it is most often of girls by male adults, though abuse of boys is common also and female adult members are not exempt from being perpetrators of abuse – takes many forms. It may start quite insidiously with undue fondling and caressing by the father (or, often, stepfather) of the girl at bedtime, leading to increasingly intrusive sexual acts up to full intercourse. It may start when the child is quite young, even in the preschool period and may continue for years. Only gradually does it dawn on the child that there is something wrong with what is happening. Once the enormity of it begins to become clear, she is then faced with the agonising question of what to do. Who should she tell? Will she be believed? Is it all her fault? What will happen to her family if she tells? And so on. Many abusers threaten or intimidate the child. They may tell her that she is 'special', that Daddy has chosen her because of the special relationship they have, and that it is to be their own secret to be shared with no-one else.

The child in this predicament may hesitate for a long time before disclosing the abuse to anyone. Indeed some never do disclose. Then, much later in their lives, it may emerge during the course of psychotherapy. Freud obtained such disclosures from his patients but was persuaded – or persuaded himself – that his patients were reporting fantasies rather than real events.

The conflicts sexually abused children may face are enormous. Such abuse almost inevitably damages their self-esteem, as well as giving them a distorted view of their own sexuality. They almost always experience feelings of guilt. They often feel that it was, at least in part, their fault that the abuse occurred. When they disclose the abuse the consequences, which may be the break-up of the family or the jailing of the abuser, seem also to be their responsibility.

Then there is the – by no means remote – possibility that they will not be believed. Many mothers refuse to believe what their daughters tell them. It is a moot point how often these mothers truly disbelieve their daughters' accounts of abuse by the fathers and how often they are unprepared to face the consequences – such as the break-up of the family and the loss of the family's breadwinner. It is also unclear how often they have been aware of what has happened – though it is certain that in some cases they are fully aware and in others there is often reason to believe that they have had their suspicions which they chose not to heed.

The feelings that children abused by adult family members have to deal with are deep, complex and distressing and they affect their adjustment in many ways. Anger is usually combined with guilt. The anger may be directed primarily towards the abusing adult or towards the parent who failed to protect the child or refused to believe her or him when told what was happening; or it may be projected on to others. The child may herself or himself become an abuser of other children or, when the anger is turned inwards, may become depressed and develop suicidal ideation or behaviour.

It is small wonder these children fail in many areas of their lives. The emotional consequences of the abuse may affect their academic performance at school. Their self-esteem may have suffered serious damage which may only be reparable over a long period of time, and their ability to form and maintain healthy relationships, especially with the opposite sex, may have been compromised.

Among the symptoms reported among sexually abused adolescents have been depression, low self esteem, suicidal ideation and behaviour, running away, playing truant from school, alcohol and drug abuse, promiscuity, compulsive masturbation, prostitution, physical fights and delinquent or criminal behaviour. Some sexually abused children themselves become perpetrators in adolescent or adult life. (See the review of Beitchman *et al.* 1991 for relevant references.) A small-scale study by Pelletier (1990), however, suggested that sexual acting out may not be an outcome specifically related to sexual abuse in those adolescent girls who remain in caring families in which the perpetrator no longer remains, and who are taken for treatment. This finding is quite in keeping with the well-known fact that children's problems, and no doubt their failures also, are multifactorial in their origin. Positive factors can counter the effects of negative ones. Thus living in a caring, secure and supportive family environment which provides suitable nurture and a haven from stress can probably counter the potentially adverse effects of many traumas and stresses.

The review by Beitchman *et al.* (1991) similarly raises questions about the precise role of sexual abuse as opposed to the many other adverse circumstances these children have faced. For the practising clinician this is not usually of paramount importance, since all possibly aetiological factors which come to light must be addressed in formulating treatment plans.

Emotional abuse often accompanies either physical abuse or sexual abuse, or all three may occur together. It can be as damaging to the psychological development of children as physical abuse can be to the body. In specific cases, though, its effects may be harder to define precisely. Physical injuries and their resulting disabilities are often plainly visible, and acts of sexual abuse are generally easier to define than the ongoing emotional abuse that many children suffer.

An important result of emotional abuse, in many instances, is damage to the abused child's self-image. It is little exaggeration to say that we are all what we believe we are. If I believe I am a worthwhile human being with my own special place in the world, I am likely to act accordingly. If I am repeatedly told I am 'dumb', 'stupid', 'a retard', 'good for nothing' or 'a slut' (and I have seen children who have been called all of these and many other derogatory things), I am likely to come to believe what I am told, especially when it is important people in my life, like my family, that tell me. These concepts then become part of my self-image. One of the most precious gifts parents can give their children is a good sense of self-worth.

There is no substitute for the warm, nurturing, affirming atmosphere of the stable, united family that welcomes the newborn child into its fold. How far this atmosphere has to be lacking for the child actually to be labelled 'emotionally abused' is perhaps more a matter of legal definition than clinical importance. It is reasonable to assume that any deficiency may have its effects. At the same time we cannot expect perfection in every parental couple and some children seem to be remarkably resilient and able to triumph over adverse circumstances in ways which can surprise us.

The interaction of factors

Most of the problems with which children present and which may cause them to experience failure in one or other area of their lives have multiple causes. The interaction between these and the strengths and protective factors in their physical, temperamental and psychological makeup is complex. One adverse factor may have little effect, especially if it is brief and occurs in the context of a basically healthy and nurturing family environment. Failure becomes increasingly likely if there are more factors operating and they continue over a longer period of time.

Failure, of course, is a relative term. Many great artists have died in poverty, only to be recognised for what they were much later. Vincent van Gogh was surely a success as an artist, but his social life was a near disaster and he died in poverty. Did he fail? During his lifetime many would surely have said so, but how many of them are remembered today?

A person who was certainly abused and deprived as a child was the jazz singer, Billie Holiday. As a teenager she was placed by her mother – unknowingly it seems – in a brothel, and her subsequent life was plagued by drug and alcohol abuse and problems with the law. Her relationships with men seem to have been disturbed and difficult and all the evidence suggests that she was anything but a happy person. Her drug and alcohol problems no doubt contributed to her decline and early death. Yet she is widely regarded as the greatest jazz singer that ever lived. Was she a failure? Artistically, certainly not. In her personal life, yes. Would she have become as great a singer as she did had she had a conventional, secure and happy middle class upbringing? This we cannot know for certain but my own view is that she would not have been able to sing with the poignancy and feeling that she did had she not had a hard childhood.

When the pianist and blues singer, Little Brother Montgomery, ran away from home at age 11, this may have looked like failure. His formal education must have suffered but he learned – the hard way – to survive in the situation in which he found himself. No doubt he had much native musical talent to help him and he subsequently had a remarkably successful career.

Failure and abuse

Perhaps we should conclude that we need a definition of failure before we can say how far abuse contributes to it. Not only is failure a relative term, it may or may not be evident in a variety of different aspects of a person's life.

Perhaps we should regard 'failure' in this context as lack of success in realising our potential. Some people's greatest potential may not lie in academic success at school, nor in the conventional 'middle-class' or 'blue-collar' life many seek for themselves and their children. Indeed too rigid insistence by parents and others on the conventional tasks of childhood – even on formal schooling – may stifle creativity. It is striking how many of the world's great artists and entertainers have had abusive or deprived childhoods. Charlie Chaplin springs to mind – abandoned by his mother and placed in an orphanage while young, he nevertheless had a somewhat successful life. It seems he turned his own self-esteem problems to advantage by playing the clown.

Lately there has been some media attention to the career of the late Josephine Baker who grew up in poor circumstances and might have been expected to have been a failure. In some senses, moreover, she was. Her relationships with men were chaotic and although at one point in her career she was immensely rich, she died in poverty because of a series of ill-judged decisions she took. Yet surely the world was a richer place for her life! On the other hand her childhood circumstances, which might be regarded as abusive, probably had results which handicapped her in realising her full potential and making wise decisions about the disposal of her great wealth.

While formal education is clearly important in our 'Western' industrial societies, it is the capacity to use our full potential in all areas of our lives which should probably be considered of the greatest importance. Abuse in any of its forms militates against this. This is perhaps the essence of failure. It could even be argued that too much pressure on a child to succeed in areas chosen by the parents – even though with the very best of intentions – is abusive. The converse – sensitivity to the child's strengths, interests and potential and an upbringing which facilitates their expression – is the non-abusive alternative for which parents and society should surely strive.

Summary

Abusive experiences, especially when they are multiple and prolonged, may adversely affect any or many areas of a child's development and thus lead to failure in those areas of development or more generally.

The physical effects of abuse may have the most obviously handicapping results, for example brain injury, mental retardation or blindness. Physical neglect and emotional abuse act more insidiously and, like sexual abuse, may profoundly damage the child's self-image. This may lead to failure in any area of life, since children who do not believe they can achieve success tend not to succeed – since the tasks with which they are faced seem hopeless to them.

Sexual abuse, especially when it is intergenerational and perpetrated by significant adults may result in arrest or distortion of psychosexual development. The results may include various dysfunctional behaviours, particularly in the area of relationships with the opposite sex. Some abused children themselves become perpetrators of abuse on others.

As a general rule, failure in one or more areas of development is more likely when various abusive and neglectful experiences are combined and operate over an extended period of time. Teasing out the effects of specific experiences is often difficult or impossible.

Failure is a relative term. What is considered success in one culture may not be so perceived in another. It is clear also that success in one area – for example in various forms of artistic endeavour – may be achieved despite, or even because of, problems in other areas of a person's life. Abuse may even be perceived by some as a challenge to be overcome.

One of the common legacies of abuse in any of its forms is a poor self image. Children who grow up being told, whether verbally or non-verbally, that they are in various ways defective often come to believe this. Such beliefs can be hard to shake once they are established. They can result in the failure of such people to achieve their potential in almost any of life's areas.

References

Barker, P. (1988) *Basic Child Psychiatry,* 5th edition. Oxford: Blackwell.

Beitchman, J.H., Zucker, K.J., Hood, J.E., daCosta, G.A. and Akman, D. (1991) A review of the short-term effects of child sexual abuse, *Child Abuse and Neglect,* 15: 537–56.

Caffey, J. (1946) Multiple fractures in the long bones of infants suffering from chronic subdural haematoma, *American Journal of Roentgenology* 56: 163–73.

Garbarino, J., Guttman, E. and Seeley, J.W. (1986) *The Psychologically Battered Child.* San Francisco: Jossey-Bass.

Government of Alberta (1984) *Child Welfare Act.* Edmonton: Queen's Printer.

Han, D.P. and Wilkinson, W.S. (1990) Late ophthalmic manifestations of the shaken baby syndrome, *Journal of Pediatric Ophthalmology and Strabismus,* 27: 299–303.

Lynch, M.A. (1985) Child abuse before Kempe: an historical review, *Child Abuse and Neglect,* 9: 7–15.

Payne, M.A. (1989) Use and abuse of corporal punishment: a Carribean view, *Child Abuse and Neglect 13:* 1389–401.

Pelletier, G. (1990) Personal communication.

Powers, J.L., Eckenrode, J. and Jaklitsch, B. (1990) Maltreatment among runaway and homeless youth, *Child Abuse and Neglect,* 14: 87–98.

Ronchetti, R., Bonci, E. and Martinez, F.D. (1990) Passive smoking in childhood – tobacco smoke, *Lung,* Supplement, 313–19.

Scott, P.D. (1977) Non-accidental injury in children, *British Journal of Psychiatry,* 131: 366–80.

Tager, I.B. (1989) Health effects of 'passive smoking' in children, *Chest,* 96: 1161–4.

CHAPTER 8

The Child from the Chaotic Family

Philip Barker

The chaotic family is well known to family therapists, social workers, psychiatrists and other mental health professionals. While we all have our clinical impressions of how the chaos in these families affects the members and especially the children, little research has addressed specifically the relationship between growing up in a chaotic family and the development – or not – of problems in the children in the family. Nevertheless there are good reasons to believe that a chaotic family environment affects adversely the children growing up in it. This chapter will review these reasons.

Before we go any further a warning is in order here. Children's vulnerability to adverse circumstances varies greatly. The factors we shall discuss do not affect all children equally; indeed the vulnerability/invulnerability factor modifies the effects of adverse situations generally. There is no reason to believe that those we will be discussing here are exceptions. Individual differences in response are therefore to be expected.

A prime function of any family with children is to promote the healthy development of the children. The main question which I will address in this chapter therefore is how an upbringing in a chaotic family may affect the development of the children in it.

Development may be viewed from many perspectives. I propose to confine myself to three of these – attachment theory, learning theory and Erikson's psychodynamic views. In each case I will consider how growing up in a chaotic family might affect development when examined from the particular viewpoint.

Chaotic families

The chaotic family was one of the family types delineated by Epstein *et al.* (1978) when they described the 'McMaster model of family functioning'. This model distinguishes four main types of 'control' in families: flexible, rigid, laissez-faire, and chaotic.

Family members are constantly influencing each other in many ways. They need to do so for many reasons, not least to establish and maintain order in the family system. This process is what is referred to by the term 'control'. Control is required both to sustain the maintenance functions of the family and also to enable it to adapt to changing circumstances and new demands. Steinhauer *et al.* (1984), discussing the 'Process model of family functioning', which is closely related to the McMaster Model, point out that:

> The maintenance component of control governs how family members continuously influence each other to ensure that the instrumental tasks and role requirements of daily life are regularly accomplished... Successful control of maintenance functioning, which often requires minor adjustments on a day-to-day basis since task and role requirements never remain constant, is essential for successful task accomplishment. Without it, there is failure of role integration and continuous role conflict, inefficient task accomplishment and the ongoing friction and tension these inevitably evoke. (p.82–83)

As well as the maintenance functions required in stable families, there is a need also for families to adapt to changing circumstances and developmental demands. Changing habitual ways of functioning is more challenging than continuing along in established ways and families vary greatly in their capacities to meet such challenges. To quote Steinhauer *et al.* (1984) again: 'The less a family can adapt its functioning to meet changing demands, the more chronic tension and interference with task accomplishment are likely to result' (p.83).

Flexible styles of behavioural control are those most often found in healthily functioning families. Such styles are predictable but constructive and change in appropriate ways in response to changing circumstances. Steinhauer and his colleagues favour a flexible style of control 'because its supportive and educational tone encourages family members to participate and to identify with the ideals and rules of the family' (p.83).

Rigid styles of behavioural control are high in predictability but low in constructiveness and adaptability. 'Rigid' families often manage maintenance functions well but do less well when adaptation to changing circumstances is required. Steinhauer *et al.* (1984) observe that: 'Under stress or when change is required, the forced and punitive aspects of this style encourage subversion, passive-aggressiveness, displacement of anger outside the home and multiple power struggles' (p.83).

Laissez-faire styles of behavioural control combine moderate predictability with low constructiveness. To quote Steinhauer *et al.* (1984) again:

> Since almost anything goes, inertia and indecision take the place of organisation and action. In such families, members can do as they please as long as they are not too disruptive, since little responsibility is assumed or exercised... role integration is unlikely, task accomplishment haphazard and communication frequently insufficient, unclear and indirect. (p.83)

The affective involvement of the family members is often low in 'laissez-faire' families and the children may be insecure and prone to attention-seeking behaviour.

Chaotic styles of control are low in both predictability and constructiveness. At times the style is laissez-faire and at others it is rigid. It varies along the continuum between these extremes in what usually appears to be a fortuitous fashion. There is typically both poor performance of maintenance functions and poor adaptation to changing circumstances and developmental needs. Steinhauer *et al.* (1984) state that typical responses in these families are hostility and/or withdrawal, resulting from the 'continual frustration, confusion and unpredictability they provide'.

Attachment issues

We will now consider the likely or possible effects on children of growing up in a chaotic family, focusing first on how such a family environment might affect the development of attachments.

The development of secure emotional attachments, most usually to parent figures, has come to be considered an important process in child development. Research aimed specifically to establish a connection between chaotic styles of family control and the types of attachment developing between children and their caregivers does not appear to have been carried out as yet. But theoretical considerations and clinical experience suggest that secure attachments between parents and their children are less likely to develop in chaotic families. The capricious and unpredictable reactions which children in such families experience, especially the alternation between strict, rigid styles and laissez faire ones, can scarcely be expected to promote secure attachments.

The current state of knowledge in the field of attachment has been reviewed by Goldberg (1991). Research since Bowlby (1958, 1969, 1973, 1980) described attachment theory has led to the delineation of four main types of attachment: secure, avoidant (dismissing), ambivalent/resistant (preoccupied) and disorganised. These appear to be related to different styles of behaviour on the part of the caregiver.

Ainsworth and Wittig (1969) and Ainsworth *et al.* (1978), using their 'strange situation' research protocol with infants and their mothers, originally distinguished only the first three of these types of attachment. In the secure variety the attachment system is activated only when the infant's security is threatened. When it is, the infant returns to his or her secure base, usually the mother.

The avoidant (dismissing) type of attachment is characterised by the child exploring without apparent regard for the attachment figure though the latter is monitored by the child. In other words, the attachment system is suppressed.

In the ambivalent/resistant (preoccupied) strategy the infant returns to the mother constantly even though there appears to be no reason why he or she should not feel safe and comfortable. Goldberg (1991) summarises the situation thus:

> In the avoidant strategy the threshold for activating attachment behaviour is very high, while in the ambivalent/resistant strategy, it is very low. In both insecure strategies, the threshold is set primarily to meet internal needs and is not adapted to the environment. However, in the secure strategy, the threshold is both moderate and sensitive to environmental conditions. (p.395)

Later research (Main and Solomon, 1986, 1990) has led to the identification of the fourth type of attachment, the 'disorganised'. Infants in this group lack a coherent strategy for coping with separations and reunions. They also display unusual and hard-to-explain behaviours which seem to reflect confusion or fear of the caregiver. Also included in this group are infants showing a 'mixed' pattern of attachment as described by Crittenden (1985) in maltreated infants.

It is tempting to hypothesise that the disorganised forms of attachment behaviour might be associated with rearing in chaotic families, though research data to tell us whether or not this is so are lacking. Nevertheless clinical experience and theoretical considerations suggest that all three non-secure attachment patterns may be more likely in infants raised in chaotic families. The conditions for the development of secure attachments seem largely to be lacking in such families.

What is the significance of all this for children's future development and the question of whether or not they will fail? There are good reasons for believing that securely attached children are more likely to grow up better adjusted psychologically than children in the other attachment categories. To quote Goldberg (1991):

> The quality of both early and later attachment influences self-concepts as well as expectations and attitudes toward social relationships. Individuals whose primary attachment relationships in childhood were satisfying and provided emotional security view themselves as lovable, expect positive interactions with others, and value intimate relationships. Individuals who experienced rejection or harsh treatment as children view themselves as unworthy of love, expect further rejection, and act in ways that elicit rejections. (p.393–4)

As Goldberg (1991) also points out, studies are beginning to show that secure infants are more competent than insecure infants in a variety of cognitive and social skills, as assessed later in childhood. The longitudinal study of Sroufe and his colleagues (1990), in which children assessed in infancy have been followed up to puberty, has shown consistently that the nature of early attachments influences social skills later in childhood.

Learning theory

Another perspective from which we may view the situation and development of children growing up in chaotic families is that of learning theory.

It is nowadays accepted by most workers in the field that children's development depends on the complex interaction of biological, especially neurological, maturation and environmental training and stimulation. Biological development is in large measure genetically programmed. Thus children reach a state of neurological maturity which enables them to walk, to talk and to achieve the many other developmental milestones that characterise their progression from helpless infant to autonomous adult. But appropriate environmental conditions are necessary for optimal development, especially of the more finely honed skills needed for living in the complex, technologically oriented environments that comprise much of the developed world today.

Put more simply, children must be taught things. In societies as complex as ours, they need to be taught many things. Unless they are in grossly understimulating institutions, they will, without much instruction, learn to walk and acquire the elements of verbal communication skills. But much more is needed nowadays. This may not be provided in chaotic families.

It is not just table manners that are not genetically programmed but social relationships generally. We are not born honest or dishonest. We either learn our society's concepts of right and wrong or we do not; and we are either taught, or we are not, the advantages of living our lives according to the rules and conventions of the particular social system into which we have been born.

Success in a complex technologically oriented society depends of course on much more than sound social relationships, helpful as these are. The acquisition of much knowledge and technical skill is also necessary.

It is generally accepted that, given biological readiness, children (and adults too!) learn by four main methods. The first three are operant conditioning, respondent (or 'classical') conditioning, and modelling. The fourth is the process of 'figuring things out' in one's mind or, in behaviour therapy terms, 'learning by cognition'.

Operant conditioning is the modification of behaviour by the response which the behaviour elicits. If one touches the cooking stove while it is hot one may get burned and if so one is unlikely to repeat the act which led to the painful burn. If preparing a tasty meal leads to fulsome praise from one's family, one is likely to be more strongly predisposed to cook a meal another day... and so on. We are all of us learning, day by day, from the consequences of our actions.

Respondent conditioning refers to the results of altering the circumstances (or 'contingencies') leading up to an action. The usually quoted example is that of Pavlov's dogs. Pavlov rang a bell before feeding his dogs and it wasn't long before the dogs started to salivate when they heard the bell rather than when their food was presented. Before the experiment began, of course, the bell evoked no such reaction.

Modelling is the imitation of the behaviour of others. Toddlers are typically modelers *par excellence*. They observe, often acutely, what others in their family, and even outside it, do and try to do the same themselves. The little boy gets hold of his daddy's tie, puts it around his neck and attempts to tie it. The girl gets hold of her mother's make-up and plasters it all over her face, and probably clothes too. Neither has been taught to do such things. They are just modelling the behaviour they have observed in their parents.

Learning by cognition is also observable in quite young children. No-one taught my two-year-old to bring a chair into the kitchen, climb up on it and gain access to the shelf on which we keep brightly coloured jars of spices which, presumably, looked such interesting playthings.

A fuller account of these learning processes is to be found in *Basic Behaviour Therapy* (Murdoch and Barker 1991). It is not difficult to understand how they may be impaired in the rearing of children in chaotic families. The consistent rewarding of desired behaviours and the punishment of undesired ones does not occur. Instead such children do not know what to expect. Anything, or nothing much, may happen in response to their behaviour. There may be no response in the family's laissez-faire moments, or excessive response at other times. These inconsistent responses represent a poor way of achieving social training, and they are liable also to arouse anxiety in the children. These children do not know what to expect but may always fear a harsh or angry response.

The behavioural model offered to children by the parents in chaotic families is also a poor one. Modelling is a powerful process by which children acquire social skills. While such skills are specifically taught in many families, even more important may be the observation by children of the behaviour of others. They learn to say 'please' and 'thank-you' because they hear their parents using these terms. Indeed much of the way they relate to others is modelled on the behaviour of those in their immediate circle. If their parents behave capriciously and inconsistently, they are likely to grow up doing so also.

What about learning by cognition? Is this liable to be affected by rearing in a chaotic family? The answer is probably yes. While children certainly figure things out without being taught, 'problem solving', as this skill is often called, can be taught. There are certain steps which need to be taken: identification of the problem, identifying possible means of addressing it, considering the merits of the different possibilities, acting on that which seems best and monitoring the result, and modifying or altering one's behaviour if the strategy used is unsuccessful. These skills may not be taught in the chaotic family as well as they might be.

In summary, children in chaotic families are apt to be disadvantaged in several ways. The responses of their parents to their behaviours, being inconsistent, may adversely affect their learning of social and other skills;

they may lack constructive role models; and they may not be taught good problem-solving skills.

Erik Erikson's 'Eight Ages of Man'

Another of the many paradigms for understanding child (and adult) development is that proposed by Erikson (1965). We will consider here only the earlier stages of Erikson's 'ages of man'. The first of these is that of 'basic trust versus basic mistrust'. Erikson writes:

> The general state of trust... implies not only that one has learned to rely on the sameness and continuity of the outer providers, but also that one may trust oneself and the capacity of one's own organs to cope with urges; and that one is able to consider oneself trustworthy enough so that the providers will not need to be on guard lest they be nipped (Erikson 1965, p.239–40)

How is this trust to be to be created? Erikson's view is summarised in the following quotation:

> Mothers create a sense of trust in their children by that kind of administration which in its quality combines sensitive care of the baby's individual needs and a firm sense of personal trustworthiness within the trusted framework of their culture's life style. This forms the basis in the child for a sense of identity which will later combine a sense of being 'all right', of being oneself, and of becoming what other people trust one will become. (Erikson 1965, p.241)

Continuity and sensitivity, two of the qualities Erikson considers babies to need in the care they get from their mothers, are liable to be absent in chaotic families.

Erikson's second 'age' is that of 'autonomy versus shame and doubt'. At this stage, Erikson states, 'outer control... must be firmly reassuring'. A 'basic faith in existence' needs to be acquired. He explains:

> Firmness must protect [the child] against the potential anarchy of his as yet untrained sense of discrimination, his inability to hold on and to let go with discretion. As his environment encourages him to 'stand on his own feet', it must protect him against meaningless and arbitrary experiences of shame and early doubt. (Erikson 1965, p.243–4)

A sense of shame is something with which many children from dysfunctional families emerge and it is a serious handicap. Doubt, Erikson says, is the brother of shame. A sense of autonomy implies substantial freedom from shame and doubt about oneself.

The third of Erikson's eight ages is that of 'initiative versus guilt'. The healthily developing child, Erikson suggests:

> is in free possession of a surplus of energy which permits him to forget failures quickly and to approach what seems desirable (even if it also seems uncertain and even dangerous) with undiminished and more accurate direction. Initiative adds to autonomy the quality of undertaking, planning and 'attacking' a task for the sake of being active and on the move, where before self-will, more often than not, inspired acts of defiance or, at any rate, protested independence. (Erikson, 1965, p.247)

Initiative is not typically encouraged in chaotic families and the harsh reactions to behaviour which may be, quite capriciously, experienced by the children are apt to foster feelings of guilt or even shame.

Why are families chaotic?

Before we consider the problems children in chaotic families may display, a brief consideration of what may be behind this form of family functioning is in order. This may assist us in devising suitable therapeutic interventions. It is generally believed that parents tend to rear their children along the same general lines as they themselves were reared by their parents. So if you grew up in a chaotic family there is a more than average chance that the family you form will be, at least in some degree, chaotic (and we must remember that there are degrees of chaos).

Other factors may operate. A common one is the abuse of alcohol and other drugs by one or both parents. The altered states of mind experienced by the drug user are almost certain to cause inconsistency in responding to children. While some children report that their father or mother is more 'mellow' or more likely to let them have their way when he or she is drunk or 'stoned', in many families the reverse is the case. The drunk father, for example, may be aggressive, violent and an object of fear, even though he is a fair and caring parent when sober.

Other psychiatric disorders in parents may foster chaos in the family, notably depression. The depressed parent may be too lacking in energy and apathetic to bother about what the children are doing – until their behaviour becomes 'too much' when he or she suddenly flares up in anger and desperation and imposes some draconian punishment which, however, the parent may not have the energy to enforce consistently.

Characteristics of children from chaotic families

We may summarise the foregoing discussion by saying that children growing up in chaotic families may suffer any of the following disadvantages. Any or all may lead to failure in various areas of their of lives:

- insecure or disorganised emotional attachments

- poor social training and consequent lack of social skills
- high levels of anxiety resulting from the inconsistent and unpredictable responses of their parents
- regression to, or fixation at, one of the early stages of emotional development described by Erik Erikson
- impaired self-esteem, since neither the laissez faire nor the rigid family control styles usually enable parents to affirm their children and to instil in them the trust in themselves and the world that healthy adjustment requires.

At the level of symptoms or syndromes, children from chaotic families may develop clinical pictures that fit the diagnostic criteria for conduct disorders, oppositional disorders or anxiety disorders. Academic failure and difficult peer relationships are other common associations.

Management

What can we do for these children? The best solution, of course, is to restore the family to a healthy mode of functioning. 'Restore' may not be the right word, though, because many of these families have never functioned well.

Family therapy designed to help the family system become more functional is probably the treatment of choice, at least in theory. A major focus will be to promote the operation of a better system of control within the family. In practice, it is often hard to engage these families in therapy. This is particularly inclined to be the case when one or more family members are alcoholics or drug addicts in denial – as they often prove to be.

If a radical change in the family system cannot be achieved, some – usually limited – success may be achieved by systematically instructing or training the parents in providing a more consistent and predictable environment for their children.

Individual therapy with these children may provide them with at least a measure of order in their lives – as provided by the therapy sessions, as well as opportunities to work through and come to terms with the anxiety and anger they usually feel as a result of their family experiences.

These children desperately need success so that structuring their school and playtime activities so that they achieve it – in games or in youth organisations if not at home – may be of real help to them.

If depression or another psychiatric disorder is found to be present in a parent this should be treated.

Summary

Chaotic families are those which provide inconsistent and unpredictable environments for their children. Behaviour control varies from rigid and punitive to laissez faire. Children growing up in such families are at risk in many ways. Secure emotional attachments to their parents may not develop, their learning of social skills may be impaired and they may not learn to trust the adult world, and they may grow up with feelings of doubt about their worth.

Families may be chaotic because the parents themselves grew up in such families and are not familiar with any other way of functioning. Parental alcoholism, drug abuse and other psychiatric disorders may also contribute. Treatment often requires work with the entire family as well as with the individual child.

References

Ainsworth, M.D.S., Blehar, M.C., Waters, E. and Wall, S. (1978) *Patterns of Attachment: A Psychological Study of the Strange Situation.* Hillsdale, New Jersey: Erlbaum.

Ainsworth, M.D.S. and Wittig, B.A. (1969) Attachment and exploratory behaviour of one-year-olds in a strange situation, in Foss, B.M. (ed.), *Determinants of Infant Behaviour.* London: Methuen.

Bowlby, J. (1958) The nature of the child's tie to his mother. *International Journal of Psychoanalysis,* 39: 350–73.

Bowlby, J. (1969) *Attachment and Loss: Attachment.* New York: Basic Books.

Bowlby, J. (1973) *Attachment and Loss: Separation.* New York: Basic Books.

Bowlby, J. (1980) *Attachment and Loss: Loss, Sadness and Depression.* New York: Basic Books.

Crittenden, J. (1985) Maltreated infants: vulnerability and resilience. *Journal of Child Psychology and Psychiatry,* 26: 85–96.

Epstein, N.B., Bishop, D.S. and Levin, S. (1978) The McMaster model of family functioning. *Journal of Marriage and Family Counselling,* 4: 19–31.

Erikson, E. (1965) Eight ages of man. *Childhood and Society,* 2nd edition. Harmondsworth, Middlesex: Penguin.

Goldberg, S. (1991) Recent developments in attachment theory and research. *Canadian Journal of Psychiatry,* 36: 393–404.

Main, M. and Solomon, J. (1986) Discovery of an insecure-disorganised/disoriented attachment pattern, in Brazelton, T.B. and Yogman, M.W. (eds.), *Affective Development in Infancy.* Norwood, NJ: Ablex.

Main, M. and Solomon, J. (1990) Procedures for identifying infants as disorganised/disoriented during the Ainsworth Strange Situation, in Greenberg, M.T., Cicchetti, D. and Cummings, E.M. (eds.), *Attachment in the Preschool Years.* Chicago: University of Chicago Press.

Murdoch, D. and Barker, P. (1991) *Basic Behaviour Therapy.* Oxford: Blackwell.

Sroufe, L.A., Egeland, B. and Kreutzer, T. (1990) The fate of early experience following developmental change: longitudinal approaches to individual adaptation in childhood. *Child Development*, 61: 1363–73.

Steinhauer, P.D., Santa-Barbara J. and Skinner, H. (1984) The process model of family functioning. *Canadian Journal of Psychiatry*, 29: 77–97.

CHAPTER 9

Racial prejudice and achievement

Gerry German

Formal educational achievement depends on open access to educational institutions, fair treatment within those institutions and an optimistic expectation of a successful outcome at the end of each stage of education. One would expect institutions to be managed in the most professionally competent way to guarantee full equality of opportunity throughout the whole of the educational process. Testing and assessment have a key role to play in facilitating the proper allocation of young people to courses and teaching groups and ensuring the kind of educational treatment appropriate to their needs and potential. Accuracy and fairness here and in the final measure of competence will be crucial in determining one's future in relation to a wide range of life chances.

However, schools and colleges are not the sole determinants of educational success. While teachers and lectures make a conscious choice to exercise their professional responsibilities as educationists, young people up to the age of 16 at least have no choice. Even after that, there is little if any space for them to negotiate the nature of their educational experiences even though they appear to be able to choose their institutions and their courses. Educational institutions do not operate in a vacuum: their participants, both teachers and taught, are also products of their conditioning – socially, culturally, spiritually, economically and politically.

We have a fairly accurate picture of the outcome of the educational process. We know how many succeed in school examinations and how many proceed to further and higher education. The male – female classification is self-evident; class distribution could be worked out; up to now, however, there have only been limited local surveys on an ethnic basis (although the recent introduction of ethnic monitoring will make that task easier in the future).

Ethnic data for enrolment are incomplete in that they reflect simply a head-count rather than the full picture of applying for and actually gaining a school or college place. However, here again there have been a few local enquiries which yield that information, generally in relation to selective schools.

What is lacking is a detailed picture of what actually happens to young people in the classroom and the lecture-room. However, there have been a number of sound ethnographic studies at infant, primary and secondary level along with student surveys which go a long way to bringing out the different black and white experiences. There are also some anecdotal records of how young black people have perceived their treatment at the hands of white people responsible for their education. The attitudes and actions of the peers are also recorded in various local and national studies as well as in personal reports.

Prejudice is arriving at a position and expressing an attitude or making a judgement before considering the relevant facts. Racial prejudice is acquired early in life and leads to unfair and unfavourable judgements which limit the chances of all the parties involved. It will limit the range of human relationships possible in Britain's multi-ethnic society and it will block open wide-ranging enquiry and obstruct the development of a healthy stimulating curiosity about the world. It would seem self-evident therefore that prejudice of any kind is likely to hinder the realisation of human potential in every field of activity. A racially prejudiced person in a management position, for example, would find it difficult to appoint and inspire a representative workforce as well as to deliver an equitable, effective service.

If education is about acquiring knowledge based on true facts, prejudice must hinder that process. One needs to ask oneself, especially as a teacher, about one's own prejudices and how they were acquired. I personally was anti-semitic before I was ten years old. I was also afraid of black people. I was terrified of Gypsies. I disliked English people and I hated rich people. On the other hand, I was not impressed either by the Welsh people or by poor people with whom I most readily identified. My prejudices were easily dredged up from a framework of early childhood conditioning.

I was suspicious of and I disliked Jews despite the fact that we had a Jewish lodger and I would go out with the Jewish travelling salesmen who occasionally stayed with us. I also worked as an errand boy for a Jewish dry-cleaning firm, and I would put on the lights and the heating in the synagogue on the Jewish Sabbath. There were also Jewish pupils in my form at the grammar school. But the lessons I had learned from listening to discussions between my father and my uncle about the Zinoviev Letter and the Zionist plot to take over the world remained unshaken by the widening contacts with Jewish people. They were really different. Some of them had funny names. The Jewish pupils stayed out of morning assembly until the announcements were due to be made. They stuck together. And in the early years of the Second World War the media seemed to justify the reservations I had about Jews. Some of my mother's cheap paperbacks portrayed them as unfeeling, mean and opportunistic. It was only much later in life that I learned that my paternal grandfather was Jewish!

While my hatred of Jews was vigorous and even destructive, my prejudice against black people was a combination of fear and superiority. From a very early age I was intimidated by my mother with warnings that 'the bogeyman would get me if I didn't get home before dark'. The Overseas Mission collections at Sunday School portrayed them as benighted heathens in need of white efforts to bring about their salvation. *Coral Island* and the *Biggles* books promoted an image of them as ignorant, superstitious and resistant to change and progress as well as inclined to slaughter and cannibalism. My regular diet of the *Rover* and the *Wizard* celebrated the glories of Empire and the inadequacies of the 'natives' in countries that we had *discovered* overseas. Our grammar school studies of the British Empire did nothing to challenge these destructive stereotypes. And in fact when we studied the Crusades, we seemed also to be laying a foundation to justify a calculated although informal use of terms like 'wogs' (and in other closely related contexts 'nigger').

We knew about a Liverpool 'half-caste' family in the district but they were said to be troublemakers and not the kind of family to mix with. The terms 'half-caste' and 'half-breed' were helpful in labelling deficiencies and in defining boundaries to social intercourse. None of their children went to the grammar school, of course. Their families presented no evidence to challenge what we had learned about the inadequacies of people who, because of mixing the races, were only halfway at most to being as good as white people!

Our prejudice against gypsies was developed in the same way. We were to be particularly careful of them because they came and went suddenly. They were likely to steal anything they wanted, including children! Kidnapping was a terrifying prospect. While we had heard about 'tinkers' and even welcomed them when they called to sharpen our knives, we were unaware of the further distinctions between 'Romanies' and 'Travellers'. 'Gippos' was the term that suited all our purposes.

In many ways the negative nature of my schooling and up-bringing made it easy for me to acquire and cling to a range of prejudices. We were distrustful of others. We were to be constantly on our guard against the influences of those who might cause us to lower our standards and behave in ways that would bring shame to our schools and families. Indeed it seemed that the general negative conditioning was the consequence of the ever-present threat of humiliation and failure. And surrounding all this there was a national ethos that projected a permanent view of white supremacy and English imperial greatness. The bodies of knowledge that were shared with us confirmed but never challenged the view that we had of ourselves as superior white people and others distinguished by the colour of their skin as different and inherently inferior. As Welsh working-class people we developed our own forms of self-hatred but we were never in doubt about our superiority as white people.

I introduce this autobiographical account because I believe that people need to examine the nature of their own prejudices and the conditioning that developed them. The latter should include not merely domestic and school factors but the range of institutional influences interacting to produce and sustain prejudiced attitudes towards other people. One needs to ask how those attitudes will influence the quality of life for oneself and for others with whom one will come into contact and for whom one may also have a professional responsibility. One needs to ask how one may avoid picking up such prejudices in the first place or how one might discard them or how one can ensure that they do not adversely affect the discharge of one's social, civic and professional duties towards others.

There has been a common belief that black people are underachieving academically. On the other hand, some commentators consoled themselves with the findings of the Rampton and Swann Reports (DES 1981, 1985a) that while pupils of Afro-Caribbean origin did not do too well in external examinations, Asian pupils did as well as, if not better than, their English white counterparts. Some have used the information to deny any inadequacy in the British educational system in its capacity to accord equality of opportunity to minority ethnic pupils. On the other hand, more detailed surveys such as those carried out by the Inner London Education Authority (Mabey 1986, Kysel 1988) reveal variations of performance and progress in the different ethnic groups. Peter Mortimore of the ILEA warned us early on about the danger of over-generalisation (Mortimore 1983).

In the same essay Peter Mortimore expresses his 'basic belief that whilst not all children can achieve the same educational level... whole groups should not fall short in their achievement. If they do, I suggest, we need to examine our educational system very carefully to make sure that the system is not, in some way, responsible' (Mortimore 1983 p.17).

Educational institutions generally display a strong sense of tradition in the way that they organise and structure themselves. Their principal task of transmitting knowledge is founded on explicit statements of what is relevant and measurable. Their systems of testing and assessment are narrowly focused on those things considered worthwhile by the high-achieving authorities of the past. Successful performance takes place within a particular kind of course culture with content, methodology and books and resources intimately related to criteria defined by individuals and organisations that uphold and are sustained by that culture.

Cecile Wright (Wright 1987) has conducted two ethnographic school studies covering the infant, primary and secondary stages in an attempt to reveal how that culture operates in the classroom, that is in the interaction between the pupil and the teacher. She also records comments made in her hearing or directly to her by teachers about pupils and their parents. She reproduces remarks made by children and their parents in discussions (often at crisis-point) with teachers. There is space too for the expression of insights into the treatment of black children as perceived by black teachers.

Black pupils, especially those of Afro-Caribbean origin, are perceived as problems. Black pupils, Asian and Afro-Caribbean, are treated differentially, disrespected, disparaged, ignored and provoked by their teachers in the classroom. They are excluded from school or suspended from the class more often than their white counterparts. They are also the subject of faulty assessment even when their classroom contribution and examination performance suggests otherwise. These studies reveal how black pupils are disadvantaged as a result of a devastating combination of negative prejudice, destructive stereotyping and low expectations on the part of teachers.

Cecile Wright also described how black pupils coped. In primary and secondary schools some challenged their teachers' overtly racially prejudiced comments. Older ones eventually entered further education colleges. The younger the child, the more likely it is that racial prejudice on the part of the teachers or the pupils will have an adverse effect on the target pupils and those most likely to identify with them. Cecile Wright describes how teacher prejudice leads to grossly discriminatory behaviour and the inhibition of language development among young Asian pupils. She gives a vivid description of a teacher's insensitive, even callous, treatment of a group of shy young Asian girls trying hard to avoid a public display when changing for games. And by drawing attention to minority ethnic pupils as a group of inadequate performers, the prejudiced teacher endorses the attitudes of racially prejudiced white pupils who join in the general disparagement with glances, nudges and snide remarks. These are *not* the circumstances in which effective learning can take place and in which one can achieve one's real potential.

Cecile Wright's studies also demonstrate that there are parents who will support their children and challenge their teachers' racially prejudiced behaviour. The importance of family support is confirmed by Mairtin Mac An Ghaill's work among black students in a sixth form college. He writes:

> Placing students at the centre of the research enables us to see how schooling for black female and male youths is a central part of an alienating social response to them, that results in their experience of a structured 'different reality' from the white population. In respect to this, they have, collectively and individually, creatively developed coping and survival strategies. (Mac An Ghaill 1989 p.273)

The students generally agreed about Britain as a racially stratified society although they reported different experiences of racism in their schooling. Some succeeded by working hard alongside significant numbers of black pupils in their schools. Others set out to prove themselves to the overwhelmingly white schools they attended. One was determined to prove her snobbish boarding school wrong about black people. They were conscious of teacher prejudice and low expectations directed both at black pupils and working-class children generally in the inner-city schools they had attended. They were aware of the stereotyping attached to Asian and Afro-Caribbean males and females. Ghaill describes how some students evolved a 'strategy of resistance within accommodation', that is, performing conventionally to satisfy the academic demands of patently biased teachers but reserving their own positions of integrity in relation to them and their racist institution. They would avoid hostile racially prejudiced teachers and seek out those they respected and from whom they might draw support in moving successfully through the system.

While we can very well ask how much better they might have performed without having to cope with prejudice of a racist kind, we must recognise that these young people were realists capable of evolving strategies and forging alliances aimed at surviving with dignity in a racist society.

Depending on the support networks, coping becomes easier as one gets older but it is in the early years that great damage can be done to children. How are they to value themselves and pupils like them if the messages they get from teachers and the system are that they are not only different but in fact strange and peculiar, not only inferior but permanently incapable of measuring up to white standards? Role models are rare, not only among the staff but also in posters on the walls, books and other resources. Fund-raising activities for people overseas confirm the inadequacy of black people. The persistence of racial harassment inside and outside the school, and the unwillingness or inability of the authorities to do anything about it are a further drain on the energies that people need to bolster their sense of confidence and well-being.

Racial prejudice is not easy to pin down and challenge, even for adults. Professional adults are often unlikely to express their racial prejudices in a grossly offensive way. Their sentiments will be expressed in sophisticated, persuasive, logical and even solicitous ways. Since they are going to have to compete in a monolingual, monocultural society – such as England really is – it would be better for them to concentrate on acquiring English skills and to forget the distraction of mother-tongue and so on! It is sometimes argued that personal attitudes do not matter very much at all – 'We don't care whether you like us' – so long as service delivery is the same for all.

Sivanandan of the Institute of Race Relations puts it powerfully when he states 'My business is not to train the policy officer out of his "racism", but to have him punished for it – that is, if he is meant to be accountable to the community he serves' (Sivanandan 1985). He goes on to say that changing the attitudes of immigration officers will achieve very little when it is really the immigration law and Home Office instructions that need to be changed. Similarly, attitude changes among housing officers will do little for over-crowded or homeless black families when housing stock is limited. Likewise, a change of heart for newspaper owners and editors will do little to counter the racist thrust that sells newspapers.

Sivanandan draws a helpful distinction between racism and racialism.

> Racism, strictly speaking, should be used to refer to structures and institutions with power to discriminate. What individuals display is racialism, prejudiced attitudes, which give them no intrinsic power over non-whites. That power is derived from racist laws, constitutional conventions, judicial precedents, institutional practices – all of which have the imprimatur of the state. (Sivanandan 1985 p.28)

Sivanandan stresses the need to make a clear distinction like this in order to distinguish the different kinds of targets in the struggle for racial justice. While

I can understand the position expressed in the argument that 'I'm not concerned with your attitude – just your behaviour' – when it concerns an adult in relation to an employer, a housing officer, a policeman, a social worker, a court official or a social security clerk – I cannot really agree that confrontation with the prejudiced teacher in school can be described as 'the lesser fight'.

The prejudiced teacher is in a powerful position to intimidate, to inhibit, to humiliate and to cause a child to fail. School pupils spend a lot of time with teachers in a variety of circumstances, both formal and informal. They will be judged on attendance, punctuality, appearance, co-operation, participation and obedience among other things. Those judgements will not be made in neutral spaces. The norms which the pupils may achieve or from which they may fall short are the product of the teacher's conditioning, involving the complex interplay of preconceived notions and ready-made, close-at-hand stereotypes to sustain and refine what might otherwise remain as vague prejudices of fear, suspicion, dislike or even outright hostility.

In the late 1960s an eight-year-old Jamaican born girl said to a visiting Jamaican teacher – at the girl's primary school in a south-of-England county town as part of her counselling course at the nearby university – that the teachers didn't like the Jamaican children: 'I doan know why but dem doan like we, Miss'. The woman head of the infant-primary school had welcomed the Jamaican post-graduate student and asked her to see the small group of West Indian [sic] pupils because their teachers were finding them a problem. The young black children did not know how to define prejudice and stereotypes or to explain imperialism and white supremacy but they were able to recognise that they were being placed at a disadvantage because they felt that they were disliked, not capriciously and casually as individuals (who might somehow deserve it) but as a group – 'dem doan like we'. And it was not just one or two of them but all of *dem* on the staff who disliked them.

The session with the black visitor from the university was confirmation of their being perceived by their teachers as a group exhibiting certain characteristics together that were different from other children and that were a cause of concern to their teachers. They were not only treated differently but evidently valued differently, to the point of dislike. The head's invitation to the black visitor to discuss the West Indians' *problem* with them, to be the intermediary, suggested a fundamental inability to relate and identify with a particular group of children identifiable by the colour of their skin, a common geographical origin and peculiar speech habits, not to mention their apparent distrust of their (white) teachers.

The racially prejudiced teacher, no matter how deep or how wide-ranging his or her prejudice, is inextricably bound up with the educational institution and its practices and procedures for assessing, classifying, allocating to teaching groups and according differential treatment and educational opportunities as a consequence. No matter how refined and sophisticated a selection system might be, so long as the selective schools exist, then it is likely that minority ethnic pupils will continue to be excluded through no fault of their own (Berkshire County Research and Intelligence Unit 1989). What about the oversubscribed denominational primary school, for example? No matter how unprejudiced or unbiased the teachers may be, minority ethnic pupils are unlikely to gain admission. As Peter Newsam, former Chair of the Commission for racial equality, said: 'I have no need to be individually racist since my institution does it so well for me!'

The current concern with testing and assessment and the wider aim of publishing results in league-table form implies standards of accuracy and validity that need constant review. The gap between the identifiable pool of ability and those selected for grammar schools, for example, suggests both an imperfect sampling as well as the failure to remove malignant cultural bias (Trafford Metroplitan Borough Council 1990).

While racially prejudiced teachers may well resort to destructive racial stereotypes in misallocating minority ethnic group pupils to ability groups (Commission for Racial Equality 1992c) it seems likely that such views and practices may become ritualised in regional and national assessment schemes. Academic achievement is related to the structure of knowledge as defined and refined by authorities whose prejudices and enlightenment those structures will reflect and within which changes can occur only in relation to a well-defined framework of references.

In a paper delivered by Dr Julia Dreyden to the National Foundation for Educational Research (Dreyden' 1989) radical suggestions are made about changing both what is regarded as relevant knowledge in a multi-ethnic society and how all members of that diverse society are fairly assessed in their grasp of that knowledge. Despite progress by test-makers in detecting and eliminating single questions which elicit differential performances by different ethnic groups, Dr Dreyden states that 'ultimately the meaning of standardised test scores rests with our dedication to a particular world view, and increasingly, groups whose talents are undermeasured in that world view challenge the legitimacy of its pervasiveness' (Dreyden 1989 p.12).

Testing for success or failure is related to the process of acquiring knowledge, that is, how learning is facilitated by the teacher. If the experiences of certain groups are excluded from that body of knowledge and the dominant world view and system of values, then underachievement and failure are inevitable for large numbers in those groups. Intimidation through exclusion or devaluing is likely to inhibit learning and performance. As Dr Dreyden puts it, 'getting past the gate keepers can be hellishly difficult'.

It is not the tests that cause discrepancies in attainment, she says; but these discrepancies are symptomatic of the educational philosophy and the underlying paradigm of knowledge. It is self-contained and grounded in the Euro-American heritage which is in turn bolstered by a reverence for the achievements of the past. Its structures and value systems place it beyond the kind of scrutiny that might lead to any fundamental change. What she says has a great deal of significance for the persistence of negative prejudice in individuals, groups and systems:

> The knowledge paradigm serves the interest of a special group, actually a minority in their own right, who are unlikely to forgo the advantages and privileges accorded by their society, or in fact, by virtue of the learning which appears to be the desirable and inevitable outcome of the loftiest ideal and most rigorous intellectual standards. (Dreyden 1989 p.12)

Dr Dreyden makes three suggestions, based on the more progressive United States practices, aimed at producing a just system of imparting knowledge and skills and assessing competence: first, 'establish a new canon' by which the 'histories and cultures of under-represented groups' can be 'recovered or constructed and infused into the curricula'. While this is recommended as a national endeavour, she says that is 'essential in school districts where children of non-European heritage predominate'. In the second place, 'teach that the insights and traditions of sub-cultures create ballast to the predominant culture; that a variety of strains in the society increases the depth and complexity of discourse and that diversity in society, as in natural evolution, enhances the chances for survival'. Third, and equally radically, she recommends that one should 'use test results with a healthy dash of professional scepticism. Recognise especially that they have a limited validity in predicting real world success'. She referred to the US Office of Employment finding that test score adjustment for specific groups qualified a percentage of minorities approaching parity in the population. 'On the job, individuals admitted under these adjusted scores performed equally well with employees admitted at normative score levels' (Dreyden 1989 p.12).

Negative prejudice operating at individual and institutional levels in the educational communities creates a hostile learning environment for young people from minority ethnic groups. They experience stresses and strains which are not shared by the majority groups whose presence, interests and abilities are so vigorously reflected in the institutions of which they are so clearly an integral part. They may then comfortably use their intelligence to cope with a range of experiences that are neither unexpected nor dislocating. As Dr Dreyden puts it, 'A normal intelligence may be said to have at its disposal limited resources to expend for self-preservation, then more disinterested motives'. However, she reminds us of the way that black children in particular have to order their priorities and deploy their energies.

> Members of the society devalued by the tradition are in the position of..having to spend limited resources on a hierarchy of priorities beginning with diffusing hostility to obtain physical security; to transforming the environment to one that is sympathetic to non-traditional experience; to establishing and extending one's own traditions. (Dreyden 1989 p.12)

The imperfections of nationally laid down assessment tests have led to the consideration of compensatory schemes designed to do justice to black pupils in particular. The report of a seminar held by the Sheffield local education authority on Recording the Achievement and Experience of Black Pupils states that its 'initiative on primary records of achievement and experience is working against a background of national legislation which fails to acknowledge fundamental needs of black children' (Desforges 1989 p.2). It draws attention to the 'curriculum framework which structures and values both knowledge and skills in an ethnocentric way'. Deficiencies with regard to language provision, the report states, will have 'a detrimental effect on the self concept and self esteem of black pupils'. The report is particularly critical of the Task Group on Assessment and Testing for making 'only a passing reference to bias in assessment'. It notes that 'the problems of fair and unbiased assessments sensitive to ethnic background and bilingualism were ignored'. The seminar noted the struggle of the black communities against 'inappropriate testing, biased assessment and racist professional judgements of its children for many years and some progress has been made. It is crucial that these small advances are not lost in the introduction of a blanket national system of testing which takes no account of linguistic and cultural diversity' (Desforges 1989 p.3).

This is where racial prejudice disadvantages black children most of all – where government introduces legislation, task forces are established, reports are produced and schemes adopted which have all the power of constitutional correctness and scholastic authority as well as the virtually unalterable permanence stemming from such procedures – but when those appointed to deliberate and those elected to legislate do not reflect Britain's multi-ethnic society or a capacity to project the variety of its experiences and aspirations. Lip service may be paid to principles of equality and there may be even ethnic representation but changes are no more than technical. Racial prejudice remains but this time with official endorsement and an even greater power to discriminate on racial grounds. Little favours and small concessions are calculated to give the impression of flexibility and magnanimity but they do very little to enhance the life chances of black people in particular. Opening the gate a little wider will not let people in when the security chain of racial prejudice is still attached.

But even when progressive schemes are introduced, the effects may still be malignant in the hands of racially prejudiced practitioners responsible for their implementation. The Working Group against Racism in Children's Resources (WGARCR) is concerned not only to ensure that good anti-racist resources are available in domestic, caring and learning situations but that adults are properly trained in using them to promote positive self-images, self-confidence and co-operation based on a view of the world as a place where all human beings are equally respected, valued and catered for (WGARCR 1990). The Working Group has also carried out a unique study of the most common texts recommended for use on child-development courses: it shows how strong the effects of racial prejudice are in ignoring, marginalising, tokenising, patronising or distorting the nature of black and minority ethnic group experiences (WGARCR 1991).

How will this cause underachievement or failure? The authors are well regarded as experts in their field. Their books are widely used, some of them running fundamentally unchanged into second and third editions. The authors will have gained their knowledge and expertise through their own studies as well as their experiences as practitioners. Their views will have received the endorsement of publishers in the first instance and the recommendation of staff in educational institutions in the second place, the latter often as a result of favourable reviews in the educational press and professional journals. The books will then be used by students whose final assessment will depend on their capacity to reflect the thinking that has gone into the texts. Those students will in turn find their way into institutions charged with caring for young children. If their prejudiced attitudes and their stereo-typical images of young black children in particular have never been challenged, they will, perhaps all unwittingly, continue the vicious circle of misunderstanding, depreciation and failure.

The Working Group's publication catalogues a series of failures by the authors of these books: an obsession with a *single* normality; no recognition of their own racism; no acknowledgement of the need to counter racism in their readers; ignorance of the fact that very young children pick up racist attitudes; lack of emphasis on the importance of mutual respect between individuals and cultures; absence of positive attitudes to physical differences; no consideration of the variety of ways in which child-development concepts are transmitted; lack of attention to hair and skin care as a unique positive issue; no discussion of specific physical conditions and their treatment; no attention to the ways in which parents may be intimidated by professionals.

What the authors have failed to do is to consider fully what kind of texts are needed on child-development courses in a multi-ethnic society that is at the same time fundamentally racist. There is no way in which the authors could be described as wilfully prejudiced. But they have produced books which can be described as prejudicial to the interests of black people in particular. While those books will have contributed to the students' successful completion of their studies, they will have failed to convey a full and balanced picture of child development across different groups in Britain's multi-ethnic society. This constitutes a disservice not only to children visible by the colour of their skin but also to the white group whose so-called normality in a self-evidently dynamic multi-ethnic society must also be vastly different from what it was half a century ago in a time of unchallenged ideas of white supremacy. The success of biased, prejudiced white authorship and scholarship in facilitating academic competence measured on white terms is bought at the expense of children of minority ethnic groups whose energies must be directed at survival and the preservation of individual integrity in circumstances created in part by their teachers and carers whose qualifications place them in authority over them and their parents.

The damage to children occurs early in life and can be permanent. There is evidence that three-year-old children will already have shown the ability to distinguish differences in skin colours and invested them with different values (Milner 1983). White is viewed more favourably and is more acceptable than black. White is given a high status and treated with greater respect. White is the colour of authority and the learning environment. White is the norm by which all other standards are judged. Children's stories confirm the hierarchy of values. Language has a wide vocabulary of disparagement, contempt and condemnation for black people. The media present headlines, pictures and comments that highlight black inferiority in terms of disadvantage, deprivation, division and deviousness. Internal and external walls bear symbols conveying messages of white strength and certainty juxtaposed against black vulnerability and insecurity.

But the damage is not all one-sided: a recent publication from the Commission for Racial Equality states:

> It is important to acknowledge that racism damages all concerned: black children may internalise racist messages, while white children too are limited by a narrow, ethnocentric environment which denies them the opportunity to develop positive attitudes towards other people and ways of life. *Being proud of one's culture is not the same as believing it to be superior.* (Commission for Racial Equality 1989b p.22, my italics)

In order to 'give all children the skills to succeed and to function effectively in British society', the Commission booklet stresses the need to '*recognise and eliminate racial discrimination*'. That takes various forms and the Commission deals with it under the Race Relations Act 1976 in relation to access and treatment as well as the training and employment of practitioners. The booklet talks about 'maximising each child's motivation by encouraging her or his sense of being included, personally, racially and culturally, in all aspects of the learning experience... To provide an exclusively "white" environment disadvantages all children and, in particular, those whose home language is not English'.

The task must include, the Commission states, 'avoiding another generation of white children developing a belief that they are superior or somehow more British than their black peers because of a very narrow, old-fashioned notion of what being British means'.

A report of a formal investigation by the Commission for Racial Equality (1992a) illustrates what this means in practice: parents wanting their children to be admitted to two prestigious schools in a southern county town (one for boys and the other for girls only) have to write letters in support of their applications. The investigation revealed that there appears to be a minimum number of reasons accompanying the successful applications. These in turn reflected a combination of fluency in the English language and an experience and knowledge of the English system of education which was *not* shared by a substantial number of parents of Asian applicants. Such a requirement was not known to parents. Indeed it had not even been articulated by those processing the applications. But the effects of the procedures in what had evolved over the years into an elaborate structure of applications, decisions, appeals and final decisions were *discriminatory* as far as the children of the less fluent and less experienced Asian parents were concerned.

There was no evidence of individual racial prejudice or personal racial hostility. One might of course point to the absence of black staff and curricula and resources reflecting Britain's multi-ethnic society but those might also be a feature of schools where their children were successful in gaining admission. These were, however, selective schools in that they were considerably oversubscribed. Admission criteria needed to be fairly worked out and applied. A time-consuming, heavily resourced system had been evolved covering transfer at 11 to secondary schools. But with all the checks and balances, something seemed wrong: the vast majority of the black children from the district where the schools were located did not gain admission. Consideration of applications for admission to the schools had spawned ideas about the nature and number of acceptable written reasons; these ideas in turn had permeated the procedures leading to the decisions for admission and rejection.

While the children's failure to gain admission could not be ascribed to racial prejudice in the sense that it was the result of decisions taken by officials who were motivated by an unfavourable view of black children as unsuitable or inadequate, nevertheless the decisions were taken on the grounds of written fluency and persuasiveness on the part of the parents when it was the children's competence alone that should have been considered.

In what sense could the failure of children to gain admission to schools of their choice, where their parents thought that they had the best chance of succeeding academically, be ascribed to racial prejudice? The officials concerned with the administration of the scheme and the individuals considering appeals were white (mainly) English. The language of application and appeal was English. The acknowledged ethos and structure of the schools were implicitly English and white. As applications increased, a new criterion emerged – the fluent presentation in English of a minimum number of relevant reasons for the child's admission. This was not the subject of reasoned analysis. Nor was it made known to schools and parents. It undoubtedly manifested an unfavourable view of the less fluent. It was ill thought out and irrational insofar as relevant facts were concerned. Again, insofar as the outcome was known to have been a matter of concern to black parents for some years, here was a practice that was adhered to without any attempt to seek further information or evidence on which a review of the system might be based.

Under the Race Relations Act 1976 such a system leading to this kind of outcome can be described as unlawfully racially discriminatory of the indirect kind (Commission for Racial Equality 1989a). Indirect discrimination can be described as representing a *state of affairs* while direct discrimination can be said to represent a *state of mind* (CRE 1989).

The failure of the children to gain admission to and enhance their life chances in these two prestigious institutions was no accident. It was the result of criteria introduced by individuals charged with administering and developing a fair and just system. They obviously failed to produce such a system. The racial origin of applicants was recognisable from their (South Asian) names. It was likely that they would be similarly identified from the language or style of their written submissions. On this score, one needs to consider whether racial prejudice, as usually defined, was at the root of the children's failure to gain admission, aided and abetted no doubt by a system that was fundamentally anachronistic anyway.

Just like the little Jamaican children in school in the southern county town, these people, the parents of the failures, had a feeling that something was wrong but they couldn't put their finger on it.

Similarly, some 60 black applicants for places at St George's Hospital Medical School were discriminated against annually on racial grounds (Commission for Racial Equality 1988). The computer program developed to decide which applicants to call for interview was loaded by a factor of one-third *against* black applicants. The program had been developed over a number of years to match the views and practices of individuals working together to sift out applicants for interview in the pre-computer 'eye-balling' days. Evidence was given as to how the views of participants were sought and programmed. Here, then, the racial prejudices were reproduced in the computer program. Those who failed to be called for interview were unaware of the fact that they were being discriminated against on racial grounds and that the system employed to consider their applications was based in some degree on individual racial prejudices.

These were high academic performers who could neither guess the reasons for their failure nor blow the whistle on a system they were desperately eager to enter. An investigation of alleged racial discrimination at a Scottish university revealed some significant evidence but failed to enlist people who were willing to stand up as witnesses for fear of risking their careers (Commission for Racial Equality 1992b). At another Scottish university there seemed to be evidence to suggest that overseas black students were marked down in their final honours years when their qualifications upon admission and their marks during the first three years of the course were generally better than those of their native white peers (Commission for Racial Equality 1985). While enquiries failed to provide conclusive evidence, the pattern of the results suggested that the race element might have had some bearing on the final assessment. A more recent case concerned a young student of working-class Pakistani origin at a prestigious college in a highly regarded south-of-England university – he had been unable to sit the end of year examinations because he had been hospitalised due to what he contended was a racist attack when he was walking alone in the town at night. The police and the college authorities refused to concede that it was a racist attack. While he was in hospital efforts were made to persuade him to follow the ordinary degree course rather than the honours course. He had previously walked out of a tutorial as a result of what he considered to be a tutor's bigoted behaviour towards him – as a result of his stand, the tutor apologised to him and the rest of the group. His determination was rewarded and his appeal against the ordinary degree recommendation was successful. One should note, however, his view that he would not have had to expend energy on such a struggle if he had not been a *working-class* Asian student! (Commission for Racial Equality 1991)

At every level of the educational system black pupils and students in particular are likely to meet obstacles to self-fulfilment and academic achievement. Young people who complain, or whose parents complain on their behalf, find it difficult to get a fair hearing. Charges of racial harassment against teachers are difficult to sustain even when clear proof seems available. Because of the fear of possible *consequences*, charges may not be made in the first place or they may be dropped in the face of the intimidating use of institutional powers and procedures against the complainant. When it comes to more subtle forms of discrimination, such as down-grading marks or misallocation to teaching groups, the 'victim' hardly knows where to begin.

At the organisational level, institutional practices and procedures will have evolved over the years into almost sacred customs which are applied impersonally and universally. Some argue that they were developed for what was seen as a homogeneous society suited to their time but still not yet critically regarded as perhaps anachronistic, especially in view of the clear demographic and epistemological changes taking place in Britain and the world. The failure of substantial numbers of young people from different ethnic groups to *conform* or *make the grade* – their bunching in significant patterns or clusters in lower bands or sets and non-examination forms, their disproportionate presence among those suspended or excluded from school, their individual and group experiences of racial abuse, graffiti and bullying – while these are a concern of young people and their parents, they seem less urgent for people in authority.

The slow inadequate nature of change is tolerated and excused for a number of reasons. One reason is that that is the essential character of change, especially in the field of education. Another is that individuals are products of their conditioning with little control over the processes that have moulded their ideas and attitudes. And while racial bigotry can often be readily recognised (but not so quickly dealt with even then) there is an unconscious, unintended level of racial prejudice and stereotyping in the way in which individual teachers act – that will need understanding, patience, tact and time to remedy! Finally, what the institutions do in discriminating against young black people, is the outcome of the slowly and subtly evolving *ritualisation of racial prejudice* for which no one can be blamed!

However, racially hostile attitudes and practices on the part of individuals and institutions whereby black people fail because they are *black*, are the direct, immediate responsibility of policy-makers and practitioners as far as their removal is concerned.

The complex nature of the problem of black, particularly African-Caribbean academic failure or underachievement is illustrated by Professor Bhiku Parekh's evidence to the Swann Committee (DES 1985b) when he lists the factors that have been suggested from time to time to account for such failure. He refers to *genetic intellectual inferiority*, a 'view...far more widely held than is realised'; *family structure*; the *materially and culturally disadvantaged* West Indian home; *racism in school and society*; the less intellectually demanding *structure and ethos* of modern schooling; *education authority* failure to meet particular educational needs; *several other explanations* which 'are also advanced from time to time' (pp.4–5).

He goes on to explain why such an argument is so confusing and unsatisfactory. 'First, the debate is vitiated by what I might call the *fallacy of the single factor*. The participants tend to look for one specific factor, be it class, racism, West Indian family, West Indian culture, the school or educational system, to explain the fact of underachievement. *This is obviously an inherently impossible enterprise*' (p.5).

'Second, the debate is led astray by two false assumptions, namely that *all* West Indian children fail and all Asian children succeed'. He points out that some people take this as proof that failure is not the result of racism. He comments that this argument is invalid because 'it wrongly assumes that the same factor must always produce the same results' (p.5).

He refers also the weaknesses caused by the highly abstract level of much of the debate, some participants' obsessive commitment to specific theories and the ideologically defensive response of groups which feel that particular explanations point an *accusatory finger* at them.

Parties to the dispute might gain some consolation from Professor Parekh's argument: it might appear to them that racism is but one likely factor while lower intelligence and less positive family support might be others. On the other hand, *all* these factors may well be informed by racism, especially the idea of genetic intellectual inferiority, long discredited but still often rearing its ugly head. There are differences in home and family life but there is no general absence of love and support for children in black families. Modern schooling is different but that is not solely because of the presence of black children in them. And if education authorities have failed to recognise and make provision for special educational needs, may it not be because differences (of language, culture and religion for example) are regarded as unimportant or even as weaknesses rather than as extra ingredients of interest and potential in the classroom mosaic?

This has been the experience of countless black people, and it is well articulated by bell hooks in her description of the experiences of black people in graduate schools in the United States (hooks 1989). She reports that she was never taught by a black woman English professor at the four universities where she studied. There were only two black male professors who taught her though 'both were reluctant to support and encourage black female students'. She appreciated them as proof that black people could, however, fill these academic roles 'despite their sexism and internalised racism'. She describes how white professors 'terrorised' black student undergraduates through various humiliations aimed at shaming them and breaking their spirit. Other white students sympathised but ascribed the mistreatment to dislike rather than racism or sexism.

In graduate school she found most of the courses she was obliged to choose were taught by 'quite racist' professors. Confrontation was undermined by the absence of people willing to take the accusations seriously. 'Individual white professors were supported by white-supremacist institutions, by racist colleagues, by hierarchies that placed the word of the professor above that of the student' (p.57).

She makes another interesting point: 'It was often in the very areas of British and American literature where racism abounds in the texts studied that would encounter racist individuals' (p.57). While she is talking about overtly and destructively prejudiced individuals, it is interesting to speculate about the relationship between teachers and courses taught by them which do not challenge racism in the knowledge they are imparting or in the texts and other resources used to facilitate that course. Here is an example of racist inertia failing to do justice to the young minds presenting themselves innocently for guidance, instruction and awakening.

bell hooks describes the compromises entered into by black and white graduate students in order to succeed. The difference was that white students were able to play this 'game' because most of them came from privileged class backgrounds which sustained their integrity and sense of self-worth in the face of their authoritarian initiation into post-graduate work. 'Clearly those students who played the game best were usually white males and they did not face discrimination, exploitation and abuse in many other areas of their lives' (p.59).

She contrasts the support networks developed for overseas students by institutions which have become aware of the dilemmas experienced by those students as a result of the institutions' failure to acknowledge cultural differences with the absence of similar support for native American black students whose 'cultural codes' are different from those of the white institutions where they are enroled. She describes the personal pressure on black students who are aware of the implications of their success or failure for the future enrolment of other black students. On the other hand, the maladjustment or failure of individual white students do not have the same implications for all white students!

bell hooks also reports on the support that she has found, however, in otherwise racist and sexist institutions. She emphasises the importance of writing and talking about discriminatory and oppressive experiences in order for people 'to know that they are not alone, that the problems that arise, the obstacles created by racism and sexism are real – that they do exist – they do hurt but they are not insurmountable. Perhaps these words will give solace, will intensify their courage, and renew their spirit' (p.61).

hooks, Wright and Ghaill describe the growth of self-awareness and shared group knowledge in developing coping strategies. There are examples too of original analysis and research to lay the basis for sustained campaigning. But the final aim is not coping with racism, with racially prejudiced individuals and racially biased and discriminatory systems – the purpose is to remove racism as an obstacle to equality of opportunity and the full realisation of human potential. Dreyden (1989) illustrates the wastefulness of having to expend one's energy and exercise one's intelligence to survive in a racist educational, social, economic and political framework. Sivanandan (1985) points the way to the radical transformation of society if racial justice is to be achieved.

Unfortunately in education, despite the growth of individualised curricula and of collaborative exercises for heterogeneous groups, there seems to be a state-inspired backlash in the direction of education in the basic skills for largely homogeneous ability groups subsequently formally tested for their grasp of a relatively narrow body of knowledge – with some succeeding and others failing. The numbers failing and succeeding are predictable, of course: where there is selection at eleven-plus, the number of pupils assessed as capable of benefiting from a grammar school education exactly matches the number of places available! In Wales, for example, in the pre-comprehensive stable-population era, the cut-off point was set at 40 percent of the eleven-plus population each year. Failure was accepted. Sixty percent of the pupils were just not good enough. On reflection, they had never done as well in primary schools as those who had been selected for grammar schools. And they did not expect to do as well as their more fortunate peers in the future either. The old primary school–neighbour–district friendships gave way to new social divisions not only between but even within schools where status depended on academic performance.

But performance is the outcome of a process predetermined by the dominance of the tidy and symmetrical curve of the distribution of ability. As a result of tried and tested theories, intelligence is neatly distributed along that curve. There is an accuracy and a permanence about it with hardly the slightest variation from year to year. Nationally, regionally or county-wide, institutionally across year groups and tutor groups, performance follows the curve with teachers facilitating pupils and students with a clear recognition of their position in relation to others and a clear expectation of what their performance will be.

Some succeed while others *have* to fail! Within such a framework, many young people will find themselves occupying points on the curve which have little to do with their ability but more to do with the negative prejudice, the stereotypical views and the low expectations of their teachers. After all, if some have to fail, is it not to be expected that it will be those about whom the power-broker or the decision-maker have a negative view. When there are limited places for which people must compete, it is not unexpected to find that ideas of male superiority, white supremacy and class structure will ensure that academic success is gained by members of the white, male, middle and upper classes while those are black, female and working class will find themselves among the underachievers and failures.

One recalls Dr Dreyden's suggestion that test results be used 'with a healthy dash of professional scepticism' (Dreyden 1989 p.13). One needs to go further in describing and analysing the system for all those affected by it – practitioners, young people, parents *and* policy-makers. Most of all its shortcomings need to be exposed so that all the participants in the educational charade can ask why such a system is so revered and why it is preserved. The ultimate goal of the debate is of course the abolition of a system that so ruthlessly disables such a substantial proportion of people of diverse skills and abilities.

Racial prejudice needs to be debated in similar ways, especially in empowering young people and their families and wider communities to understand its harmful effects on both the holders of prejudice and their targets. Practitioners in particular need to understand how prejudices are formed and sustained in British society and what can be done to counter them at all stages of education. Racial prejudice needs to be understood as one of the prime elements in British institutional structures which have evolved as part of the racist design to preserve British white supremacy. The records of racist oppression need to be told and retold by the story-tellers of the oppressed so that young people can gain inspiration and sustenance from their accounts of determined struggle and dignified survival. Above all, it needs to be understood that the resistance movement is aimed at improving the quality of life for all members of the society, black and white, so that all may be accorded equal value and respect and thus achieve their full potential.

References

Berkshire County Research and Intelligence Unit (1989) *The Performance of Children from Different Ethnic Groups 1986/87*.

Commission for Racial Equality (1985) Unpublished record of informal attempts to investigate allegations about the Engineering Faculty of a Scottish University.

Commission for Racial Equality (1988) *Medical School Admissions: Report of a formal investigation into St Georges Hospital Medical School*. London: CRE.

Commission for Racial Equality (1989a) *Code of Practice for the Elimination of Racial Discrimination in Education*. London: CRE.

Commission for Racial Equality (1989b) *From Cradle to School: A Practical Guide to Race Equality and Childcare*. London: CRE.

Commission for Racial Equality (1991) Unpublished record of successful informal negotiations with a constituent college of a Southern England University.

Commission for Racial Equality (1992a) *Eleven Plus for Parents. Report of a formal investigation into the selection procedures operated by the Hertfordshire LEA in relation to the Watford Grammar Schools.* London: CRE.

Commission for Racial Equality (1992b) *Annual Report–reference to agreement between Commission and Glasgow University School of Dentistry. London: CRE.*

Commission for Racial Equality (1992c) *Against the Stream.* London: CRE.

Commission for Racial Equality (1992d) *Don't Fidget, Marcus. An Ethnographic Study of a Selected Number of Nursery and Primary Schools.* London: CRE.

DES (1981) *West Indian Children in Our Schools* (Interim Report of the Committee of Inquiry into the Education of Children from Ethnic Minority Groups) Cmnd 8273. London: HMSO.

DES (1985a) *Education for All* (Final Report of the Committee of Inquiry into the Education of Children from Ethnic Minority Groups) Cmnd 9543. London: HMSO.

DES (1985b) *Education for All. A brief guide to the main issues of the Report* by Lord Swann, Chairman of the Committee of Inquiry into the Education of Children from Ethnic Minority Groups. London: HMSO.

Desforges, M. and Grant, R. (1989) *Recording the Achievement and Experience of Black Pupils,* a half-day exchange of views and experiences between the PRAE team and primary SUMES staff. Sheffield: LEA.

Dreyden, J. (1989) *Multiculturalism and the Structure of Knowledge: A Discussion of Standardised Tests,* a paper given at the National Foundation for Educational Research.

hooks, b. (1989) Black and Female: Reflections on Graduate School, in Hooks, B. *Talking Back Thinking Feminist – Thinking Black.* London: Sheba Feminist Publishers.

Kysel, F. (1988) *Ethnic Background and Examination Results,* Educational Research Volume 30 Number 2.

Mabey, C. (1986) *Black Pupils' Achievement in Inner London,* Educational Research Volume 28 Number 3.

Mac an Ghaill, M. (1989) 'Coming-of-age in 1980s England: reconceptualising black students' schooling experience', *British Journal of Sociology of Education* Volume 10 Number 3.

Milner, D. (1983) *Children and Race: Ten Years On,* London: Ward Lock Educational.

Mortimore, P. (1983) 'Under achievement: A framework for debate', *Journal of Community Education* Volume 2 Number 2.

Sivanandan, A. (1985) *Racism Awareness Training and the Degradation of the Black Struggle.* London: Institute of Race Relations.

Trafford Metroplitan Borough Council (1990) *An Independent Inquiry into the Secondary Assessment Procedure* operated by the Metropolitan Borough of Trafford carried out by D.T.E. Marjoram between May and October 1990.

Working Group Against Racism in Children's Resources (1990) *Guidelines for the Evaluation and Selection of Toys and other Resources for Children WGARCR*, 460 Wandsworth Road, London, SW8 3LX.

Working Group Against Racism in Children's Resources (1991) *Guidelines for the Selection and Evaluation of Child-development Books.* London: WGARCR.

Wright, C. (1987) Black students – white teachers, in Troyna B. (ed.) *Racial Inequality in Education.* London: Tavistock.

CHAPTER 10

The Lack of Proper Social Relationships in Childhood Failure

Clive R. Hollin

Failure is a strong word, sounding with a terrible ring of finality; perhaps even more so when used to describe children. My task here is to look at the place of social relationships in how and why children fail, however, before doing this there is an important point to make. Failure is a relative term, an agreed social label for certain clusters of behaviours: it follows from this that failure is not solely a quality that resides within the individual child, rather it is the consequence of an interaction between the individual child and his or her social world. Yet further, we need to decide what the child has failed at: is it academic failure, is it poor family relations, is it a lack of friends or even the wrong friends, is it all or none of these?

To understand failure, however defined, in the context of social functioning, it is necessary to consider the child's social competence alongside and in relation to their social environment. Using the example of anti-social and delinquent behaviour, the first part of this chapter will be concerned with social functioning; the second part will then look at the role of social relationships in childhood failure.

Social competence and failure in childhood

One of the major developmental tasks all children must tackle is the development of skills to facilitate effective communication with other people. In order to communicate effectively each child must learn to convey information about their own needs and intentions; while at the same time learning to comprehend the messages given by other people. The learning of this process of social communication necessitates mastering the complexities of a verbal language that involves both the written and spoken word, together with the subtleties of *non*-verbal communication. Argyle (1983) discusses the many different forms of non-verbal communication including gesture and posture, facial expression, bodily contact, and eye contact. The child who has developed effective social communication skills, the socially competent child, is able to blend these discrete elements of verbal and non-verbal behaviour, sometimes termed *micro-skills*, to form more complex aggregates of social behaviour such as holding a conversation, being assertive, expressing thoughts and feelings, and making friends. Such amalgams of micro-skills are often referred to as *macro-skills*. Macro-skills are used to achieve the social goals we desire in life: for the child these goals may be to form friendships, to maintain family relationships, to cope with school and so on.

Following the original social skills model (Argyle and Kendon 1967), the suggestion has been made that social skills consist of three related components – social perception, social cognition and social performance (Hollin and Trower 1988). As the child develops so these social skills are learned and refined. The size of the task is daunting. The child must acquire the social perception skills that will enable them to 'decode' other people's non-verbal messages. Simply, the child must learn that if someone smiles then they are happy, if someone shouts they may be angry or upset. Of course, non-verbal messages are often a great deal more complex than this with many subtle shades of meaning, thereby demanding sophisticated social perception skills. In total, a socially perceptive person is aware of which messages to attend to, and understands the shared meaning of those messages. Social cognition, in the sense used by Argyle and Kendon, is analogous to social problem solving.

Having perceived and understood the communications from other people, the child must translate their perceptions into action. This process of translation or problem solving demands that the child has to consider the range of options they can take in a given situation, evaluate the likely consequences of these options and select the course of action that will produce the desired outcome. Finally, the child must acquire their own verbal and non-verbal social performance skills to allow him or her to express their own feelings and communicate effectively with other people. However, as this is a *social* account of behaviour, it must take into account the social impact of the child's actions: other people will, in turn, perceive the child's actions and respond accordingly... and so the sequence rolls on. The concept of social skills therefore involves a dynamic interaction between the child and his or her social world, in which the child's thoughts, feelings, and actions are continually changing to suit the demands of the situation; while the situation changes as the child's actions impact upon other people.

For the majority of children the acquisition of social skills is a relatively smooth process, so that the child is able to manage most social encounters without too much difficulty. However, the child that fails to develop appropriate social skills at any or all of the three levels discussed above will be greatly disadvantaged. That child might be insensitive to the social cues delivered by other people; might not be able to 'think through' a social situation; might not have the performance skills necessary to communicate their needs and intentions to other people. Such problems with social skills have been seen to pay a role in many childhood difficulties and failures, ranging from loneliness and peer rejection, through school and family problems, to aggression and other forms of anti-social behaviour (Furnham 1986, Herbert 1986).

The reasons for the poor development of social skills can be numerous: the child him or herself may have a learning difficulty; or they may live in an impoverished social setting that fails to provide the modelling and encouragement needed to develop fully functional social skills; or they may be part of a social group or culture that encourages the type of behaviour that the majority consider socially unacceptable.

To amplify the thesis developed above I have selected the research on anti-social and delinquent behaviour to illustrate the argument. What is known about the social perception, social cognition and social performance skills of children who display this form of social failure?

Social skills and anti-social behaviour

Social perception

McCown *et al.* (1986) investigated the ability of delinquents to recognise emotion from facial expression. They found that compared to non-delinquents, the delinquents could recognise happiness, anger and fear equally well; but were less able to detect sadness, surprise and disgust. Further, there is a body of research evidence to suggest that aggressive children and adolescents are much more likely than their non-aggressive peers to misinterpret social cues in a hostile manner (Slaby and Guerra 1988). A study by Stefanek *et al.* (1987) showed this to be the case even with very young children. Stefenak *et al.* recorded the self-talk of the children when they were in social contact with other young children: it was found that aggressive children were more likely to describe events to themselves in a hostile fashion, using statements such as 'That child doesn't like me', and 'They want my toys'.

As well as difficulties with the recognition and labelling of social cues, it is also known that aggressive children search for and perceive *fewer* social cues than non-aggressive children (for example Dodge and Newman 1981). So that, in total, the aggressive child is perceiving only a limited number of social cues; while those which are perceived may be wrongly interpreted and understood.

Social cognition

As noted above, the translation of perception into action demands the ability to generate feasible courses of action, consider alternatives and make plans towards achieving the desired outcome. A number of studies have suggested that children and adolescents who display anti-social behaviour experience difficulties with this aspect of social cognition, sometimes called *social problem solving* or *social information processing* (Akhtar and Bradley 1991). For example, Freedman *et al.* (1978) found that delinquents gave less competent responses than non-offenders to a series of social problems, as assessed using the Adolescent Problem Inventory (API). The delinquents used a more limited range of alternatives to solve interpersonal problems, and tended to rely on the use of verbal and physical aggression as a means of resolving difficulties. Similarly, Gaffney and McFall (1981) developed the Problem Inventory for Adolescent Girls (PIAG), a self-report measure of social competence in dealing with awkward social situations. They found that delinquent girls gave less socially competent statements as to their probable actions in the various social situations. When this style of thinking is set alongside immature moral reasoning and a belief in the legitimacy of anti-social, aggressive behaviour, it is clear that social cognition plays a central role in understanding social failure.

It should also be noted that cognitive functioning can be influenced by emotional state. It is now generally accepted that complex reciprocal relationships can exist between emotional arousal and cognitive activity. For example, angry arousal can act to increase the frequency and intensity of hostile thoughts; while concentration upon hostile thoughts can likewise increase emotional arousal (Novaco and Welsh 1989).

Social performance

Spence (1981a) compared the social performance skills of 18 young male offenders with 18 non-delinquent controls matched for age, academic performance and social background. The delinquents showed significantly less eye contact and speech, but more 'fiddling' and gross body movements—an aggregation of behaviours known to relate to poor ratings of social skill (Spence 1981b). Indeed, on global ratings of social skill, social anxiety and employability the delinquents were rated less favourably than the non-delinquents.

In summary, the force of much of the research is that *some* delinquents do experience a degree of difficulty with all three components of social skills (Hollin 1990a). However, there are two caveats to note. Firstly, the empirical studies are not extensive and conclusions should be tentative in nature. Second, the heterogeneity of the delinquent population must also be considered: children and adolescents are a diverse group with a wide range of social skills. Overall, it would be quite wrong to assume that *all* young offenders have social skills difficulties and, indeed, that there is a systematic relationship between social skills and anti-social behaviour (Hollin 1990b).

Nonetheless, the evidence is strong enough to suggest that social skills do play some role in child and adolescent social failure. The issue that then arises is how to account for the failure to develop functional social skills. This issue can be approached in two ways: one can search for internal causes of failure such as low intelligence, biological functioning, personality type and so on; or one can turn to the social environment to see if anything here distinguishes those children and adolescents who experience failure. For the present purpose I shall focus on the latter: social explanations for childhood failure, again using the literature on anti-social and delinquent behaviour to illustrate the position.

Social influences on childhood failure

The Cambridge study of delinquent development has clearly identified a number of environmental factors associated with the onset of anti-social behaviour (West 1982). Of the various economic and social factors thus highlighted, the family featured strongly and, indeed, family functioning and anti-social and delinquent behaviour has generated a considerable research literature. Loeber and Stouthamer-Loeber (1986) completed a large-scale review of family factors and delinquent behaviour and noted a strong association between parental criminality and child and adolescent anti-social behaviour. Loeber and Stouthamer-Loeber also identified several features of family functioning that consistently characterised such problem families: these can be summarised as *parental disharmony, large family size* and a harsh, rejecting *style of parenting*. I have therefore focused on these three factors in the following discussion of family influences on the development of anti-social behaviour in children and adolescents.

The family

PARENTAL DISHARMONY

Perhaps the most obvious manifestation of parental disharmony is when the partnership between the parents ends, so producing a broken home. The search for a relationship between broken homes and anti-social behaviour in the children thus affected has a long research history. Slawson (1923) suggested that delinquents were twice as likely as non-delinquents to come from a broken home. Similarly, research carried out up to the late 1950s consistently concluded that broken homes were more common among delinquents than non-delinquents (for example Merrill 1947, Monahan 1957, Shaw and McKay 1932). The data for these studies were typically gathered from court records, court referrals or from institutionalised young offenders.

Studies carried out more recently have confirmed the findings of the earlier research for *convicted* offenders. For example, Stratta (1970) reported that 46 percent of a sample of 361 imprisoned young offenders came from broken homes; while, also with a convicted delinquent sample, Bottoms and McClintock (1973) found just over half the young offenders in their sample came from homes in which the parental relationship was disrupted because of death, desertion or separation.

Nye (1958) pointed out two potential sources of error with research conducted with convicted young offenders. First, the measurement of delinquency relies on official indices of offending which may not be absolutely reliable. Second, there may be sampling problems in that courts might select adolescents for custody on the basis that they come from a broken home, thereby artificially inflating the broken home rate among convicted young offenders. (This selection for custody is not as harsh as it might appear: when there was a belief in the rehabilitive powers of time spent in an institution, to send a delinquent to custody may have been intended as a positive gesture. Whether this was misguided or not is another matter.)

In addition to the quantitative question of the incidence of broken homes, there is also the qualitative issue of the process by which the home is broken: does a break caused by the death of a parent have the same effect as a break precipitated by divorce or desertion? Yet further, from a contemporary standpoint, the concepts of 'home' and 'family' are heavily ideologically loaded. The 'traditional' home and family is often defined according to the terms that would be understood in white, Western society: such a family would consist of a married, heterosexual couple living together under the same roof and acting as parents to their own biological offspring. However, this is only one type of home and family and many legitimate variations exist in, for example, the marital and sexual relationship between the parents; whether one, either or both of the parents are the biological parents to the children; and single-parent families. Indeed, over the past decades it seems likely that society has shifted in its conception of what constitutes a home and family. Such a change, in turn, may have affected social and legal perceptions and reactions to family breakdown; if this is the case, it is possible that the impact of a broken home on delinquency rates would be less now than, say, 40 years ago.

In an attempt to overcome some of the problems set by concentrating research efforts on convicted young offenders, Nye used a self-report methodology to gather details about delinquent behaviour among American high school students. In contrast with previous studies, Nye found only a slight relationship between self-reported criminal behaviour and broken homes in this non-delinquent (i.e. unconvicted) population. This finding using a self-report methodology has been replicated in more recent research (for example Hennessy et al. 1978).

A number of commentators have suggested that broken homes may have different effects on male and female children (Offord 1982). However, the outcomes from the empirical evidence is mixed: some studies suggest that broken homes have a greater impact on males (for example Peterson and Zill 1986); others that the impact is greater on females than on males (for example Biron and LeBlanc 1977); while others do not record any such difference (for example Rankin 1983). Similarly, other factors have been seen as important in mediating the effect of a broken home: these include the race of the family (for example, Monahan 1957), and the age of the child at the time of the breakdown (for example, Glueck and Glueck 1950).

In an attempt to resolve some of the ambiguities that result from the varying methodologies and definitions of variables in this field of research, Rosen and Neilson (1982) reanalysed the findings of 15 studies of male delinquency published between 1932 and 1975. This reanalysis used a standard statistical procedure to convert the findings of the 15 studies to a common measure of the relationship between delinquency and broken homes. Their reanalysis led Rosen and Neilson to conclude that: 'Despite the variation in time, locale, sample size, nature of population, definitions of both delinquency and broken home, and in basic research design, the conclusion is clear: the strength of the relationship [between broken homes and delin-quency] is very small' (p.128). The tactic adopted by Rosen and Neilson of applying a common statistical standard to empirical studies of the same topic but which used different measures, subject populations and so on is an early step in the development of a methodology that offers a considered overview of a large body of research evidence.

Until very recently the narrative research review was the standard means by which to assess and integrate a large body of research. With this narrative approach the reviewer identifies either all or a sample of studies in a given area, describes and evaluates their findings, and finally offers a synthesis and conclusion. While the narrative review is of undoubted importance, it is not without its drawbacks. These drawbacks include reviewer bias in selecting the studies; 'vote counting', that is listing the numbers of studies for and against a specific effect without taking account of variations between studies; the qualitative rather than quantitative nature of any conclusions; and the subjective and theoretical slant inherent in the work of most reviewers. However, over the past few years the more rigorous method of *meta-analysis* for reviewing a large body of experimental research has been developed. As Wells and Rankin (1991) explain, meta-analysis 'Treats the findings of prior studies as empirical data points in a new, second-order analysis, resulting in a statistical summary of the prior studies that is more precise, quantitative, objective, and replicable than the traditional narrative review' (p.72). Now, while it would be a mistake to believe that meta-analysis is the answer to all the shortcomings of the narrative review, it is none the less an important advance in review methodology.

Wells and Rankin (1991) identified 50 studies of broken homes and delinquency published between 1926 and 1988, and conducted a meta-analysis thereby producing a quantitative summary of the outcome of these studies. Wells and Rankin divided the findings from the meta-analysis into *methodological* and *substantial* outcomes. The principal methodological find-ing was the 'official' samples of delinquents and measures of delinquency produced inflated estimates of the size of the relationship between broken homes and delinquency. This is in keeping with the idea of a 'selection effect' with respect to convicted samples of delinquents.

As for the substantial findings, Wells and Rankin concluded that taking everything into account across all 50 studies there is a real impact of a broken home: 'The prevalence of delinquency in broken homes is 10–15 percent higher than in intact homes' (p.87). However, to add some fine details to this broad summary, the relationship is stronger for less serious status offences than for serious index offences; and the type of break has an effect in that the link with delinquency is slightly stronger when the break is caused by divorce or separation than by the death of parent. However, there is no consistent pattern of impact of broken homes according to the sex or race of the child, or according to the age of the child at the time of the breakdown; step-parents do not produce any special effect on delinquency rates; and there is no evidence of any historical shift in the magnitude of the effect, in other words the relationship between broken homes and delinquency has remained stable over time.

As Wells and Rankin make clear, their meta-analysis is not the final word on broken homes and delinquency. However, given the thoroughness of their meta-analysis, it is also likely to be the case that future efforts at such reviews will give diminishing returns for the time, money and effort expended.

FAMILY SIZE

Family size, like broken homes, has had a long-held association with the anti-social behaviour in childhood: a number of studies have consistently found that delinquents belong to larger families than non-delinquents (for example Glueck and Glueck 1950, Hirschi 1969, Nye 1958, Weeks 1940, West and Farrington 1973). This finding of a link between family size and delinquent behaviour holds true for studies using either official or self-reported measures of delinquency. With respect to the definition of 'large', it is apparent that the what constitutes large has changed over time. For example in 1950 Glueck and Glueck reported that the average number of children in delinquent families was 6.8 as compared to 5.9 in non-delinquent families; however, in 1973 West and Farrington defined a large family as four or more siblings (and hence small as fewer than four siblings). It follows from this that as the definition of what constitutes a large family has changed considerably, the long-standing association between large family size and delinquency is unlikely to be simply due to absolute numbers of children. Could the effect be due to one or more elements of family composition? Several studies have found that the large family size effect on delinquency is more marked for males than for females (see Offord 1982). Further, within large families the birth order of the delinquent and the sex of his or her siblings appear to play but a marginal role; however, a *delinquent* sibling seems to be of significance (West and Farrington 1973).

Why should large families have an increased likelihood of producing a child who displays delinquent behaviour? A number of hypotheses have been advance: first, family size may be related to social disadvantage and paucity of income and resources; second, in large families each child receives less parental attention, monitoring, supervision and control; and third, 'contagion' through association with delinquent siblings. In an attempt to determine the relative influence of these factors, many studies have in their analysis controlled for variables such as socioeconomic class and parental supervision to attempt to partial out their effect on the association between family size and delinquent behaviour. The outcome of such analyses is summarised by Fischer (1984):

> There can be little doubt that large families are related to greater delinquency. The relationship has been noted when a number of variables, i.e., income, socioeconomic status, parental criminality, family composition, e.g., age, sex have been controlled. The higher birth rate for lower classes does not appear to be an adequate explanation for the relationship between family size and delinquency, nor do 'less close parent-child affectional ties' or less parental supervision, although all of these may have some influence. The presence of an 'infectious example' seems partially to account for the relationship. (p.532)

Thus, while the presence of a delinquent sibling is significant, giving some weight to the 'contagion' hypothesis, it seems that there is unlikely to be one clear explanation for the relationship between family size and delinquency.

STYLE OF PARENTING

A number of family sociodemographic characteristics, such as a broken home and large family size, have been associated with the development of delinquent behaviour. While these factors are important indicators of the circumstances of the family, they do not say anything about family *functioning*. Another body of research has been concerned with patterns of family interaction and anti-social behaviour: there are several reviews of this extensive research literature (for example Henggeler 1989, Patterson 1986, Rutter and Giller 1983, Snyder and Patterson 1987), and a brief overview is given below.

Control

At some time or another all parents will be faced with a situation in which they have to control their child's behaviour. The way in which parents manage this process of disciplining their child is known to play a role in a number of family problems, for example, physical child abuse (Frude 1991), of which anti-social behaviour is but one. Those parents who are able to discipline their children successfully show a number of characteristics: they are able to define the behaviour to be controlled, to watch for occurrences of that behaviour and to use effective, but not harsh or physically punitive, strategies to inhibit the child's behaviour and bring it under control. The studies that have looked at parental discipline in families that contain children who display anti-social behaviour show that this pattern of effective parental control is not evident. The parental style of discipline in 'delinquent families' is typically lax, erratic, inconsistent, harsh and overly punitive: as Patterson (1986) comments, 'In discipline confrontations, the parents of problem children have been shown to threaten, nag, scold, bluster, and natter, but they seldom follow through on their threats... At infrequent intervals, parents explode and physically assault the child' (p.436).

The link between ineffective discipline and anti-social behaviour can follow one of two paths. With the first of these, called an *enmeshed* disciplinary style, the parents continually reprimanding their child's every move through the use of verbal threats and expressions of disapproval. Such a disciplinary style sets up coercive patters of family interaction: when the child behaves in certain ways, other family members respond in a negative, aversive fashion; the child responds in turn in a negative way, and this pattern continues until one side gives in. Thus a situation exists in which family functioning consists of cycles of aversive interactions. This is then compounded when the child acts in this coercive fashion outside the family, say with peers and school-teachers, so setting the scene for further problems. The second problematic style of discipline is termed a *lax* disciplinary style. As the name suggests, this is characterised by very low levels of parental control over the child's behaviour, so that the child does not learn to curb their anti-social and delinquent actions. While one of the tasks facing parents is to exert discipline, the other side of the coin is to be positive in reinforcing pro-social behaviour.

Encouragement

As discussed above, the development of social skills and social competence is a fundamental part of the process of socialisation. It is well established that parents have a crucial role to play in the child's acquisition of social skills, and that this aspect of a child's development requires both the modelling and reinforcement of appropriate behaviours (Herbert 1986). Parents must strive to provide models of skilled behaviour and when interacting with their child they should focus on the positive aspects of their child's actions, providing consistent positive feedback to the child for his or her achieving normative social goals. Thus for optimum socialisation, parents will talk regularly with their children, take an interest in their activities, and act in a caring and supportive manner. Of course, parents who do this are likely themselves to be reinforced by their child's words, actions and achievements. It is a consistent finding in the family functioning research literature that compared to the parents of non-delinquents, the parents of delinquents are less supportive and affectionate, spending less time with their children in shared tasks and interests. In other words, the parents fail to provide good role models and fail to reinforce the child's socially competent actions. The crucial theoretical question is how these difficulties with social skills exactly lead to anti-social behaviour. Snyder and Patterson (1987) suggest a complex chain of events:

> The relationship between skills deficits and antisocial behavior is recip-
> rocal. Conduct problems during childhood interfere with the develop-
> ment of skills and may lead to rejection by normative socialization
> agents. This lack of skills reduces further socialization opportunities and
> fosters association with deviant peers which, in turn, promotes contin-
> ued antisocial behavior. (pp.223–4)

Supervision

The administration of discipline and the giving of reinforcement and encouragement means that parents must be aware of their child's actions. Effective supervision means a clear setting of the boundaries for what is and is not permissible, and crucially taking the time and trouble to make sure these boundaries are being respected. With a young child who spends most of their time at home, supervision is relatively easy; it is as the child grows older and begins to spend increasing amounts of time away from home that supervision becomes more difficult. With children over ten years of age, parents are forced to begin to change their style of supervision, looking to other indicators of their child's behaviour such as school attendance and achievement, peer group members and activities, and the use of cigarettes, drugs and alcohol. Parents who are able to monitor effectively their child's behaviour will be in a better position to detect and, assuming they have the necessary skills, intervene if something does go awry. The majority of studies have found that parents of children and adolescents who show anti-social behaviour have poorer monitoring skills than parents of non-delinquents. It follows therefore that parents of delinquents are less likely to detect their child's delinquent behaviour in order to attempt to remedy matters.

Managing conflict

Most families will at times face disputes and crises that place family members under stress and in positions of conflict. In such a situation the family is faced with a problem that it must solve in order to overcome conflicts and reduce stress. The research conducted with 'delinquent families' strongly suggests that such families are characterised by high levels of parental conflict. It is a commonplace finding that families in which there are excessive arguments, conflict and unhappiness are much more likely to contain children who display anti-social behaviour. Further, the longitudinal studies suggest that such family conflict is antecedent to the anti-social behaviour: this in turn indicates that the conflict is more likely to be a contributory factor to the development of delinquent behaviour rather than being the result of the presence of a delinquent child in the family.

When it comes to problem solving, again the research consistently shows that in families with a delinquent child problems are faced with anger, blame, denial of responsibility and less co-operative talk. In itself, this may appear relatively trivial and not uncommon, however, it should be seen in the context of the characteristics of family functioning already described. In other words, it is necessary to consider the way in which all the family variables – parental criminality, control, encouragement, supervision and managing conflict – interact to culminate in the child's anti-social behaviour. The development of complex, multivariate models of the relationship between family functioning and the development and maintenance of anti-social behaviour is now at a reasonably advanced stage (for example Loeber 1990, Patterson 1986).

Peer influences

As with broken homes, another long-standing research finding is that children and adolescents with delinquent friends are significantly more likely themselves to behave in an anti-social manner (for example, Elliott *et al.* 1985, Hirschi 1969). The predictive power of peer influence remains strong with both self-report and official measures of anti-social behaviour; in studies using both longitudinal and cross-sectional research designs; with a range of offences; and when other factors such as social class or age are controlled (Henggeler 1989). However, if the effect of mixing with delinquent peers is known, an understanding of the processes involved remains elusive: *how* exactly do delinquent peers turn a child or adolescent to involvement in anti-social behaviour? A number of theoretical accounts have been advanced that incorporate social factors.

Differential association theory argues that the learning of anti-social behaviour occurs within intimate personal groups (Akers 1985). Through the formation of close relationships with a delinquent peer group, the young person learns both the attitudes favourable to anti-social behaviour and the skills to carry out specific acts. Following from differential association theory, differential reinforcement theory and social learning theory elaborate on the social processes by which peers can influence behaviour (Hollin 1989). It is well established that peers, especially those the individual accords a high degree of status, are powerful models for future behaviour (Bandura 1977). However, Brownfield (1990) found that there were two sides to adolescent status: measures of popularity among peers such as dating, drinking and smoking were associated with higher levels of self-reported delinquency; while more conventional measures of status such as popularity with teachers, responsibility at home and good academic performance correlated with lower levels of self-reported delinquency. It is not difficult to imagine the model presented by those with high delinquent status set against those with high conventional status. As well as providing role models for the acquisition of delinquent attitudes and skills, peer groups are also a potent source of both tangible and social reinforcement for anti-social behaviour. Indeed, the delinquent peer group can become an institution itself in the form of a gang, with its own social organisation, rules and ethics (Goldstein 1991). Such powerful forms of social cohesion can, as Fagan (1990) notes, 'offer a wide variety of opportunities and services: status, economic opportunity, affiliation, and protection' (p.211). Of course, not all delinquent groups reward the same type of delinquent activity. Yablonsky (1963) outlined three different types of gang: *social* gangs that share some common interest such as sport or music; *delinquent* gangs as characterised by the commission of crimes of acquisition such as burglary and theft; and *violent* gangs that carry weapons and commit crimes against other people such as assault. The social rewards and structures differ across the three types of gang. In the first two types, that is social and delinquent gangs, the gang members are able to form stable relationships with each other and a coherent group structure is evident. However, the violent gang is more likely to be characterised by conflict between members and an unstable social structure.

While membership of a delinquent peer group or gang can be a rewarding experience, there is strong evidence to suggest that young people who deviate markedly from the norm are *less* popular among their more conforming peers. Children who are persistent absentees from school have few school friends and tend to be unpopular among their peer group (Reid 1984); while peer rejection in childhood is itself a good predictor of delinquent behaviour in adolescence (Parker and Asher 1987). Overall, the hypothesis can be advanced that, for whatever reasons, some children fail to form attachments to conventional agents of socialisation such as school, family or conforming peers. This failure to establish social bonds and the associated rejection by peers, means that the young person must seek social contact elsewhere – the most obvious place being with others outside the conventional mainstream. Thus we arrive at the apparent paradox of some young people being accepted and popular within a delinquent counter-culture, yet at the same time rejected and unpopular among their more conforming, socially bonded, peers.

When it comes to tests of this hypothesis, as Agnew (1991) points out, empirical investigations of peer influences on anti-social behaviour have been rather simplistic in their methodology. The typical methodology in this area of research is to identify individual adolescents and then count their delinquent friends and the frequency with which these friends commit delinquent acts. However, by their very nature, social groups consist of more than just numbers of people and their frequency of contact. Agnew highlights three aspects of group dynamics that play an important role in mediating the effects of groups on their individual members: these are *attachment, contact* and the *extent* of peer delinquency. The argument for attachment as an important influence rests on the premise that with high attachment and emotional closeness to a delinquent peer group, so delinquents will be more attractive role models and more powerful sources of both reinforcement for anti-social behaviour and of punishment for being straight and conforming to social rules. It follows that the more contact there is between the adolescent and the delinquent group (and hence the greater the extent of the delinquent behaviour), so the likelihood is increased of the delinquent peers modelling, observing and rewarding the adolescent's anti-social attitudes and behaviour. Further, it would be predicted that the relationship between these group dynamics would be interactive: for example, greater amounts of contact might lead to greater levels of attachment.

In order to search for such interactive effects Agnew (1991) carried out a study of delinquent peer group functioning looking at factors such as peer attachment, time spent with friends, peer approval for delinquency and peer pressure for deviance. Agnew further classified delinquent peers as 'minor', that is indulging in acts such as vandalism, petty theft and bullying; or 'serious' in that they sold hard drugs, committed burglary and stole large amounts of money. Agnew's data were gathered from the National Youth Survey, conducted in the state of Colorado in the USA, based on self-reported information from a sample of 1725 young people aged 11 to 17 years. From a thorough and sophisticated analysis of the data, Agnew arrived at two key findings. The first is that 'The results are compatible with previous research: peer delinquency is the best predictor of delinquency' (p.62). However, the second suggests that this relationship is not so straightforward as it might seem:

> The impact of Delinquent Friends (Serious) on delinquency is strongly conditioned by the measures of peer interaction. When the peer interaction variables are at their mean or lower levels, Delinquent Friends (Serious) has no effect or in some cases a negative effect on delinquency. When these variables are at high levels, Delinquent Friends (Serious) has a strong positive effect on delinquency. The measure of Delinquent Friends (Minor), however, is largely unaffected by the peer interaction variables. (p.68)

Thus delinquent peers do have an influence, but only in certain circumstances: it is when an adolescent forms strong relationships with delinquents who commit serious offences that peer-group influence exerts its strongest influence. Adolescents who associate with peers who perform minor delinquent acts or who do not form strong attachments to their delinquent peer group do not appear from Agnew's findings to be at increased risk of becoming delinquent themselves. Agnew conducted further analyses of the data, looking at the influence of a range of control variables such as the demographic factors of age, sex and race, community size and socioeconomic status; and measures of parental attachment and school achievement. However, these factors had a minimal impact on the pattern of results described above: the finding remains that the prediction of delinquency is dominated by the effects of peers.

While there can be little doubt that peers exert a considerable influence, it would be a mistake to assume that *all* anti-social acts are a product of peer-group pressure. Agnew (1990) offers another empirical study looking at young peoples' accounts of the origin of their delinquent events. The methodology used in this study involved interviewing a sample of 1395 adolescents, asking if they had engaged in any of 17 different delinquent acts (grouped for the purpose of analysis into the four categories of violent offences, property offences, drug offences and the status offence of running away). When a positive reply was given, the adolescent was then asked, 'What led you to do this?' and their reply recorded. The majority of responses fell into one of three categories: first, responses that reflect a rational choice in that the delinquent act was carried out for some positive benefit such as money or kicks; second, responses that are a reaction to a negative event such as anger or provocation; and third, responses that suggested the delinquent behaviour was carried out because of peer pressure to conform, or to impress friends and gain their approval. The main part of Agnew's analysis was to see if the delinquents' explanations for their actions varied according to the type of delinquent act. This was found to be the case. Violent offences were most often committed for retaliation or revenge following an insult or other provocation; property offences were most often carried out in a rational search for personal gain, although the gain was more often fun and thrills than hard cash; drug offences were most often seen as being committed because of social pressure; finally, running away was most often precipitated by some negative event and carried out to avoid punishment or to exact revenge on other people. The explanations for the different crimes remained constant when the seriousness of the offence was taken into consideration.

In conclusion, while most delinquents mix with other delinquents and, of course, commit some crimes with their delinquent friends, it would be a mistake to assume that all delinquent acts are carried out because of peer pressure. While delinquent peers are a strong predictor of delinquency, it is clear that much remains to be uncovered about the dynamics of this relationship.

Social process and social structure

While we can point to a complex social interaction between the child and their family and peers, it would be wrong to think that this is the end of the story. The interaction reaches beyond the individual child and their immediate family to the very fabric of society as reflected in social processes and social structure. For example, there is a well-established association between school and anti-social behaviour that extends beyond the social relationships between the child and their peers and teachers. The climate of individual schools, educational policies, funding and resources, and levels of teacher training must also be considered (Hawkins and Lishner 1987). The importance of social structure is perhaps most sharply highlighted when considering the relationship between poverty and criminal behaviour. Alongside individual, family, peer-group and school influences, many studies have pointed to indices of poverty, such as parental unemployment, low income and poor housing, as important antecedents to the onset of anti-social behaviour (for example West 1982). It is difficult to establish the nature of the relationship between social structure and individual behavior – as illustrated in the long-running debate about whether economic factors such as unemployment cause crime (Field 1990) – which suggests that this is an area in which there might be a fruitful collaboration between psychologists and sociologists.

Summary

The theme developed in this chapter, using the example of anti-social and delinquent behaviour, has been that while childhood failure is undoubtedly related to close social relationships, the nature of this relationship is both complex and poorly understood. It is evident that a child's behaviour is intimately connected to his or her own individual social skills, and also to family and peer-group functioning. Yet, at one and the same time, the child's functioning and that of their immediate social environment is affected by broader social factors, or *meta-contingencies* as they are sometimes called (Lamal 1991). In seeking an explanation and remedy for childhood failure it would be quite wrong to look for a 'single-factor solution' such as social relationships: the child's social relationships are important but they must be seen in the context of both individual differences and social and cultural meta-contingencies.

References

Agnew, R. (1990) The origins of delinquent events: An examination of offender accounts. *Journal of Research in Crime and Delinquency*, 27: 267–94.

Agnew, R. (1991) The interactive effects of peer variables on delinquency. *Criminology*, 29: 47–72.

Akers, R.L. (1985) *Deviant Behavior: A Social Learning Approach* (3rd edn). Belmont, CA: Wadsworth.

Akhtar, N. and Bradley, E.J. (1991) Social information processing deficits of aggressive children: Present findings and implications for social skills training. *Clinical Psychology Review*, 11: 621–44.

Argyle, M. (1983) *The Psychology of Interpersonal Behaviour* (4th edn). Harmondsworth: Penguin.

Argyle, M. and Kendon, A. (1967) The experimental analysis of social performance, in Berkowitz, L. (ed.), *Advances in Experimental Social Psychology*, Vol. 3. New York: Academic Press.

Bandura, A. (1977) *Social Learning Theory*. Englewood Cliffs, NJ: Prentice-Hall.

Biron, L. and LeBlanc, M. (1977) Family components and home-based delinquency. *British Journal of Criminology*, 7: 157–68.

Bottoms, A.E. and McClintock, F.H. (1973) *Criminals Coming of Age*. London: Heinemann.

Brownfield, D. (1990) Adolescent male status and delinquent behavior. *Sociological Spectrum*, 10: 227–48.

Dodge, K.A. and Newman, J.P. (1981) Biased decision-making processes in aggressive boys. *Journal of Abnormal Psychology*, 90: 375–9.

Elliott, D., Huizinga, D. and Ageton, S. (1985) *Explaining Delinquency and Drug Use*. Newbury Park, CA: Sage.

Fagan, J. (1990) Social processes of delinquency and drug abuse among urban gangs, in Huff, C.R. (ed.), *Gangs in America*. Newbury Park, CA: Sage.

Field, S. (1990) *Trends in Crime and their Interpretation: A Study of Recorded Crime in Post War England and Wales*. London: HMSO.

Fischer, D.G. (1984) Family size and delinquency. *Perceptual and Motor Skills*, 58: 527–34.

Freedman, B.J., Rosenthal, L., Donahoe, C.P., Schlundt, D.G. and McFall, R.M. (1978) A social-behavioral analysis of skills deficits in delinquent and non-delinquent adolescent boys. *Journal of Consulting and Clinical Psychology*, 46: 1448–62.

Frude, N. (1991) *Understanding Family Problems: A Psychological Approach*. Chichester: Wiley.

Furnham, A. (1986) Social skills training with adolescents and young adults, in Hollin, C.R. and Trower, P. (eds.), *Handbook of Social Skills Training, Volume 1: Applications Across the Life Span*. Oxford: Pergamon Press.

Gaffney, L.R. and McFall, R.M. (1981) A comparison of social skills in delinquent and non-delinquent adolescent girls using a behavioral role-playing inventory. *Journal of Consulting and Clinical Psychology*, 49: 959–67.

Glueck, S. and Glueck, E.T. (1950) *Unravelling Juvenile Delinquency*. New York: Commonwealth Fund.

Goldstein, A.P. (1991) *Delinquent Gangs: A Psychological Perspective*. Champaign, IL: Research Press.

Hawkins, J.D. and Lishner, D.M. (1987) Schooling and delinquency, in Johnson. E.H. (ed.), *Handbook on Crime and Delinquency Prevention*. New York: Greenwood Press.

Henggeler, J.Q. (1989) *Delinquency in Adolescence*. Newbury Park, CA: Sage.

Hennessy, M., Richard P.J. and Berk, R.A. (1978) Broken homes and middle-class delinquency: A reassessment. *Criminology* 15: 505–28.

Herbert, M. (1986) Social skills training with children, in Hollin, C.R. and Trower, P. (eds.), *Handbook of Social Skills Training, Volume 1: Applications Across the Life Span*. Oxford: Pergamon Press.

Hirschi, T. (1969). *Causes of Delinquency*. Berkeley, CA: University of California Press.

Hollin, C.R. (1989) *Psychology and Crime: An Introduction to Criminological Psychology*. London: Routledge.

Hollin, C.R. (1990a) *Cognitive-Behavioral Interventions With Young Offenders*. Elmsford, NY: Pergamon Press.

Hollin, C.R. (1990b) Social skills training with delinquents: A look at the evidence and some recommendations for practice. *British Journal of Social Work*, 20: 483–93.

Hollin, C.R. and Trower, P. (1988) Development and applications of social skills training: A review and critique, in Hersen, M. Eisler, R.M. and Miller, P.M. (eds.), *Progress in Behavior Modification*, Vol. 22. Newbury Park, CA: Sage.

Lamal, P.A. (ed.) (1991) *Behavioral Analysis of Societies and Cultural Practices*. New York: Hemisphere.

Loeber, R. (1990) Development and risk factors of juvenile antisocial behavior and delinquency. *Clinical Psychology Review*, 10: 1–41.

Loeber, R. and Stouthamer-Loeber, M. (1986) Family factors as correlates and predictors of juvenile conduct: Problems and delinquency, in Tonry, M. and Morris, N. (eds.), *Crime and Justice: An Annual Review of Research*, Vol. 7. Chicago: University of Chicago Press.

McCown, W., Johnson, J. and Austin, S. (1986) Inability of delinquents to recognise facial affects. *Journal of Social Behavior and Personality*, 1: 489–96.

Merrill, M. (1947) *Problems of Child Delinquency*. Boston: Houghton-Mifflin.

Monahan, T.P. (1957) Family status and the delinquent child: A reappraisal and some new findings. *Social Forces*, 35: 250–8.

Novaco, R.W. and Welsh, W.M. (1989) Anger disturbances: Cognitive mediation and clinical prescriptions, in Howells, K. and Hollin, C.R. (eds.), *Clinical Approaches to Violence*. Chichester: Wiley.

Nye, F.I. (1958) *Family Relationships and Delinquent Behaviors*. New York: Wiley.

Offord, D.R. (1982) Family backgrounds of male and female delinquents, in Gunn, J. and Farrington, D.P. (eds.), *Abnormal Offenders, Delinquency, and the Criminal Justice System*, Vol. 1. Chichester: Wiley.

Parker, J.G. and Asher, S.R. (1987) Peer relations and later personal adjustment: Are low-accepted children at risk?. *Psychological Bulletin*, 102: 357–89.

Patterson, G.R. (1986) Performance models for antisocial boys. *American Psychologist*, 41: 432–44.

Peterson, J.L. and Zill, N. (1986) Marital disruption, parentchild relationships, and behavior problems in children. *Journal of Marriage and the Family*, 48: 295–307.

Rankin, J.H. (1983) The family context of delinquency. *Social Problems*, 30: 466–79.

Reid, K. (1984) Some social, psychological and educational aspects related to persistent school absenteeism. *Research in Education*, 31: 53–82.

Rosen, L. and Neilson, K. (1982) Broken homes, in Savitz, L. and Johnston, N. (eds.), *Contemporary Criminology*. New York: Wiley.

Rutter, M. and Giller, H. (1983) *Juvenile Delinquency: Trends and Perspective*. Harmondsworth: Penguin.

Shaw, C. and McKay, H.D. (1932) Are broken homes a causative factor in juvenile delinquency? *Social Forces*, 10: 514–24.

Slaby, R.G. and Guerra, N.G. (1988) Cognitive mediators of aggression in adolescent offenders: 1. Assessment. *Developmental Psychology, 24: 580–8*.

Slawson, J. (1923) Marital relations of parents and juvenile delinquency. *Journal of Delinquency*, 8: 280–3.

Snyder, J. and Patterson, G.R. (1987) Family interaction and delinquent behavior, in Quay, H.C. (ed.), *Handbook of Juvenile Delinquency*. New York: John Wiley & Sons Ltd.

Spence, S.J. (1981a) Difference in social skills performance between institutionalised juvenile male offenders and a comparable group of boys without offence records. *British Journal of Clinical Psychology*, 20: 163–71.

Spence, S.J. (1981b) Validation of social skills of adolescent males in an interview conversation with a previously unknown adult. *Journal of Applied Behavior Analysis*, 14: 159–68.

Stefanek, M.E., Ollendick, T.H., Baldock, W.P., Francis, G. and Yaeger, N.J. (1987) Self-statements in aggressive, withdrawn, and popular children. *Cognitive Research and Therapy*, 11: 229–39.

Stratta, E. (1970) *The Education of Borstal Boys*. London: Routledge.

Weeks, A.H. (1940) Male and female broken home ratios by types of delinquency. *American Sociological Review*, 5: 601–9.

Wells, L.E. and Rankin, J.H. (1991) Families and delinquency: A meta-analysis of the impact of broken homes. *Social Problems*, 38: 71–93.

West, D.J. (1982) *Delinquency: Its Roots, Careers and Prospects*. London: Heinemann.

West, D.J. and Farrington, D. (1973) *Who Becomes Delinquent?* London: Heinemann.

Yablonsky, L. (1963) *The Violent Gang*. New York: Macmillan.

CHAPTER 11

Gender and failure
A motivational perspective

Colin Rogers

In considering the nature of the relationship between gender, educational failure and motivation it is clearly necessary to begin with some basic definitions. While not wishing to labour the point, it is quite easy to demonstrate that none of the three key terms (gender, failure and motivation) is as straightforward as might at first appear.

While most people will be prepared to accept that the concepts of failure and motivation both need some clarification, it might be thought that gender is rather more straightforward. In many respects this is the case, but it is worth making the point at the outset that a distinction needs to be drawn between 'gender' and 'sex'. Delamont (1990) amongst others makes the point that we need to differentiate between those things that are biologically determined and those that are the product of culture or society. As Delamont's own introductory discussion makes clear, it is not always easy to disentangle the biological from the cultural and any arguments about the 'natural' differences between males and females are often likely to generate more heat than light. Difficult though it may be to make the distinction, and to consistently maintain it, it is certainly one that is worth making.

As there are clear biological differences between the sexes it is tempting to infer that these 'natural' differences are related to the differences that we see between the two genders. The fact that a typical man may be taller and more muscular than a typical woman is often associated with the greater degree of aggressive behaviour that men are assumed to display in our culture. Tempting though it may be to claim that both differences (those in physiognomy and those in behaviour) have the same biological root, the connection needs to be demonstrated rather than assumed. Indeed the more one looks at different cultural patterns that exist for men and women in various parts of the world, the clearer it becomes that gender is not the same as sex.

In this chapter then the term 'gender' will be used to refer to those aspects of behaviour which might be assumed to be cultural in origin rather than biological. 'Sex differences' will refer to the biological.

This approach will leave us with many potentially contentious issues of classification. Suppose for example, that we find evidence to suggest that girls achieve less well than boys in maths, and boys less well than girls in modern languages. Are these to be treated as gender differences and therefore regarded as cultural, or as sex differences and therefore to be regarded as biological, relating in some way to differences between the sexes in terms of brain functioning? Attempting to answer this question by direct reference to the best available evidence each and every time it occurs lies well beyond the scope of this chapter. Throughout what follows, the assumption will be made that observed differences are gender issues, rather than sex differences, unless very clear evidence exists to the contrary. There is one very good reason for adopting this stance.

Schools are to do with changing people. Any parent would have very good grounds for complaint if their child came out of the school system at 16 exactly as they were when they went in at 5! Schools also make a difference to pupils' life chances (see Smith and Tomlinson 1989 Mortimore *et al.* 1988; Galloway *et al.* 1982 for varying accounts of research into school effectiveness) in that some institutions bring about greater and more beneficial change than others. Now while the amount of and the nature of change and development that occurs with respect to any one pupil will be to some degree determined by biological factors, it is at best unlikely that this will be the case when one considers differences between schools in terms of the impact that they have upon their pupils. Here we are surely dealing with the social and the cultural. Consequently it is sensible to place the accent in this chapter upon those things over which the schools might be able to exercise some degree of influence.

Failure is also a somewhat problematic concept and one can approach the task of defining it in a number of different ways. The particular interpretation focused upon will have a considerable impact upon the conclusions that one might draw. Let us briefly consider some of the options.

First, failure can be defined in normative terms – how well any one person or defined group, is doing in comparison to others. Educational performance is often assessed in this manner, so that doing well means doing better than others often irrespective of the absolute level of performance obtained.

Second, failure can be assessed against a pre-established criterion. The British Driving Test and the graded examinations of the Associated Boards of the Royal Schools of Music are familiar examples of this approach. A standard is set prior to the performance that is to be assessed being undertaken. One succeeds if the standard is met or surpassed, one fails if it is not. On a good day, everybody could pass, on a bad day nobody will.

Third, we could in theory attempt to assess success and failure against some idea of what is possible. Just imagine that it were actually possible to assess precisely the maximum level of performance attainable in any given curriculum area for any given child. To the degree that a child undershoots this potential the child, or the system, can be said to have failed. This would be so even if the child out performed all other children and met other criteria that may have been laid down for the performance.

Failure in relation to gender can be considered in any or all of the three ways discussed above. We can examine the normative performance of boys and girls in relation to each other and in relation to the combined population, we can assess the degree to which boys and girls succeed in reaching pre-established criterion levels of performance, and we could attempt to assess the degree to which each gender group succeeds in reaching the limits of their potential. In this chapter an attempt will be made to discuss two of these approaches, the normative and the potential. The details of this will be presented later but for present purposes let it suffice to say that we shall be looking at normative approaches to success and failure as a gender issue by looking at recent trends in public examination results and that in respect to assessments of potential we shall be looking at motivational processes.

This naturally draws us into the third issue of definition: what is the nature of motivation? This will be examined in much more detail than the other two, as it really forms the core concern of this chapter.

The school effectiveness literature, referred to briefly above, offers the notion of school ethos as a possible explanation of the differences in levels of effectiveness between schools. This is as yet a relatively unelaborated and poorly understood term, but it would seem to include reference to factors relating to pupil motivation. A school with a 'good' ethos is one that encourages pupils to have high, but still realistic expectations, to have a good degree of self-confidence, to enjoy good relationships with members of staff and so on. None of these factors would influence the levels of ability of pupils, but may well influence the degree to which the potential represented by that ability can be exploited to the benefit of the pupil. Let us simply for the moment adopt the view that motivation is *the* one factor that determines the degree to which the potential of any one child might be exploited. Further, let us also adopt the view that there are no differences between the two sexes in terms of their abilities. In other words, boys and girls enter the school system with equal ability levels and therefore equal potential. Differences emerging between the sexes in terms of performance would represent, therefore, differences in motivation.

This would still not allow us to determine the degree to which the school itself could be held to account for any gender differences in performance level that might be observed. If motivation is the key to determining the differences then, in order to show the degree to which schools may be responsible, we would need to be able to demonstrate that schools themselves are responsible for determining levels of motivation. To do this we need to have a clear idea as to the nature of motivation.

To summarise the position so far. A case has been made to support the view that schools ought to be concerned with issues about which they can do something. In as much as gender differences in attainment might be established this implies that there is relatively little point in schools concerning themselves with considerations of the degree to which those differences can be attributed to biological/genetic factors. Rather, schools should concentrate most on those areas where action might be taken, and this is likely to include reference to motivation. Motivation itself, however, would only be a useful concept for schools to employ in an attempt to enhance performance, if it implied that the schools themselves will have a bearing on the type of motivational patterns displayed. If motivation is considered to be something established prior to school, or predominantly outside of school, then motivation, like ability, can be seen as a factor over which the schools have no control.

The nature of motivation

The last decade or so has seen a considerable increase in the level of interest shown by educational researchers in motivational processes. To some degree this has reflected the concerns shown by most Western governments over this period with standards of educational attainment (in the US, for example, the federal government has officially indicated that the study of motivational processes ought to be a major focus of research effort), but it has also reflected the advantages that have followed from theoretical developments. The next section of this chapter will set out, albeit briefly, the nature of these developments, and it will then be possible to examine the implications as regards gender.

In breaking out of the constraints of their behaviourist period, psychologists have rediscovered the importance of cognition in the determinants of human behaviour. At its simplest this reflects the belief that the behaviour of any one person is best understood by making some reference at least to that person's view of the situation. Rather than seeing people as organisms that respond directly to environmental stimuli, people are seen as reacting to those stimuli as they themselves understand them.

This broad approach to the conceptualisation of motivation is often referred to as a qualitative rather than a quantitative one. The distinction has been best developed by Carol Ames (1987) and her work would provide a very useful source for those who wish to explore the distinction further. For present purposes the following brief points ought to suffice.

A quantitative approach to the definition of motivation would tend to focus upon concepts such as drive levels and energy. In short, the determinants of motivational differences between people are to be found in variations in the amount of something that those different people have. The highly motivated individual has more energy or a higher drive level than someone else. Just as a torch with weak batteries glows more dimly, so the pupil with lower drive levels offers less 'sparkle'.

Quantitative conceptions tend to relate fairly closely to the everyday conceptions of motivation that teachers and other people have (Rogers 1990). It is worth noting at this point that such an approach can help to influence attitudes towards differences between certain kinds of pupils in that a quantitative view of motivation could be associated with a belief that performance differences were relatively fixed and beyond the control of the teacher (Cooper and Good 1983).

A qualitative approach to motivation places the emphasis on the ways in which people think. Differences in motivation as displayed in a particular setting are seen as resulting from differences in these ways of construing. One implication of the adoption of the qualitative approach is that it leads to an interest in the longer-term aspects of motivation, in that changes to the way an individual conceptualises an aspect of their life can have implications for their behaviour in a number of settings over a period of time, whereas changes in the quantitative factors of, for example, energy level, can be seen to be relatively short lived.

But as Ames (1987) in particular has argued, the adoption of a qualitative view also leads one to see motivation as something akin to a skill. Differences in motivational patterns are less to do with different endowments of the raw ingredients that determine energy or drive levels but have more to do with different learning patterns that have led to the establishment of different degrees of skill. Some of the further implications of this view point will be returned to later.

Aspects of the qualitative approach

There are many variations on the theme of the qualitative approach to motivation and the interested reader is advised to examine the series edited by Ames and Ames (1984, 1985 and 1989) to explore these variations in much more detail. It will be useful here to focus attention on two aspects of the qualitative approach under the headings of goals and self-efficacy.

As I have argued elsewhere (Rogers 1990) the current concern with qualitative aspects of motivation reflects in many ways the earlier concerns of Atkinson (1964, Atkinson and Raynor 1978). While Atkinson's work had, perhaps, little direct relevance to the teacher, the ideas he generated are worth examining briefly.

For Atkinson, motivation was essentially about the resolution of conflicts between different concerns and interests. At one level this conflict arises when there is more than one thing to which we feel attracted. We have all experienced the difficulty involved in maintaining concentration on one task, while there is another that also calls for our attention. As the attention given to one waxes and wanes so the attention received by the other also varies. However, Atkinson's more enduring contribution has been to draw attention to the importance of considering the possible conflicts that might exist between different goals held by the same person at the same time.

Atkinson developed variations on this theme but the core idea remains a simple one. An individual is not considered to be simply motivated to achieve one thing, for example the successful completion of a task. Instead that individual is also motivated to avoid being seen to fail. These are not simply the mirror opposites of each other. The motive to achieve positively draws someone into an achievement setting. The motive is essentially a desire to succeed on the task for its own sake, to gain the sense of accomplishment that will follow. It is not dependent upon the maintenance of a programme of rewards or reinforcements. The motive to avoid failure, on the other hand, acts as a positive inducement to avoid achievement settings as this is the most effective way of avoiding failure. Again, the concern is with the intrinsic aspects of the motive; the failure itself and the self-doubts that may come with it are what one seeks to avoid, not the opprobrium of others that might follow. In any achievement setting where success, and therefore failure also, is possible, Atkinson suggests that one is likely to be faced with a conflict between the desire to engage in the task in order to satisfy the motive to succeed, and the desire to avoid the task in order to satisfy the motive to avoid failure. Different people may develop characteristic ways of dealing with these conflicts.

More recently the notion of goals in motivated behaviour has been taken up and explored further by researchers such as Dweck and Nicholls (Dweck and Elliot 1983, Nicholls 1983, 1989). While different authors have used different terms, and would tend to define their own concepts as being different from others, there is a considerable degree of commonality involved between the different constructions.

Nicholls (1989) talks of the difference between task and ego-related goals, while Dweck and Elliot (1983) discuss the distinction between learning and performance goals. When an individual is working towards a task or learning goal, their attention is directed towards the task itself and its successful completion. They are likely to be intrinsically, rather than extrinsically motivated and to be concerned with the development of their skills in respect to the task. Challenging tasks are seen as opportunities to learn; set-backs (they are less likely to be defined as failures) will be used as opportunities for analysing possible shortcomings in skill employment; and success is likely to be seen as being contingent upon the degree of effort exerted and the effectiveness of the strategies employed.

When working towards an ego or performance goal an individual is more likely to be concerned with the degree of success they are perceived (by themselves and others) to have had. Success is important because it demonstrates the presence of ability, failure is equally important as it demonstrates its absence. The emphasis is now less on acquiring mastery over a task and more on showing what one can do. As Nicholls (1989) demonstrates, the ego-oriented individual is most likely to experience problems when confronted with a failure. While failure need not threaten the task-orientated person (after all, such a lack of success provides one with an opportunity for further development), for one working towards an ego-related goal failure is likely to be threatening. In closely related work Covington (1984) has suggested that people fearful of failure, because it is seen to reflect poorly on their ability and therefore on their sense of self worth, will develop strategies that are designed to protect themselves as much as possible from this possible damage. It is important to note that these strategies are designed to be self-defensive rather than self-enhancing. That is, under these conditions one is not seeking to develop strategies that will maximise learning, or even strategies that are designed to minimise failure, but rather strategies that will minimise the *consequences* of failure. So the strategies identified by Covington include procrastination and the reduction of effort, neither of which are likely to lead to improved learning, but which do help to provide excuses for failure which direct attention away from ability ('I failed because I only started working on the project at the last moment; had I made an earlier start you would have seen better. Therefore neither you nor I can use this failure as evidence of low ability').

Self-efficacy

The second motivational construct to be examined in a little detail is that of self-efficacy. Stemming from the work of Bandura (1982) and Schunk (1990), self-efficacy theory brings together the concerns of self-concept and motivational theorists. Essentially, the work has concerned the role played by beliefs held by individuals in their own capabilities with respect to specific tasks in determining performance levels at those tasks. Collins (1982), for example, has demonstrated that self-efficacy beliefs relate to performance in mathematics independent of ability. Children within a number of ability groups were shown to perform at higher levels if they had higher levels of self-efficacy. Furthermore, it was clearly the case that efficacy beliefs varied within ability groups. Not all high-ability children saw themselves as having a relatively high level of self-efficacy, neither did all low-ability children see themselves as lacking efficacy.

Given the part played by efficacy beliefs in helping to determine performance levels it is clearly important to develop some understanding of the ways in which these beliefs are generated. Schunk has provided a number of thorough reviews of this work (1989 1990) and the focus of attention here will be strictly limited to only one of the relevant factors.

In addition to factors such as the availability of differing peer role models, the setting of easy or difficult, short-term or long-term goals and the provision of strategy instruction, one important determinant of self-efficacy is the pattern of attributional feedback made available to an individual. Attributions are the explanations offered, either by oneself or by others, for various events, by way of attributing the event to a particular cause or combination of causes. In this case the events will be those related to success or failure. Weiner (1986) has inspired much of the research into the role of attributions within the process of motivation and has developed his own theoretical approach, suggesting a somewhat different role for attributions than that argued for by Schunk. Schunk maintains the view that it is self-efficacy beliefs which have the more direct role to play in determining motivation, but that these efficacy beliefs are influenced by the attributional process.

In one of a number of studies, Schunk (1984) compared the effects of attributional feedback that highlighted ability as a cause of success ('You have done well because you are clever') and feedback that highlighted the role of effort ('You have done well because you have worked hard'). The order in which the feedback was provided was also systematically varied so that some pupils received effort feedback prior to ability feedback, and others vice versa. The significant finding here is that it was early ability feedback that has the most positive effect on self-efficacy. Other studies have shown that effort feedback can have a beneficial effect on motivation (Weiner would argue that this is due to the belief that effort is something that can be controlled by the individual and therefore successes linked to effort are more likely to be reproduced), but Schunk's work suggests that prolonged emphasis on effort can lead to a fall in self-efficacy. Simply, if one comes to believe that relatively high effort levels continue to be necessary for success, one is likely to start doubting one's level of ability.

Let us now return our attention to gender issues. Some indication of the parameters of the debate needs to be given. There are of course a number of different ways in which performance within the school system could be examined as a function of gender, and each of these could require extensive exploration in order to present a fully accurate and justified picture. Again, it is necessary to be highly selective by focusing attention on two aspects of school-related performance. The first performance in public examinations up to the point of leaving school, and the second a consideration of the incidence of referrals for children experiencing behavioural difficulties.

While it is accepted that data associated with performance levels at public examinations (GCSE, GCE and so forth) does not tell all that we would want to know concerning performance variations as a function of gender or any other means of classification, they are nevertheless an important source of information. Given that the DFE provides an annual statement of outcomes for school leavers it is possible to examine the current situation in the light of recent trends. The interested reader will find much more relevant data in the Statistics of Education, School Examinations (DES 1991 and previous years).

In the following section the figures given represent the percentage of school pupils in the year 1988/89 and in earlier years for comparison, obtaining varying levels of qualification. The data are presented separately for boys and girls. In addition, the difference between boys and girls in percentage points is given so that a minus figure represents a higher level of achievement for boys and a plus figure a higher level for girls.

At a very simple level the data suggest that girls do better in school than boys. For example, consider the figures in Table 11.1, showing the percentage of school leavers who left with given levels of qualification.

Table 11.1: Percentage of leavers with at least one A-level pass

Year	Girls	Boys	Difference
1979/80	12.7	12.57	+0.13
1988/89	17.42	16.09	+1.33

**Table 11.2: Percentage of leavers with no
GCE, CSE, GCSE qualifications**

Year	Girls	Boys	Difference
1979/80	11.20	14.28	-3.18
1988/89	7.09	9.81	-2.71

We can see, then, that a slightly higher proportion of girls obtain at least one A-level pass and that a somewhat smaller proportion of girls avoid leaving school essentially unqualified. It is also worth noting that over the last decade during a period in which growing proportions of pupils enjoyed some success at public examinations, girls have slightly increased their lead over boys with respect to minimal A-level performance. We shall see in Table 11.3 further data supporting such a trend.

Other analyses of gender differences in examination performance (for example Rogers 1990) have indicated that performance differences can vary considerably depending on the particular area of the school curriculum under consideration. This is an important observation and one that is worth illustrating with the latest batch of DFE statistics.

Table 11.3: GCE, CSE and GCSE passes by subject

Subject	Year	Girls	Boys	Difference
English	1979/80	42.0	31.6	0.4
	1988/89	51.5	38.6	12.9
Maths	1979/80	23.2	29.2	-6.0
	1988/89	32.1	36.8	-4.7
Science	1979/80	23.2	33.9	-10.7
	1988/89	30.9	34.4	-3.5
Modern	1979/80	18.7	11.5	7.2
languages	1988/89	26.2	15.8	10.4

The differences shown to exist between the two genders in the four main curriculum areas of English, mathematics, science and modern languages follow the well-established trends, with girls being over-represented in English and modern languages and under-represented in maths and science.

However, it is also clear that over the last decade the comparative disadvantage experienced by girls in maths and science has decreased, while the comparative disadvantage experienced by boys in English and modern languages has increased. It is also worth noting that for both boys and girls maths and science are currently less popular than English.

We can also explore the pass rates for the two genders in these areas of the curriculum. One of the stated objectives of the National Curriculum is to encourage all pupils to continue studying across a wide range of subjects during the years of compulsory schooling. It is possible that up to now schools have selectively placed pupils for examinations in a gender biased way. Thus in an area like physics, a girl would need to demonstrate considerably greater talent in order to be put in for a GCSE than would be the case in English. If this is so, then the pass rates for girls and boys ought to differ, with each gender scoring higher pass rates in those subjects that they are less likely to take. Table 11.4 gives some data relevant to this.

Table 11.4: Percentage of pupils taking GCSE in 1988/89 obtaining grade A – C passes

Subject	Girls	Boys	Difference
Physics	52.9	48.8	4.1
Maths	36.9	42.7	-5.8
English	57.0	43.4	13.6
French	54.0	49.2	4.8
Biology	43.1	49.4	-6.3

We can see that the pattern emerging is more complex than our simple hypothesis would have suggested. Girls do have a higher pass rate in physics, in which they are under-represented, and so too do boys in biology, where they are under-represented. However, girls have a lower pass rate in maths (where they are under-represented) but higher pass rates in both English and French (where they are over-represented).

Finally, let us take a look at the destinations of school leavers during the 1988/89 year. Where a pupil goes to on leaving school tells us something about their level of qualification (you can only get on to degree-awarding courses if you have reached given levels) but also something about their levels of aspirations and their levels of confidence about what they might be able to achieve or simply cope with (in short, you won't get on to a degree-awarding course unless you have the confidence to apply for a place).

It can be noted from the data in Table 11.5 that boys are generally more likely than girls to go on to degree courses for any given level of qualification. (There are some exceptions to this, for example, girls are more likely than boys to take up degree courses leading to a teaching qualification.) However, it can also be seen from Table 11.5 that the degree of difference varies according to the level of qualification and whether the degree course is at

Table 11.5: Destinations of 1988/89 leavers as a function of qualification level

Level of qualification	Destination	Girls	Boys	Difference
At least 3 grade C A-level passes	University degree course	63.1	66.1	-3.0
	Polytechnic degree course	7.1	6.8	0.3
No grade C or better but 3 other A-level passes	University degree course	16.6	24.2	-7.6
	Polytechnic degree course	25.0	28.6	-3.6

university or polytechnic. The difference is most notably in favour of boys when we are looking at relatively poorly qualified students, by degree course standards, going on to university courses. The difference favours boys least, and actually shifts to favour girls, when relatively well-qualified students are going on to degree courses at polytechnic. The figures clearly indicate that for the 1988/89 leavers, degree courses at university carry higher status. It is not unreasonable to suggest that taking up a place at the higher status alternative with marginal qualifications requires a higher degree of confidence than taking up a place at the lower-status alternative with relatively high qualifications. By this analysis, girls at this stage have lower levels of confidence. (Of course, a fuller analysis here would also look at the subjects to be read in these degree courses. Boys are more likely than girls to read science, and the A-level requirements are currently lower in the sciences than in the arts. Paradoxically, the sciences are also regarded as being more difficult, so the inference of differences in confidence levels would still stand.) As the reader will be aware, the distinction between university and polytechnic, as institutional titles, has now largely disappeared. A similar examination of destination figures far 1994 or so onwards ought to help to determine the degree to which these variations in destination reflect the apparent prestige of the institution or the relative attractiveness of the type of courses which each offers.

Before moving on to the final section of this chapter which will attempt to draw out the rudiments of what is needed for the development of a motivational perspective on gender and failure, there is one other area of study that ought to be highlighted. While interest in the study of disturbing children (that is those that regularly disturb classroom activities to a degree that disrupts not only their own education but that of their classmates) tends to wax and wane, it has consistently been the case that disturbing behaviour is seen to be a phenomenon associated with boys (for example Galloway *et al.* 1982). This in itself is a result of a number of processes which will include the perceptions and preconceptions of teachers as well as the actual behaviour of boys and girls.

Differences between the genders relating to disturbing behaviour also relate to differences in diagnoses relating to special educational needs. Croll and Moses (1985) found that, in the junior school sector, nearly twice as many boys as girls were perceived to have special educational needs. In the same research study, Croll and Moses also provide evidence to show that boys are more likely to have emotional problems underlying discipline issues, and that boys are both seen to have greater problems with learning to read, as well as being more likely than girls to have low reading ages. In a more recent article Croll and Moses (1990) argue that differences between boys and girls in terms of interaction patterns with teachers can also be accounted for by reference to the greater proportions of boys perceived to have behavioural difficulties.

One of the 'established truths' of gender research in classrooms is that girls receive less attention from teachers than boys do (for example, Kelly 1988, Spender 1982). This seems to be especially so when teacher–pupil interactions concerned with discipline matters are the focus of attention. Writers such as Spender (1982) have argued that this general imbalance between the sexes is the result of the generally held views about the relative importance of the two sexes. In short, it is the case that our culture places a lower value on girls and their achievements than it does on boys and their achievements. Therefore girls are less deserving of teacher attention. Croll and Moses's own review of the literature suggests an alternative explanation. First, they argue that the available evidence indicates that clear cut gender differences with respect to teacher–pupil interaction are more likely to be found in small-scale rather than large-scale studies (it is worth noting that Delamont (1990) has noted that feminist research has tended to be overwhelmingly qualitative and therefore small scale in nature, and calls for more quantitative and therefore possibly larger scale studies). Croll and Moses go on then to argue that the evidence from larger scale studies (for example Mortimore *et al.* 1988, NFER 1987, Tizard *et al.* 1988) indicates that there are only small and unreliable differences in teacher–pupil interaction as a function of gender. The differences often found in smaller-scale studies may be a reflection of the particular classrooms examined. For Croll and Moses the issue of gender differentiation with respect to teacher–pupil interaction is essentially one of classroom management.

> If it is not the case that there is a general pattern whereby all or most boys get slightly more attention than all or most girls, but rather a pattern whereby a few boys get very much more attention than all other pupils, then the gender imbalance is best seen as a problem of classroom

management rather than necessarily a problem of sexist bias. (Croll and Moses 1990, p.198)

It is intriguing to ask what the relationship between these variations in levels of classroom disruption as a function of gender, and possible differences in motivational processes might be. One prediction that could be derived from the work on the differences between the motivational goals of the ego-involved and the task-involved, would be that the ego-involved would be more likely to resort to disruptive behaviour as a means of protecting themselves against the ego-threatening effects of failure. Variations in the incidence of disruption might suggest that boys experience greater ego-threat in the school setting.

However, such an interpretation is again likely to prove to be too simplistic. As Galloway and Goodwin (1987) point out, while boys tend to react to failure by becoming disruptive, girls tend to react by becoming withdrawn. Both strategies can be seen as ways of developing protection from the threats to self-esteem implied by failure, but it will be the response of the boys that will attract the greater teacher attention.

These relations with ego-threat themselves imply variations in self esteem. If self esteem is strong and positive then presumably there is less need for defensive strategies to be employed. Variations in self esteem between the two sexes, however, are again complex.

In her comprehensive review of the then extant literature, Wylie (1979) concluded that there were no overall differences between the sexes in respect of general self-concept. More recent research suggests that this might simply reflect the relatively low informational content of studies relating to general self-concept. Marsh and his colleagues (Marsh 1986, Marsh et al. 1988), following the earlier work of Shavelson et al. (1976), have provided evidence to support the view that general self concept measures produce only weak relationships with academic attainment, whereas measures of self concept relating to more specific aspects of performance are more indicative. Consequentially, if girls have more positive self concepts than boys in some areas, but lower self concepts in others the actual effect of self-concept differences across different areas of the curriculum might be substantial, while overall differences in a general self concept could average out at near to zero.

Marsh's research (1989) seems to broadly support this view, suggesting that differences between boys' and girls' self concepts in specific areas are broadly in line with sex stereotypes (for example boys having higher self concepts than girls in maths). It has been further argued that these differences in self concept, themselves determined by sex stereotypes, can influence performance. However, Skaalvick and Rankin (1990) provide evidence to indicate that when self concepts are assessed in respect to the expectations one holds for future performance (i.e., a higher level of expectation indicates a higher self-concept) the gender differences tend to disappear. Expectations for specific tasks are not influenced by variations in self-concept, but are instead a more direct result of differences in attainments.

At each turn we seem to find the waters muddied. While some clear differences in attainments can be identified, these are clearly subject to change over time, and are certainly not as one-sided as may have been presumed. Differences in motivation, self-efficacy and self-concept are also difficult to identify clearly. In an attempt to point to a clearer way forward, let us look finally at some further research examining gender, motivation and success and failure.

Helen Farmer (1987) has also concluded that research looking for gender differences in motivation has generally been characterised by a 'now you see it, now you don't' quality. Her own work suggests that this may well be due to important variations across different contexts. In her work she examines motivation in respect of aspirations (including career aspirations) and mastery motivation. The level of each of these types of motivation will be affected by differences in background factors, such as gender, social class, ethnic group and so forth; personal factors such as academic self-esteem, preferred explanations for success and failure; and aspects of the immediate environment such as the degree of support perceived to be given by teachers, parents and the workplace.

While acknowledging that research such as that of Hackett and Betz (1981) indicates differences between the sexes in self-efficacy (in this case boys have greater feeling of efficacy in maths with this gap increasing with age), Farmer claims that the aspirations of the two sexes tend to be much the same until the workplace is entered. This observation reflects the one made above in respect of the different destinations of school leavers with similar qualifications. Here we noted that girls are still less likely to go on to degree courses at university even though their background qualifications are clearly good enough.

These differences in aspiration are seen to be influenced by background factors, including gender. However, the background effects are not always direct but instead work their way through other variables in the current environment. Critically, for girls/women, it is the level of support seen to be offered by teachers and the degree of support available for working women that mediated the background variable of gender. Mastery motivation was also affected by the level of support seen to be given to girls by teachers.

Farmer's work, and the other studies she cites, reveal yet another complex pattern with further unexpected twists. For example, Farmer and Fyans (1983) found in a study of adult women returning to education that the less support they reported themselves as having at home the stronger was their mastery motivation. They also found that relatively high levels of fear of success were positively associated with aspiration motivation. However, one important conclusion to be drawn is that variations in motivational patterns are likely to be highly specific to the particular environment within which people are working.

This is very much the conclusion that one might draw from a general appraisal of the implications of a cognitive approach to motivation. Both the theoretical developments within self-efficacy theory and within theories to do with different goal states place an emphasis upon what the individual might learn from a particular environment and how the challenges and threats of a particular environment will produce particular responses. It would follow from this that major changes in the expectations held by a society over time would lead to major changes in what people do (witness the changes in attainments levels over just the last decade). It would also follow that schools will affect their pupils differently. Schools seen to be highly supportive of achievement in areas atypical of one gender, ought to get the higher levels of performance aimed for. Schools that avoid creating ego-threatening environments for both boys and girls ought again to obtain higher levels of performance. All of this implies that we ought to stop looking for general differences between the sexes, and look instead at the ways in which performance variations as a function of gender themselves vary as a function of the characteristics of a school, or indeed of any other setting.

This is not just a conclusion that says that schools matter (Mortimer *et al.* 1988) but also one that says that you cannot necessarily blame schools for differences that emerge elsewhere. Differences between the sexes in terms of success levels are now greater in higher education, further education and the workplace than they are in school. While it is possible to suggest that motivational patterns learned in school only have their impact later (when there are fewer constraints imposed upon people, in the sense that it is left up to them increasingly to decide what to do and what to aim for) it is also possible to suggest that motivation is constantly influenced and to a considerable degree by the immediate environment. If gender differences in schools are decreasing, at least in some areas, this implies that schools are increasingly providing environments that support members of each sex. It is important to ensure that institutions are only held to account for that for which they might be responsible.

References

Ames, C. (1987) 'The enhancement of student motivation', in M.L. Maehr and D.A. Kleiber, (eds), *Advances in Motivation and Achievement, Vol. 5. Enhancing Motivation.* Greenwich, Conn: JAI Press.

Ames, R.E. and Ames, C. (eds) (1984) *Research on Motivation in Education, Vol. 1. Student Motivation.* London: Academic Press.

Ames, C. and Ames, R.E. (eds) (1985) *Research on Motivation in Education, Vol. 2. The Classroom Mileu.* London: Academic Press.

Ames, C. and Ames, R.E. (eds) (1989) *Research on Motivation in Education, Vol. 3. Goals and Cognitions.* London: Academic Press.

Atkinson, J. (1964) *An Introduction to Motivation.* Princeton, NJ: van Nostrand.

Atkinson, J. and Raynor, J. (1978) *Personality, Motivation and Achievement*. Washington, DC: Hemisphere.

Bandura, A. (1982) Self-efficacy mechanism in human agency' *American Psychologist*. 37: 122–47.

Collins, J. (1982) 'Self-efficacy and ability in achievement behavior'. Paper presented at the meeting of the American Educational Research Association, New York, March.

Cooper, H.M. and Good, T. (1983) *Pygmalion Grows Up: Studies in the Expectation Communication Process*. New York: Longman.

Covington, M.V. (1984) 'The motive for self-worth', in R.E. Ames, and C. Ames, (eds), *Research on Motivation in Education, Vol. 1. Student Motivation*. London: Academic Press.

Croll, P. and Moses D. (1985) *One in Five: The assessment and incidence of Special Educational Need*. London: Routledge and Kegan Paul.

Croll, P. and Moses, D. (1990) 'Sex roles in the primary classroom', in C. Rogers and P. Kutnick, (eds), *The Social Psychology of the Primary School*. Lodnon: Routledge.

Delamont, S. (1990) *Sex Roles and the School*. 2nd edition. Routledge: London.

Department of Education and Science (1991) *Statistics of Education: School Examinations GCSE and GCE, 1989*.

Dweck, C.S. and Elliot, E.S. (1983) 'Achievement motivation', in P. Mussen (ed.), *Handbook of Child Psychology Vol. 4*. New York: Wiley.

Farmer, H.S. (1987) 'Female motivation and achievement: Implications for interventions', in M.L. Maehr, and D.A. Kleiber, *Advances in Motivation and Achievement: Vol. 5, Enhancing Motivation*. Greenwich Conn.: JAI Press.

Farmer, H.S. and Fyans, L. (1983) 'Married women's achievement and career motivation: The influence of some environmental and psychological variables, *Psychology of Women Quarterly*. 7: 358–72.

Galloway, D., Ball, T., Blomfield, D. and Seyd, R. (1982) *Schools and Disruptive Pupils*. London: Longman.

Galloway, D. and Goodwin, C. (1987) *The Education of Disturbing Children: Pupils with adjustment and learning difficulties*. London: Longman.

Hackett, G. and Betz, N. (1981) 'A self-efficacy approach to the career development of women' *Journal of Vocational Behaviour*. 18: 326–39.

Kelly, A. (1988) 'Gender differences in teacher–pupil interactions: A meta-analytic review' *Research in Education*. 39: 1–23.

Marsh, H.W. (1986) 'Verbal and maths self-concept: An internal/external frame of reference model' *American Educational Research Journal*. 23: 129–49.

Marsh, H.W. (1989) 'Age and sex effects in multiple dimensions of self-concept: Pre-adolescence to early adulthood' *Journal of Educational Psychology*. 81: 417–30.

Marsh, H.W., Byrne, B.M. and Shavelson, R.J. (1988) 'A multi-faceted academic self-concept: Its hierarchical structure and its relation to self-concept' *Journal of Educational Psychology.* 80: 366–80.

Mortimore, P., Sammons, P., Ston, L., Lewis, D. and Ecob, R. (1988) *School Matters: The Junior Years.* Wells: Open Books.

National Foundation for Educational Research (NFER) (1987) *Teaching Styles and Pupil Performance at the Primary Level.* Slough: NFER mimeo.

Nicholls, J.G. (1983) 'Conceptions of ability and achievement motivation: A theory and its implications for education', in S.G. Paris, G.M. Olson and H.W. Stevenson, (eds), *Learning and Motivation in the Classroom.* London: LEA.

Nicholls, J.G. (1989) *The Competitive Ethos and Democratic Education.* Harvard London: University Press.

Rogers, C. (1990) 'Motivation in the primary years', in C. Rogers and P. Kutnick (eds), *The Social Psychology of the Primary School.* London: Routledge.

Schunck, D.H. (1984) 'Sequential attributional feedback and children's achievement behaviours' *Journal of Educational Psychology,* 76: 1159–69.

Schunck, D.H. (1989) 'Self-efficacy and cognitive skill learning', in C. Ames, and R. Ames, *Research on Motivation in Education, Vol. 3. Goals and Cognitions.* London: Academic Press.

Schunk, D.H. (1990) 'Self-concept and school achievement', in C. Rogers and P. Kutnick (eds), *The Social Psychology of the Primary School. London: Routledge.*

Shavelson, R.J., Hubner, J.J. and Stanton, G.C. (1976) 'Validation of construct interpretations', *Review of Educational Research.* 46: 404–41.

Skaalvick, E.M. and Rankin, R.J. (1990) 'Math, verbal and general academic self-concept: The internal/external frame of reference model and gender differences in self-concept structure', *Journal of Educational Psychology.* 82: 546–54.

Smith, D.J. and Tomlinson, S. (1989) *The School Effect: A study of multi-racial comprehensives.* London: Policy Studies Institute.

Spender, D. (1982) *Invisible Women: The Schooling Scandal.* London: Writers and Readers Publishing Co-operative.

Tizard, B., Blatchford P., Burke, J., Farquhar, C. and Plewis, I. (1988) *Young Children at School in the Inner City.* London: Lawrence Erlbaum.

Weiner, B. (1986) *An Attributional Theory of Motivation and Emotion.* New York: Springer-Verlag.

Wylie, R.C. (1979) *The Self-Concept, Vol. 2.* Lincoln, NA.: University of Nebraska Press.

CHAPTER 12

Inappropriate Curricula, Teaching Methods and Underfunctioning

Carl Parsons

If you're gonna come to school you may as well do something relevant in an interesting way where you know you've learnt something useful. (15-year-old TVEI pupil)

Introduction

Translated into education jargon the pupil is talking about content, process and outcomes. It is a plea for more relevant and interesting curricula. In the traditional educational setting schools have tended to *create* failure in the classroom by the selection of content which holds little relevance or interest for the pupils concerned, by the use of inappropriate teaching methods and by adopting approaches to assessment which tell pupils hardly anything about their individual strengths and weaknesses but simply reinforce normative comparisons with their peer group. This leaves less able children in little doubt about their status as 'failures' in an education system which has offered few lifelines along which non-academic children can begin to climb to success. They are stuck in classrooms where young people of school age are compelled to go. Legally they have no choice. It is an experience through which some pupils *feel* success and are *formally credited* with success; many more, however, are 'written off' in academic and, quite often, in personal terms, as *failures* and abandoned to while away their time in fruitless, irrelevant and boring activities which pass for 'schooling'. It was into this scenario that the Technical and Vocational Education Initiative[1] was introduced in 1982 and much of the work undertaken under its auspices since then has been directed towards alleviating the problems presented by the provision of inappropriate curricular experiences for pupils in the upper

1   The Technical and Vocational Education Initiative was funded by the then Manpower Services Commission, a department of the Department of Employment. The first round of LEAs funded from September 1983 numbered fourteen; these consisted of consortia of schools (usually four or five) and a further education college in each of the fourteen LEAs. With these consortia as with later rounds 'TVEI Centres' were set up usually with a director and advisory teachers to support developments. By 1988 every Local Education Authority in England, Wales, Scotland and Northern Ireland had a funded TVEI pilot or preparatory project.

secondary (14–18 years) age group. After discussing the main features and problems of the *traditional 'alienating' curriculum* the rest of this chapter will look at the *background to the Technical and Vocational Education Initiative* and *learning the lessons of TVEI* particularly as they relate to the pupils who have failed under the traditional curriculum, and finally some *concluding comments*.

The traditional 'alienating' curriculum

There has been a long tradition of elitist (Leach, 1973) content-focused curricula upon which ROSLA[2] and the Newsom Report (Ministry of Education 1963)[3] made little impact. Indeed, the screams of anguish from teachers over the imposition of a National Curriculum seem overdone. The 1944 Act passed control of the curriculum largely into the hands of the teaching profession. The teaching profession could not or did not exploit this *de facto* power. If examinations boards were seen as taking control away from the upper secondary school curriculum then it was with the complicity of teachers. Teachers wanted examinations associated with their subjects because of the status this association brought with it. The subject had greater currency with pupils if formally certificated and had advantages in career terms for those with higher-status subject attachment (Goodson 1985, Ball and Goodson 1985).

Despite examples of innovative, integrated, 'relevant' pupil-centred courses in secondary school the framework which dominated the secondary school curriculum was essentially that list of ten subjects plus RE that comprise the core and foundation subjects of our National Curriculum (DES 1988); this long-existing, crude structure has, in search of elegant apologists, been linked with Hirst's (1965) liberal–humanist forms of knowledge and attendant principles. The point is that the change in content brought about by the National Curriculum is rather slight, and this particularly so at Key Stage 4 (14–16-year-olds).

This knowledge-based curriculum claimed intrinsic merit for itself. The claim was that learners inducted into these ways of knowing were equipped to move on to be autonomous thinkers, socialised into an epistemological community. It comprises a status culture where learning is for its own sake and its intrinsic worthwhileness. Oakshott (1974) writes of acquiring understanding 'lodged within an already existing idiom of activity' (p.60). It is consistent with his earlier view of education as 'orderly initiation into an intellectual, imaginative, moral and emotional inheritance' (Oakeshott 1971 p.72). From a similar high culture stance Scruton asserts that 'In education a child learns to pursue things that must be pursued for their own sakes'

---

2 ROSLA (Raising of the School Leaving Age) in 1970 had brought in the Certificate of Secondary Education (CSE) and a range of Schools Council curriculum development projects aimed to accredit and cater for the less able.

3 Ideas and practical proposals contained in the report acknowledged the lack of appeal of much existing curricula for that 'half our future' which had chosen not to stay on at school.

(Scruton 1980 p.148). This view does not succumb to the smutty notions of social relevance Midwinter (Midwinter 1975) fought for, nor does it allow in practically oriented work for the 'unacademic mass' (as Bantock 1968 would have us see them). It gives little place either to the free child progressives (Dewey 1956 and Kelly 1982) who were loved for the optimistic pleasantness of their prose rather than widespread evidence of Plowdenesque practice. Still less did one find the radical curriculum, one which was so socially relevant that students were equipped to go forth from schools to right wrongs and generally reconstruct (Skilbeck 1982). Something as outrightly segregated as Ozolins' (Ozolins 1982) 'Working Class Curriculum' never got on to any agenda but remained an ignored Open University reading.

The writings of Lawton (1975) with his notion of the school curriculum being a 'selection from culture' are probably the best representative of a soft-left liberal curriculum. Examining the reality of this one has to confess that the 'selection from culture' that we actually witness in schools is partial and unrepresentative; indeed one must question Lawton's notion of a 'common culture'. It is not going too far to claim that the curriculum in most of our schools has represented for a significant proportion of children an alien culture and an alienating experience. It is a curriculum which, for upper secondary pupils (now years ten and eleven), has lacked perceived relevance and utility. 'Utilitarian' and 'Instrumental' are words not associated with a status education. The curriculum is not logically derived from some intrinsic analysis of 'knowledge' or 'contemporary culture'. It is a social construction. It is constructed out of various alliances and conflicts and services sectional interests. Ball (1990) writes of 'conflict and incoherence within the state... general and particular disputes over – the meaning of education... pedagogy, curriculum and assessment... and thus what it means to be educated' (p.21). It is out of this mêlée that the curriculum experience for pupils emerges. It is not a surprise that it lacks appeal and perceived relevance for the least influential social groupings.

Curriculum-development models traditionally point to three sources for our educational aims; Kerr's representation is but one – society, knowledge and the pupil. 'Society' is such an unwieldy concept that is difficult to see it used analytically as a source of aims. Industry needs workers with particular skills and HIV is a contemporary danger pupils must be educated about; that seems to be about the undifferentiated level of debate. It is similarly crude with regard to the pupil. Usually it is reference to *ability* which dominates and HMI documents (DES 1989b) in particular have considered 'match' in that respect. Programmes of study developed by the Schools Council for ROSLA such as Geography for the Young School Leaver tried to acknowledge more local and immediate interests of less academically interested adolescents while maintaining that the key ideas were of merit to all pupils. The acknowledgement of the interests of these young people did not extend very far.

Even Hirst a prime exponent of the knowledge analysis approach, agrees. 'Decisions about the content of courses cannot be taken without careful regard to the abilities and interests of the students for whom they are designed' (Hirst 1983 p.4). Learning theory is currently all about constructivism.[4] In von Glasersfeld's (1989) view the learner is an active agent assimilating and accommodating, interpreting and reinterpreting, information and stimuli according to personal mental schema. The issue is not about how much control of their own learning to give students but that they inevitably have this control. Whatever as teachers we transmit, whatever learning experiences we facilitate, the learner, to put it crudely, controls what goes in, where it goes and how long it stays there. Current Open University courses and modules make great play with this theoretical position at present (E271, E819) (Open University 1990) but underplay motivation. The practical management of learning in our school curricula arguably as scant regard for this theoretical position.

Returning to a sociological theme, we have not learned from Lacey (1970) and Hargreaves (1967), nor from Willis (1977) and Corrigan (1979). These authors have recorded how groups of adolescents, usually working class, have developed a resistance to what school offers. That we have working-class 'successes' excuses the continuation of a status culture by which failure was assured for many. Whatever Scruton (1986) might say about cultural relativism, culture can seem fairly relative to some groups, and fairly irrelevant.

What is so lamentable is the inertia and injustice of such an alienating curriculum. At upper secondary level school may justifiably be seen to have custodial and certification roles stronger than educational roles.[5] Bell (1980) writes: 'Teachers are often unsure what they want pupils to learn, about what it is the pupils have learned and how, if at all, learning has actually taken place' (p.188). If that degree of uncertainty exists one wonders at the motives for sticking with such a curriculum. Yet it has remained relatively impervious to attempts to change it. Of all the forces that have harnessed sufficient power to make inroads Dale's, (Williams 1961, Dale 1986) 'industrial trainers' have done best. The vocational education lobby, backed through the Department of Employment, has given the curriculum an injection of resources, challenging principles and targets.

An odd alliance operated in the genesis of TVEI. It involved free marketeers ('Break the hold of LEAs and higher education'), industrial trainers ('Give us trained manpower') and progressive educators ('New teaching

---

4   Constructivism is a model of 'knowing' with its roots in the work of Piaget but associated with other major theorists such as Vygotsky and Bruner. The essence of the model is that the learner builds up out of available elements conceptual structures that 'fit'; the learner is an active agent interacting with people, experiences and ideas and the resulting conceptual structures are tested out (sometimes) in further interactions.

5   Numerous authorities have pointed to the primacy of custodial and certification roles (see Dove, R.P. (1976); Montgomery, R.J. (1965); Parsons, C. (1989); Schmuck, R.A. and Runkel, P.J. (1972)).

styles and relationships'). Aimed at the whole ability range yet spurned proportionately more by the most academic, TVEI may have unwittingly delivered (very much a 'Training Agency' word) a more relevant and appealing curriculum to 14–18-year-olds and collaborated in assessment procedures more likely to record success for the many.

Background to the Technical and Vocational Education Initiative

In November 1982 the educational establishment was rocked by the unexpected announcement in Parliament of the intention of starting vocational and technical courses with 14-year-olds.[6] The subsequent introduction in 14 pilot LEAs of the Technical Vocational Education Initiative brought swift and unfavourable comment from many educators and fuelled the long-standing debate between liberal and vocational education. High investment (£2m per pilot project) selectively applied (up to 30% of the 14–18 curriculum, usually up to six institutions in an LEA and a cohort in each year numbering about 200 across the consortium) made it attractive to schools.

As pilot projects became established much of the criticism of TVEI dissipated and substantive claims were made about its beneficial impact on the experience, innovation, learning and success of pupils, in particular those traditionally seen as non-academic, unmotivated and sometimes non-attending. As an attempt to turn the curriculum towards the useful and applied it appears now to be a forgotten experiment. Since the advent of the National Curriculum TVEI has to a large extent been washed away – it has been noticeably absent from the educational press in 1990 and 1991 – and it may be difficult to preserve its legacy within the current tide of change.

The aims of TVEI were stated in the following form:

> In conjunction with LEAs to explore and test ways of organising and managing the education of 14–18-year-old people across the ability range so that:

(i) more of them are attracted to seek the qualifications/skills which will be of direct value to them at work and more of them achieve these qualifications and skills;

(ii) they are better equipped to enter the world of employment which will await them;

(iii) they acquire a more direct appreciation of the practical application of the qualifications for which they are working;

(iv) they become accustomed to using their skills and knowledge to solve the real-world problems they will meet at work;

---

6   The Prime Minister herself made the announcement to parliament. TVEI was a dramatic intervention from within the Department of Employment, by-passing the Department of Education and Science with public prime-ministerial backing.

(v) more emphasis is placed on developing initiative, motivation and enterprise as well as problem-solving skills and other aspects of personal development;

(vi) the construction of the bridge from education to work is begun earlier by giving these young people the opportunity to have direct contact and training/planned work experience with a number of local employers in the relevant specialisms;

(vii) there is close collaboration between local education authorities and industry/commerce/public services, etc., so that the curriculum has industry's confidence. (MSC 1983 Annex A)

The rest of this chapter will look for changes in curriculum content, pedagogy, approaches to assessment and student achievement. It will draw on evidence from the national evaluation of TVEI, other available commentary and the reports produced by the Christ Church College Evaluation Unit over a six-year period (1985–1991) through its evaluation contracts with seven LEA pilot or preparatory schemes for TVEI. There are lessons to be learnt from the experiences of those who worked in the more generously funded pilot projects. Some of these lessons relate to the impact on the less academically successful.

Learning the lessons of TVEI

Curriculum content

In examining this area one is particularly drawn to the appeal of the *non-traditional subject* matter and the *practical, applied, instrumental, utilitarian, relevant* character it had. Official TVEI publications (*Insight, TVEI Developments*) are full of references to new courses and new modules and of taster sessions, orientation programmes and thematic events. There is also the variation in location – in school, in residential centres or in workplace and the community. Technical and vocational it may be but the titles appeared to suggest that little was ruled out. 'Communication through Expression', 'Conservation' along with 'Micro-processor Control and CDT'. Within CDT, 'Robin's Scooter' emerged in the 'design and make' section, a vehicle designed to help the mobility of a child in a special school (Insight 1988).

Pupil reaction to these courses, in the TVEI official publications, is, of course, reported as positive. The general view communicated by most is that students liked their TVEI courses. This is borne out by the NFER evaluation (Pole 1987) reporting that 95 per cent of nearly 4000 students questioned were 'very pleased' or 'quite pleased' that they had chosen TVEI. Our evaluations yielded corresponding results on smaller samples varying from 60 per cent to 80 per cent offering this affirmative view (Christ Church College Evaluation Unit 1988). The relation to work and what happens in the 'adult world' appears to be a key ingredient in this. Parents, too, approved of the novelty of the curriculum contents and its work relatedness (The

Table 12.1 Five pilot TVEI schemes evaluated by Christ Church College Evaluation Unit (14–16 Curriculum)

LEA 1 (Round 4) Started Sept 86	LEA 2 (Round 4) Started Sept 86	LEA 3 (Round 4) Started Sept 86	LEA 4 (Round 3) Started Sept 85	LEA 5 (Round 3) Started Sept 85
6 schools and 1 technical college	4 schools and 1 technical college	4 schools and 1 technical college	5 schools and 2 technical colleges	4 schools and 1 technical college
Three Common areas: Common core (PSE, careers, etc), Business Studies, and IT, technology	A core: Business Studies, Information Technology, Technology. Options offered independently (students limited to choice in own institution): food studies, graphics, modular technology, auto/electrical eng., office technology, design and realisation, CGL1365, French, media studies, modular science, modular humanities.	Construction and maintenance studies, personal services, catering services, technical studies, industrial and commercial studies, information technology, technology, business technology.	Range of options offered independently. Students limited to options in own institution. Options include: technical, graphics, business studies, catering, electronics, computer studies, history, geography, physics (enhanced) City & Guilds (background to technology) IT, construction, British Industrial Society.	12 TVEI options provided across the consortium – community health/welfare, community theatre, computer studies, creative technology distribution, electronics, film, TV and media studies, horticulture, hospitality and tourism, IT and administrative practice, multi-media art, visual presentation.

National Confederation of Parent Teacher Associations (1987). The NFER study quotes a pupil as saying: 'I would recommend it to anyone. I have seen what work is like and like and have a chance to get a qualification related to a job for a change' Stoney (1987).

Table 12.1 indicates the variety of content and structure amongst five LEA pilot projects. LEA 1 had only three common areas in all its six schools. LEA 2 had a core offered in all schools and diverse options. LEAs 3 and 4 allowed an approach where individual schools had their own set of options while in LEA 5 the consortium arrangements allowed students to opt for subjects offered in other schools or the technical college. However organised, new content had arrived and was being 'delivered'. The range of subjects being offered in the five schemes can be seen and while some are obviously of the technical and vocational sort, other much less obvious candidates for developing 'occupational skills and competencies' have been developed to accord with TVEI criteria. Technology in various forms is present in all the schemes.

Looking at the conventional science, technical and craft subjects taught in schools one is struck by the 'high science' at one extreme and the hobby and home economy content at the other. TVEI has moved the focus in some of these subjects from the relatively abstract and non-applied to a practical plane. On the other hand, it has shifted other practical subjects away from the domestic kitchen, garden shed or workbench to an industrial·level.

TVEI has taken Home Economics and made it Catering or Food Studies, sometimes with Tourism and Leisure. Child Care has become Community Health and Welfare. Woodwork and Metalwork which used to be about making stools, matchbox holders and pokers is now increasingly redundant, with the use of materials and equipment not to be found in the garden shed or garage. Craft, Design and Technology has an increasing emphasis on Design and Technology. Subjects which have retained their name have undergone quite radical changes with Physics *enhanced with Technology* to give it the applied flavour, or transformed into Electronics.

Business Studies is nearer the model found in real offices with students using in some cases £2000 Xerox word-processors, maintaining their own filing systems, setting up companies, marketing products, and so on. Technology has had its input of new equipment for electrical and hydraulics work. 'Flamefast' benches and computer-controlled lathes now abound. Rural Studies/Gardening has become Horticulture and Agriculture. 'Re-formed' History, Geography and French figure in some TVEI schemes for 14–16-year-olds. Personal and Social Education with extensive opportunities for active approaches to learning have been introduced. In all this one sees a shift away from the hobby or home-economy curriculum and a significant adjustment of the liberal curriculum towards a more industrially or commercially related content.

As can be seen in Table 12.1 the choice of subject areas included in TVEI pilot schemes does not seem unduly constrained. LEA 1 had Personal and

Social Education as a care. LEA 2 had Modula Humanities and LEA 4 had History and Geography. Community Theatre and Multi-Media Art figured in the scheme for LEA 5. The demands that MSC imposed – work experience, industrial partnership, vocational relevant – in no way compromised the curriculum offered. 'Vocationally relevant' was not narrowly interpreted and other industrial or commercial links had been found by teachers and students to be an interesting enhancement. Shilling's (1986) charge about the 'production of alienation in work-related programmes' may prove the reverse with some groups. The perceived and demonstrated utility and instrumentalism of what they have learned about in the courses can actually lead to students being *less* alienated from school. Arguably the *extreme* subcultures that Willis (1977) and Shilling (1986) studied are not the majority in what is anyway a differentiated group of 'non-academic' pupils.

There is much that can be learned which meets criteria of 'worthwhile-ness'. As educators talk increasingly about *generic* skills and *transferable* knowledge, 'worthwhileness' becomes a vaguer and less discriminating criterion. The academic, inevitably elitist, content of education gave way a little in some TVEI pilot schemes to admit matters seen as immediate, relevant and useful. This slackening of the academic, and-in-itself-curriculum has shifted advantage towards those who applied a criterion of utility to their educational experience.

Pedagogy

It is in terms of new approaches to teaching and learning that teachers spoke most highly about TVEI. Smaller groups and new equipment made many things easier. But the novelties of the new curricula in action were striking. The sorts of learning experiences introduced included:

- more problem-solving and active learning
- industry and enterprise days where the timetable was suspended for sustained group practical projects
- industrial and commercial contacts where work done was related to a *real* problem in the world of work or an industrialist came in to advise or judge work done
- work experience
- residential experience
- counselling, profiling and negotiation.

One consortium reports that: 'the central philosophy calls for work to be student centred, with self-directed learning taking place in a cross-curricular format. A key feature is the negotiation in which the students have to involve themselves' (Williams n.d. p.6). The reported effect on a teacher from one school was: 'I was getting cynical about youngsters. TVEI has given me an understanding of how kids tick. I've never been used to talking to them on a one-to-one basis' (Insight 1990). The result has been, as reported by some: 'All the teachers found that TVEI pupils in general worked hard, were better motivated, had a positive attitude and greater maturity. Trust and responsibility were offered and accepted' (Cross n.d. p.VIII). The NFER evaluation reported: 'The high degree of importance to "being treated like an adult"... a majority of students considered this to be a key distinguishing feature of TVEI lessons' (Stoney 1987 p.66). The increased experience of collaboration, control over their work and the practical project basis were fundamental ingredients in increased student enjoyment. Modular schemes were also strongly favoured by students because of the variety and choice this arrangement brought to their studies (Christ Church College Evaluation Unit 1987d).

Barnes and colleagues (1987) reported as part of the national evaluation that the shift from 'controlled' through 'framed' to 'negotiated' approaches to lessons was not as extensive as the informal and more partisan reports suggested. However, they give examples of increasingly relinquished teacher control.

The Christ Church College evaluations noted in observations the 'working unit' in TVEI and non-TVEI classes across two LEAs. A similar continuum from teacher directed through framed/negotiated to student directed was also applied. Table 12.2 reproduces these findings.

Table 12.2 Variations of working unit and teacher-directed activity (Davidson and Parsons 1990)

	Non-TVEI	TVEI		Non-TVEI	TVEI
Individual	64%	9%	Teacher directed	100%	49%
Pair	3%	0%	Framed/negotiated	0%	25%
Groups	0%	38%	Student directed	0%	27%
Class	33%	53%			

In non-TVEI lessons the norm was for pupils to be working by themselves (64%) on teacher-directed tasks. In TVEI lessons it was more common for pupils to collaborate in groups (38%) or be part of a whole-class collaborative working unit (53%).

In general in TVEI lessons in all of the schools there was a characteristic social style and atmosphere based on an informal relationship between pupils and teachers and freer interactions between the pupils themselves, the emphasis tending towards co-operation rather than competition. The degree of interaction that pupils had with the teacher and other pupils varied but on the whole was greatest in TVEI lessons, particularly when pupils were engaged in small group work. The less formal atmosphere of many TVEI lessons encouraged spontaneity and increased the level of participation of pupils. Non-TVEI lessons observed were all teacher directed while TVEI lessons included substantial proportions that were framed/negotiated or student directed. Formal forms of address and rituals such as raising hands were still common and could be said to create an atmosphere of teacher authority. Some teachers seemed to be trying to adopt a more open style of teaching in that they released control over content but somewhat incongruously often maintained an authoritarian stance over classroom discipline.

Not all studies have reported that pupils have liked TVEI lessons more than non-TVEI lessons. Hazelwood (1990) reports the opposite but offers the correction in that re-analysis, comparing groups of students reporting the most and least experiential approaches, suggested that experiential learning was associated with increased enjoyment.

The NFER questionnaire-based evaluation observed that:

> a majority of students agreed that using hi-tech equipment, engaging in a variety of learning activities, being treated in an adult fashion and receiving individual attention were also commonly-occurring characteristics of TVEI lessons. Perhaps significantly, only a minority of respondents considered that they had to listen to the teacher or take notes frequently in the TVEI classroom. (Stoney 1987 p.68)

The Christ Church College evaluation yielded evidence of TVEI students favouring situations where there was 'more practical work, more responsibility, more equipment and greater independence'. TVEI lessons in one LEA were described as follows:

> Teachers work predominantly with individual students or small groups, rather than 'lecturing' the whole class. When teachers do address the whole class, it tends to be for very brief periods (i.e. less than three minutes) for specific purposes, e.g. to give general advice/instruction, or to provide a brief review/summary.

> Students are required to make choices and decisions in their work and to have to take responsibility for various aspects of the organisation of their work. (Christ Church College Evaluation Unit 1989)

There are numerous examples of impressively managed individual learning experiences. The *case of the mashed potato that sank* was described as follows:

> A student in a Food Studies class was comparing Shepherd's Pies made from a variety of natural and processed ingredients. One pie used tinned mince, which the manufacturer claims, was ideal for several purposes, including making Shepherd's Pie. However, when the mashed potato was put on top of the mince it promptly sank. The student was clearly upset, immediately blaming herself for the 'failure' and trying vainly to get the potato to stay on top of the pie. After some reassurance from the teacher the student was able to consider other explanations for the results obtained. The object was to evaluate the *quality of the ingredients* rather than to make perfect Shepherd's Pie, and the dawning realisation

that you cannot always believe what is written on the side of a tin seemed to constitute a real 'learning experience'! (Christ Church College Evaluation Unit 1987a p.8)

The changed teacher role is evident here. The tightrope between over-protecting or over-guiding and allowing freedom to learn by costly mistakes is a difficult act for teachers. Challenge, direction, encouragement and reassurance are key roles for the teacher with much less reliance upon instruction. In some classrooms, albeit a minority, one would find a relaxed and informal atmosphere with students involved simultaneously in a range of different tasks. Students worked both individually and in co-operation in small groups with the teacher spending most of his or her time dealing with individuals or small groups in an atmosphere which is not confrontational.

Students were involved in problem-solving exercises which they were party to defining, for example designing equipment for disabled people; designing commercial packaging; organising a day trip to France. They were involved in negotiating with teachers the focus and timing of their work. Furthermore, students were involved with evaluating the quality of what they had done. Negotiating and evaluating are complex skills which pupils take time to develop. Undoubtedly the different relationship with teachers, partly made possible by smaller groups, helped in developing and sustaining these new skills.

'Teachers aren't enemies anymore' and 'Teachers are more like friends', (Christ Church College Evaluation Unit 1987c) may not have been voiced universally by students but it occurred frequently.

The considerable resources available to TVEI pilot schemes made smaller classes possible in most cases. Increased and interesting resources and novel learning opportunities were also funded. This made more open, student-centred approaches easier to embark upon and manage. Students responded more positively even to the point of raising attendance on days when TVEI subjects were on (Christ Church College Evaluation Unit 1987c). Pupil comments corroborate this: 'You feel like coming to school a lot more' (16-year-old student) (Christ Church College Evaluation Unit 1987b). It is particularly those who may drop out and those who habitually fail who appear to be positively affected by these developments.

Assessment procedures

Continuous assessment has become far more common. Students preferred this: 'not sweating over the exam, that is the best part' (Christ Church College Evaluation Unit 1987). BTEC and City and Guilds qualifications, with their competency-based framework, were appearing but not making great inroads into the traditional GCSE structure. The biggest development in assessment was in Records of Achievement. This was widespread, prompted by a government pilot scheme, local initiative and school-based versions Profiles and Records of Achievement of all sorts have been important features of TVEI.

A key aspect of the most fully fledged profiling systems was their interactive nature. So often in the past assessment has been a number or letter grade passing judgement on the learner. Profiling has usually involved a tutorial, a formative review, agreed statements on progress and attainment and target setting. It is even advocated for junior age children (DES 1989a)! Murphy and Torrance record the absence of formative approaches in most traditional forms of assessment and lament:

> The widespread practice of not returning examination scripts or test papers to students, and not revealing marking procedures, or entering into any kind of post-assessment discussion of the work of individuals... which emphasises the "rites of entry" selection function and destroys most, if not all, educational benefits which could be derived from it. (Murphy and Torrance 1990 p.172)

The alienating effect of this approach to assessment has been challenged in TVEI pilot schemes. Furthermore, Records of Achievement have usually made positive statements about what pupils know, understand and can do. This valuing of achievement is counter to the deficiency model that has prevailed and goes some way to keeping pupils in the education fold.

Heavy reliance upon coursework and the fairly fast feedback students can get in modular courses has also served this course well. The recent government move to restrict the continuously assessed element may set this trend back.

Student achievement

National findings do not suggest that TVEI students gain more examination passes and thus compete in the employment market more successfully. Evidence that students had acquired other useful skills relies on 'soft' data, self-report and small samples. Fitz-Gibbon (1990) actually report *poorer* GCSE results amongst TVEI pilot students compared with non-TVEI students. Even statistical corrections fail to explain away this finding. A major point to note is the lower reported ability of those opting for TVEI and that they report the intention of staying on at school post-16 with less frequency; they probably would gain poorer GSCE passes wouldn't they? Teachers and students themselves testify to improved performance in other ways.

In a recent follow-up study (Christ Church Evaluation Unit 1991) 30 TVEI school leavers were asked how TVEI courses had helped them to get their job. More than one-third felt that TVEI had not helped them very much. Conversely, almost two-thirds felt that it had been a positive influence and proposed a variety of ways in which it had helped them. Almost one-quarter referred to their GCSE qualifications in TVEI subjects, whilst even more said that they had been enormously helped in the interview situation by understanding how to present themselves and 'make a good impression' as a result of simulated interviews conducted during their TVEI course. Almost one-fifth reported enhanced self-confidence during the interview which they attributed to the influence of TVEI, in particular the more participatory learning process which 'encourages you to think and speak for yourself'. One-fifth of recruits said that TVEI had given them a much greater and clearer understanding of the business and commercial world. One interviewee was particularly grateful to TVEI for giving him an understanding of the language of the business world, 'Now I know what an entrepreneur is, and what demand and supply, the market place, and so on mean, so I can talk about it more easily.' Work experience and mini-enterprise were mentioned by some recruits as contributing to their success in gaining employment. One recruit particularly referred to very good reports from his employers following two work-experience placements, which he produced at interview. Inevitably, perhaps, a very few recruits found permanent employment where they had undertaken a work-experience placement. The young person at school was able to demonstrate competence at work and the employer was given the opportunity to conduct an extended interview, to their mutual satisfaction.

Concluding comments

TVEI pilot projects were designed to inject vocational relevance into the 14–18 curriculum of all abilities. They have unwittingly been a curriculum transformation likely to shift some advantage towards those who commonly fail to draw benefit from their educational experience. One expects that those with least success in education should see least stake in it and have least say in its development. Thus continues a structurally shaped cycle of educational disadvantage. It appears likely that the advantages the five-year TVEI pilot projects fortuitously offered have been diluted in TVEI Extension. TVEI Extension is destined for *all* secondary schools and across the whole 14–18 curriculum with the obvious dilution of investment, focus and effort. Furthermore, TVEI pilot developments so expensively promoted figure scarcely at all in that other high-profile central initiative presented in the government's National Curriculum. There certainly seem to be grounds for seeing TVEI pilot and extension as concerned with attitude, awareness and general skills rather than specific vocational competencies. Intended or not it would appear to be the pseudo-aristocratic, gentrified, anti-industrialist culture that Wiener (1981) writes of which TVEI is intended to counter. However, qualifications other than GCSE and A-level are rare and traditional examination measures are vital indicators of the success of the scheme.[7]

However it is viewed, TVEI was the United Kingdom's most lavishly funded innovation in education in the modern era. It cost the Department

---

7   There has been encouragement to use City and Guilds, BTEC, RSA and even locally devised
    certificates of achievement or competence.

of Employment, up to April 1990, well over £150 million in grants to schools. With the Extension funding to enable TVEI to be 'replicated' across each participating education authority in the extension phase, the bill in 1991 was in the order of £90 million and likely to continue on that scale for the duration of the ten-year Extension projects.

By comparison, the science curriculum development following Sputnik and indeed, the totality of Schools Council and Nuffield Foundation curriculum development were chicken feed. While almost every LEA was involved by the end of 1987 in TVEI, pilot and preparatory projects involved less than 5 per cent of the 14+ age groups directly and then for 30 per cent of their time except where 'extension' had begun.

Put simply, the TVEI pilot was launched with the aim of making curriculum content and classroom practice more relevant to modern industrial life and, incidentally, more relevant to young people for whom 'utility' is a prime requirement. Specifically, David Young, then Chairman of the MSC, wrote of TVEI in his letter to Directors of Education in January 1983:

> Each project would be capable of providing a four year course, commencing at 14 years, of full-time general, technical and vocational education including work experience. Courses would be for young people across a wide ability range, and would lead to nationally recognised qualifications. With this framework, young people would be encouraged to develop broadly based occupational skills and competencies. The purpose of each project... is to explore and test methods of organising, delivering, managing and resourcing readily replicable programmes of education of this nature and the kind of programme, curriculum and learning methods required for success.[8]

The letter also mentioned the objectives 'to widen and enrich the curriculum', 'help young people prepare for the world of work' and help students to learn'. Furthermore, the eight criteria by which proposals were assessed by the MSC included stress on equal opportunities, assessment and profiling, work experience and a four-year curriculum with progression.

All this seems a far cry away now with the implementation of the national curriculum proceeding. The generously funded TVEI pilot schemes in a few schools gave way to much more thinly spread resources over all subjects in all schools. We are fast losing sight of a scheme which set out to 'explore and test... programmes of education (and) curriculum and learning methods required for success'.[9] The habitual failures who inadvertently were the main beneficiaries are marginalised again in what Ball calls the 'incoherence in the dynamics of decision-making' (Ball 1990 p.48). The short-lived high-invest-

8   Letter from David Young to all directors of Education in England and Wales, dated 28th January 1983, reproduced as Annex 1 in MSC (1983) *TVEI Operating Manual*

9   Aims of the New Technical and Vocational Education Initiative, Annex 2, in MSC (1983) *TVEI Operating Manual.*

ment strategy of the TVEI pilot project brought in a perceived 'useful' curriculum, 'relevant' experience taught in more 'negotiated' ways and assessed in less sterile ways. It will be sad if we do not learn the lessons of this initiative, saddest for those alienated by a formally managed liberal curriculum who will then, predictably, continue to fail.

Acknowledgements

I would like to thank colleagues who have worked with me in the Christ Church College Evaluation Unit since 1985 gathering data on the seven TVEI local evaluation projects: Keith Howlett, Gill Davidson and Peter Stagg. I am also grateful for the efforts of Rob Povey in urging me to complete the chapter quickly and helping to make it more readable.

References

Ball, S. (1990) *Politics and Policy-making in Education: Explorations in Policy Sociology*, London: Routledge.

Ball, S. and Goodson, I.F. (1985) *Teachers Lives and Careers*. Lewes: Falmer.

Barnes, D., Johnson, G., Jordan, S., Layton, D., Medway, P. and Yeomans, D. (1987) *The TVEI Curriculum 14–16* Sheffield: MSC.

Bell, L.A. (1980) The School as an Organisation: A Reappraisal. *British Journal of the Sociology of Education* 1.2. pp.183–192.

Carrigan, P. (1979) *Schooling the Smash Street Kids*. London: MacMillan.

Christ Church College Evaluation Unit, Report A(f) (1987a).

Christ Church College Evaluation Unit, Report F (1987b).

Christ Church College Evaluation Unit, Report F(b) 1987c).

Christ Church College Evaluation Unit, Report F(c) (1987d).

Christ Church College Evaluation Unit, Reports D and E (1988).

Christ Church College Evaluation Unit, Report I (1989).

Christ Church College Evaluation Unit, Report L (1991).

Cross, J. (n.d.) Development TVEI: Foreword in TVEI Developments 4 – Case Studies. Sheffield: MSC.

Dale, R. (1986) Examining the Gift-horse's Teeth: A tentative analysis of TVEI. In Walker, S. and Barton, L. (eds.) *Youth, Unemployment and Schooling*, Milton Keynes: Open University Press.

Davidson, G. and Parsons, C. (199) Evaluating Teaching and Learning Styles in TVEI. In Hopkins, D. (ed.), *TVEI at the Change of Life*. Cleveden: Multilingual Matters.

DES (1988) *The National Curriculum*. London: HMSO.

DES (1989a) *Records of Achievement, The Report of the Records of Achievement, National Steering Committee*. London: HMSO.

DES (1989b) *The Curriculum from 5–16, 2nd edition*. London: HMSO.

Dewey, J. (1956) *The Child and the Curriculum*, Chicago: University of Chicago Press.

Dove, R.P. (1976) *The Diploma Disease*. London: Allen and Unwin.

Fitz-Gibbon, C. (1990) Learning from unwelcome data: lessons from the TVEI examination results. In Hopkins, D. (ed.) *TVEI at the Change of Life*. Clevedon: Multilingual Matters.

Glasersfeld, E. von (1989) Learning as a constructive activity. In Murphy, P. and Moon, G.B. *Developments in Learning and Assessment*. London: Hodder and Stoughton.

Goodson, F. (ed.) (1985) *Social Histories of the Secondary Curriculum*. Lewes: Falmer.

Hargreaves, D.H. (1967) *Social Relationships in the Secondary School*. London: Routledge and Kegan Paul.

Hazelwood, R.D. (1990) Outcomes of change in teaching and learning styles. In Hopkins, D. (ed.) *TVEI at the Change of Life*. Clevedon: Multilingual Matters.

Hirst, P.M. (1965) Liberal education and the nature of knowledge. In Achambauld, R.D. (ed.) *Philosophical Analysis and Education*. London: Routledge and Kegan Paul.

Hirst, P.M. (1983) *Education Theory and its Foundation Disciplines*. London: Routledge and Kegan Paul.

Insight (1988) Robin's Scooter. *Journal of the Technical and Vocational Initiative*, No. 14. p.7.

Insight (1990) Introduction. *Journal of the Technical and Vocational Initiative*, No. 18.

Kelly, A.V. (1982) *The Curriculum: Theory and Practice*. London: Harper Row.

Lacey, C. (1970) *Hightown Grammar*. Manchester: Manchester University Press.

Lawton, D. (1975) *Class, Culture and the Curriculum*. London: Routledge and Kegan Paul.

Lawton, D. (1989) *Education Culture and the National Curriculum*. London: Hodder and Stoughton.

Leach, E. (1973) Education for What? In Bell, R. *et al.* (eds.) *Education in Great Britain and Ireland*. London: Routledge and Kegan Paul and Open University Press.

Midwinter, E. (1975) *Education and Community*. London: Routledge and Kegan Paul.

Ministry of Education (1963) *Half Our Future*. Central Advisory Council for Education, London: HMSO.

Montgomery, R.J. (1965) *Examinations: An Account of their Evolution as Administrative Devices in England*. London: Longman.

MSC (1983) *TVEI Operating Manual*. London: TVEI Unit.

Murphy, R. and Torrance, H. (1990) The Need for Change. In Horton, T. (ed.) *Assessment Debates*. London: Hodder and Stoughton.

Oakeshott, M. (1971) Education: the engagement and its frustrations. *Proceedings of the Philosophy of Education Society* 5.1.

Oakeshott, M. (1974) *Rationalism in Politics and Other Essays*. London: Methuen.

Open University (1989) *Course E819: Curriculum Learning and Assessment*. Milton Keynes: Open University Press.

Open University (1990) *Course E271: Curriculum and Learning*. Milton Keynes: Open University Press.

Ozolins, U. (1982) Lawton's 'Refutation' of a Working Class Curriculum. In Horton, T. and Raggatt, P., *Challenge and Change in the Curriculum*. London: Hodder and Stoughton and Open University Press.

Parsons, C. (1989) *The Curriculum Change Game*. Lewes: Falmer Press.

Parsons, C. (1980) Geography for the young school leaver. In Stenhouse, L. *Curriculum Development and Research in Action*. London: Heinemann.

Pole, C.J. (1987) Students Views and Expectations upon Entry to a TVEI Scheme. In Hinkley, S.M., Pole, C.J., Sims, D. and Stoney, S.M., *The TVEI Experience: Views from Teachers and Students*. Sheffield: MSC.

Schmuck, R.A. and Runkel, P.J. (1972) *Handbook of Organisational Development*. Palo Alto, Calif: National Press.

Scruton, R. (1980) *The Meaning of Conservatism*. Harmondsworth: Penguin.

Scruton, R. (1986) The Myth of Cultural Relativism. In Palmer, F. (ed.) *Anti-Racism: An Assault on Education and Value*. London: The Sherwood Press.

SEAC (1990) *Records of Achievement in Primary Schools*. London: SEAC.

Shilling, C. (1986) Implementing the contract: the technical and vocational education initiative. *British Journal of Sociology of Education*, 7.4, pp. 397–414.

Skilbeck, M. (1982) Three educational ideologies in Horton, T. and Raggatt, P., *Challenge and Change in the Curriculum*. London: Hodder and Stoughton and Open University Press.

Stoney, S.M. (1987) Consumer Reactions Two Years On. Fifth Years' Perceptions of TVEI. In Hinkley, S.M., Pole, C.J., Sims, D. and Stoney, S.M. *The TVEI Experience: Views from Teachers and Students*. Sheffield: MSC.

The National Confederation of Parent Teacher Associations (1987) *Parental Perceptions of TVEI*. Sheffield: MSC.

Wiener, M. (1981) *English Culture and the Decline of Industrial Spirit*. Cambridge: Cambridge University Press.

Williams, R. (1961) *The Long Revolution*. London: Chatto and Windus.

Williams, R.P. (n.d.) Greenfield School in *TVEI Developments 4 – Case Studies*, Sheffield: MSC.

Willis, P. (1977) *Learning to Labour*. Farnborough: Saxon House.

CHAPTER 13

The Dyslexic Child

Robert Povey and Janet Tod

A middle-class child with reading problems is dyslexic. A working-class child with reading problems is a lazy little sod!

This cynical comment from a headline in the *Guardian*[1] sums up the scepticism with which the concept of 'dyslexia' has been viewed by many teachers and educational psychologists since the term first came into fashion in the mid-twentieth century.[2] Despite the fact that the word 'dyslexic' means simply *difficulty with words* ('dys' = difficulty with, 'lexis' = words) the concept has been at the centre of a fierce professional battle during the past 30 years or so in which doctors have been accused of invading educational/psychological territory and vice versa (Gulliford 1971 and Clark 1979). In general, the medical profession has maintained that it is possible to identify in some children a syndrome called 'developmental dyslexia' (Critchley 1964). Many educational psychologists, on the other hand, have argued that no such syndrome exists, that the label is often simply a convenient way of 'explaining away' the poor scholastic performance of children of predominantly vociferous, middle-class parents, and that what we are dealing with is a continuum of learning difficulty rather than a discrete condition (Bryant and Bradley 1985, Presland 1991).

In the middle of this often acrimonious debate, however, stands the child with *real* learning difficulties who is failing within the school system. Typically such a pupil is one whose reading and written work is a long way behind his or her general intellectual capabilities. The pupil is struggling to cope with the demands of the school curriculum which becomes increasingly dependent upon written language. The most *persistent* problems are usually apparent in *spelling* (rather than reading) and the pupils also sometimes exhibit marked difficulties with the retention and manipulation of symbols as, for example, in numerical calculations. The disorder is more prevalent amongst boys than girls. It is characterised by poor short-term recall (including difficulties in

---

1 Headline in the *Guardian*, 25 March 1986.
2 The term 'dyslexia' itself does, of course, pre-date its adoption as a *fashionable* concept and several research studies into the condition were reported in the late 19th century. For details see Thomson (1990)

the recall of sequences of letters or digits), planning and organisation difficulties, and orientation problems (for example, distinguishing left from right, b from d, 'was' from 'saw', 6 from 9). One often also finds slow and disordered writing, and difficulty in repeating polysyllabic words. From the parent's point of view such children have been described as 'bright in some things but with some sort of block in others', 'unable to retain a sequence of verbal instructions', 'disorganised and untidy', 'forgetful' ('he never knows what day it is'), 'floating around in time', 'dependent on others to plan his day (and his school bag!)'. There is sometimes a history of delayed speech and language development, poor motor co-ordination and a family history of similar learning difficulties. It is this type of problem with which this chapter is concerned; and even if we cannot agree about the precise nature of the disorder or the name by which we prefer to call the range of cognitive difficulties associated with it, to ignore the *manifestation of the problem* is to keep the pupil at risk of continuing failure.

In this chapter we shall start by looking more closely at the concept of dyslexia and follow this by a consideration of the nature of failure in the school system as it relates to the dyslexic child. We shall continue with an examination of the ways in which dyslexic pupils who are failing in school have been traditionally identified (or, frequently, *not identified*), followed by an examination of the problems inherent in the traditional approach. Finally we will consider the possibilities of curriculum-based assessment as a way forward. We will argue that such an approach should help to reduce failure by providing a way of identifying the dyslexics' problems and initiating appropriate teaching strategies in the context of the curricular demands which are placed upon them.

The concept of dyslexia

There can be no doubt that many children fail to master the complexities of written language in the early years of schooling. For some of these children such failure is consonant with their slow progress in other areas of the school curriculum and they would probably not be considered 'dyslexic' by most educational psychologists. On the other hand, there are a number of children with quite satisfactory patterns of development in other areas of attainment who find *specific* problems with written language. It is these pupils who would usually be considered to be contenders for the label 'dyslexic'. However, defining the criteria which provide eligibility for the label has been, and remains a contentious issue.

During the 1960s a large-scale study of children's reading (Morris 1966) failed to offer support for the idea that specific developmental dyslexia could be identified as a syndrome distinct from the more general concept of reading backwardness. Similarly, in 1972 the advisory committee set up to consider *Children with Specific Reading Difficulties* chaired by Jack Tizard, concluded that considerable doubt existed over the identification of 'specific developmental dyslexia' (DES 1972). They suggested that it was preferable to think of a continuum of reading difficulties with the term 'specific reading difficulty' being reserved for children with the most recalcitrant problems. The 1978 Warnock Report on *Children with Special Needs* (DES 1978) also accepted this view and suggested abandoning the use of categories of handicap in favour of the concept of *special educational need*.

With the advent of the 1981 Education Act (HMSO 1981) the term *specific learning difficulty* became a recognised educational concept and dyslexia has begun to find itself a respectable 'parenthetical' home as 'specific learning difficulties (dyslexia)' (Pumfrey and Reason 1991). Even hitherto reluctant local educational authorities are now beginning to accept the term 'dyslexia' provided it is seen within their own parameters. This usually means that they see dyslexics at the extreme end of a continuum of written language difficulties whilst at the same time accepting that they exhibit a relatively clear profile of learning difficulties which come within the remit of the 1981 Act. In summary, the Act states that children have such special needs if they have significantly greater difficulty in learning than the majority of children of their age or if the difficulties interfere with their ability to make use of the usual educational facilities provided for children of their age group in that particular local authority. In such cases the pupils would be eligible for *special educational provision*, i.e., provision additional to or different from normal educational provision for children of their age in that particular LEA.

We take the view that there *are* children who can be reasonably labelled as having *specific* learning difficulties in written language. These are children whose difficulties are confined to certain areas of attainment in which they show a markedly depressed and discrepant pattern of performance *compared with their own profile of attainment in other areas*. These areas of attainment are those which typically involve the retention, manipulation and reproduction of coded material especially where some degree of sequential processing is required. The pupil's difficulties become apparent in such classroom activities as reading, spelling, copying from the blackboard, generating written ideas (particularly in a timed context), learning a foreign language, remembering lists of words (or digits) and in some computational tasks. Such pupils often show a constellation of related traits, as described earlier, including general sequencing and orientation difficulties, problems in organisation and planning and difficulties in pronouncing polysyllabic words. It must be appreciated, however, that any group of 'dyslexic' pupils will be relatively heterogeneous in terms of the number and type of symptoms exhibited. They will all show the distinctive pattern of discrepant performance already described, but the range and severity of associated symptoms will differ from individual to individual. Along with other definitions of dyslexia (Thomson 1990) we would also wish to stress that the disorder can occur within the full range of intellectual abilities and that it is independent of cultural or emotional causation. For such children the term 'dyslexic' seems to represent a useful shorthand description of their problems and one which is certainly more elegant and less cumbersome than 'specific learning difficulties (dyslexia)'!

As far as the aetiology of developmental dyslexia is concerned this is still an unresolved question. *Acquired dyslexia* in adults arises as a direct consequence of specific brain damage whereas *developmental dyslexia* in children is more generally described as a problem in 'cerebral organisation' which tends to run in families and for which there may be some genetic pre-disposition (Pumfrey and Reason 1991).[3] This does not mean that the condition is irremediable but if the child's failure to cope with written language is ignored then the condition will become more recalcitrant and increasing failure in school is an inevitable consequence. Lack of identification is, therefore, often a key factor in explaining why dyslexic children enter into a downward spiral of failure as they progress through the school system; and this is why much of the present chapter concerns itself with a consideration of ways of recognising the 'failing' dyslexic child within the mainstream school.

Failure in the school system as it relates to the dyslexic child

Traditionally *failure* in an educational setting has been seen as the obverse of *success* which, in turn, has been evaluated in terms of certification (CSE/GCE, O-level/GCSE, A-levels, university entrance, diplomas/degrees and so forth). In spite of recent movements towards continuous assessment and project work in the GCSE, and the development of cumulative Records of Achievement, the traditional examination approach seems set to exert its influence just as strongly in the near future. Thus the DES *Parent's Charter* (1992) clearly states that tables of examination results and National Curriculum test results will be a published performance indicator against which parents can evaluate and compare their local schools; and the inclusion of Standard Assessment Tasks (SATs) in the National Curriculum assessment framework will provide additional national data against which to compare an individual pupil's progress at the ages of 7, 11, 14 and 16.

The concept of educational 'success' or 'failure' is therefore inextricably linked with the nature and level of performance *expected* of the child at different stages in educational development. At the pre-school level, monitoring of progress is the official responsibility of the health visitor who uses knowledge of *normative* developmental 'milestones' to assess the child's level of functioning. In general, screening procedures at this stage will tend to pick out children whose overall pattern of development is delayed together with those with some noticeable dysfunctioning as, for example, in cerebral palsy or speech impairments. On the other hand, less obvious discrepancies in

---

3   For a useful discussion of evidence relating to the possible effects of genetic factors in dyslexia see
    Thomson (1990)

developmental patterns which one might expect from 'embryonic' dyslexics would not be so easily identified. Case histories of children who have been diagnosed as dyslexic at a later stage reveal that language and motor problems were evident at the pre-school level (Newton 1970), but our knowledge of the *predictive* significance of such symptoms is still very incomplete. What is expected of the pre-school child is that he or she should develop self-help skills and a level of social and language behaviour which will facilitate a smooth transition to the Infant School. Detecting 'failure' in a pre-school child usually means, therefore, that only those children well outside the normal range of development will be identified as having problems.

On school entry the child is quickly expected to acquire basic word recognition and phonic skills, to demonstrate an understanding of number concepts, to draw, and to produce written symbols in response to orally presented material. By the age of seven years the child who has difficulty in these areas will be causing concern to both parents and teachers. Children with *specific* problems in written language may sometimes stand out but they may be placed inappropriately in the all-round *slow learner* category. The move towards an increasing dependency on paper-and pencil tests in the seven- year-old SATs may serve to focus attention on children who have specific written language difficulties provided that teachers and parents are on the look out for specific patterns of difficulty. Normative data collected on the 8–11 years age group, for example, reveal that the dyslexic group can be discriminated from the reading-retarded group by the discrepancy between observed and expected classroom performance and also by their cognitive ability profile which reveals relative weaknesses in the areas of short-term recall, speed and coding (Tyler and Elliot 1988).

The 8–11 years age group is, in fact, the peak period for 'dyslexic' referrals to the specialist agencies such as the School Psychological Service (Thomson 1990) and such referrals centre around difficulties in *reading*. Indeed, the term *difficulty with reading* is often considered to be synonymous with *dyslexia* and, as a consequence of this emphasis, the evolution of assessment procedures to identify 'dyslexics' (at any age) has been based upon data obtained from poor readers in the primary age group who are verbally above average (i.e. they are in the IQ range within which it is most likely that clear discrepancies between IQ and attainment will be obtained). Since such discrepant profiles are likely to be less obvious in pupils of average or below average verbal IQ, schools will be less inclined to refer such pupils to the already overloaded School Psychological Service and the pupils will 'miss out' on a full diagnostic assessment. Children who have developed the ability to decode print (i.e. they *are* able to read even though they may remain *slow readers* or *weak spellers*), are also probably less likely to be identified by classroom teachers as having specific learning difficulties at the primary stage. Indeed, to many people a dyslexic who can read adequately is seen as a contradiction in terms! Yet many dyslexics *do* learn to read quite competently (Snowling 1987) and the practice of using evidence obtained from the profiles of poor readers in the 8–11 years age range in identifying dyslexics (particularly in relation to other age groups) should be regarded as somewhat suspect. In summary, therefore, the pupils who are referred as potential dyslexics at the primary stage tend to be those having above average verbal IQ and a clear delay in level of reading attainment. Those dyslexics slipping through the net are likely to include less able pupils, together with brighter children who have learned to read to a level consonant with that of their peer group whilst still exhibiting learning difficulties in other aspects of written language such as spelling.

At the secondary school stage the assessment of failure is again made in relation to curricular demands. The ability to read is still an accepted requirement for accessing much of the secondary curriculum. But being able to read on its own is not a *sufficient* condition for such access. Now the pupil has to move from room to room, retain instructions presented at speed and often without visual clues. Pupils have to work and organise themselves to a timetable. The amount of written work increases and the ability to read is replaced by the increasing need to use the written word as an information source. These sources need to be retained, analysed and synthesised; and all these activities need to be done at speed. For the child who characteristically has difficulty in telling the time and remembering a timetable life becomes very difficult. If reading is a slow and laboured process ('I read like my mouth doesn't belong to my brain', as one dyslexic put it) then the work overload becomes too great even if motivation is sustained. If a knowledge of maths 'tables' has not been retained from primary school the demands involved in both manipulating and comprehending number computations can lead to an overload in the cognitive processing system. If slow, illegible writing and poor spelling are the residual symptoms of a dyslexic pupil's developmental problems then the poor quality of written work will condemn the pupil to failure in a context where success depends increasingly upon the effective generation of written language. In the secondary context, therefore, where speed and productivity in written presentation are paramount in tests of acquired knowledge, the dyslexic pupil is particularly disadvantaged.

The chances of a dyslexic pupil being recognised at the secondary stage, however, if his or her specific problems have not been identified during primary schooling, remain poor. If the pupil arrives at secondary school with some earlier documentation of 'reading and spelling problems requiring special help' then some sort of special needs provision may be offered. Allowances may be made for the pupil's difficulties and expectations may be lowered so that 'failure' to meet the new curricular demands may be less destructive to the pupil's self-esteem. All too frequently, however, the bright pupils will simply become part of the 'slow learning' set and begin increasingly to take on the characteristics of their less able classmates. Predictably, psychometric assessments using individual intelligence tests at this stage will tend to show a deterioration in level of verbal IQ and hence a less pronounced discrepancy between IQ and attainments. The verbal IQ is highly dependent on such sub-tests as vocabulary, verbal reasoning and general knowledge and these are likely to be inhibited by the pupil's previous educational experiences. A child who can, but does not, read by choice will have great difficulty in maintaining an improvement in vocabulary-based skills. To obtain above average scores on the verbal scales of individual intelligence tests 'dyslexic' children would have to keep pace with (and advance beyond) their peers. Children who are reared in a 'favourable' (i.e., verbally enriched) home and who exhibit above average language and reasoning skills at the nine years age level may well not have retained this advantage at the age of 12 *as a consequence of the effects of their dyslexic difficulties*. The chances of such dyslexic children being identified at the secondary stage, therefore, on criteria which are essentially the same as those used to identify primary-aged dyslexics are much reduced; 'failure' in relation to the accomplishment of predominantly written-language tasks performed at speed becomes more pronounced and the pupils' 'failures' are more likely to be attributed to poor ability, lack of motivation or effort ('the lazy little sods') than to 'specific learning difficulties'.

Identifying the dyslexic child – the traditional approach

The traditional approach to the identification of dyslexic children has involved the use of essentially the same set of criteria at whatever stage of schooling the assessment takes place. Sometimes pupils may have been screened on tests such as the Aston Index (Newton and Thomson 1976) or the Bangor Dyslexia Test (Miles 1983). Pupils suspected of having dyslexic problems will then be referred to the educational psychologist for full psychometric assessment. In this assessment the psychologist will compare 'global' and 'profile' scores on individual intelligence tests with performance on attainment tests, especially reading tests. It is assumed that this assessment will help to confirm whether the pupils' reading backwardness arises from a slow pattern of cognitive development in an all-round sense or is an example of *specific difficulties* in otherwise able pupils (i.e., the pupils are 'underfunctioning'). The IQ test has been used in this context to provide a reliable and valid estimate of 'general ability', a basis for predicting *expected levels of attainment* (for example in reading and spelling), and a diagnostic device for identifying areas of cognitive weaknesses. A tall order for even the best measuring instrument! But two tests in particular have offered a wealth of useful material (though this has been expensively produced since both tests can only be administered by qualified psychologists): these are the Wechsler Intelligence Scale for Children (WISC) (Wechsler 1976) and the British Abilities Scale (BAS) (Elliot, Murray and Pearson 1983).[4]

---

4   For a good discussion of dyslexic profiles on the WISC and BAS see Thomson (1990).

As far as the WISC is concerned this can provide a full-scale score based on the combined scores from the verbal and performance sub-scales which comprise the following items: information, comprehension, arithmetic, similarities, vocabulary and digit span (verbal); and picture completion, picture arrangement, block design, object assembly and coding (performance). No predictions of attainment are built into the test itself but, as mentioned earlier, Yule *et al.* (1982) have advocated the use of a regression formula with the WISC. The so-called ACID profile has also been proposed for use in the identification of dyslexic pupils.[5] This suggests that dyslexic children have distinctive profiles on the WISC in which their scores on arithmetic, coding, information and digit span are depressed. In a recent study of 160 cases of dyslexics, however, Congdon (1989) concludes that 'taken separately the best positive discriminator is the Coding measure and this is followed by Information and Digits Reversed. The Arithmetic and Digits Forward Tests were not found to be useful discriminators' (pp.9–10).

The British Ability Scales (BAS) has a similar range of items to the WISC. The items are designed to measure cognitive processing and the test can offer a full-scale, verbal and visual IQ. In contrast to the WISC, however, the BAS also has built-in *expectancy scores* so that it is possible to predict the expected attainment score from a given IQ. Dyslexic children tend to score less well on Speed of Information Processing, Immediate and Delayed Visual Recall, Recall of Digits, Basic Number Skills, and Word Reading (Thomson 1982).

Some problems with the traditional approach

One reason why the identification of dyslexia poses a problem is that the concept of *underfunctioning* to which the condition has been traditionally linked is itself a problematic concept. The idea that we can use IQ as a fixed measure of intellectual potential against which to judge a pupil's attainment is about as watertight as a colander.[6] The first problem is that IQ tests cannot be said to measure intellectual potential in any precise way since they consist of a selection of items (for example verbal and non-verbal reasoning, comprehension and vocabulary) which will all be affected, to some extent, by previous learning and experience. Even non-verbal items (which can lay claim, perhaps, to reflect potential more closely than most other kinds of test item) have been shown to be affected by cultural and experiential factors (Vernon 1969). Similarly, IQ scores are not fixed; they are estimates of ability, subject to the usual *standard errors of measurement*, and the scores will vary over time and with changing circumstances (Satterly 1981).

It might be argued that IQ scores are *less* affected by environmental factors such as school experience than attainment scores and of the two measures

---

5   For a discussion of the ACID profile see M. Thomson (1990)
6   For a recent critique of the use of the IQ in discrepancy definitions of dyslexia see Stanovich (1991).

IQ probably does, therefore, offer a closer reflection of all-round intellectual potential. But any comparisons between IQ and attainment clearly need to be considered with great circumspection. Furthermore, the fact that an individual's educational quotient (EQ) can be *higher* than his or her IQ presents more than a slight difficulty for the notion of IQ operating as a 'ceiling'! The presence of higher EQs than IQs (as well as lower EQs than IQs) is predicted, however, by the operation of a statistical artefact called 'regression' (see Figure 13.1) (Lewis 1967). Thus for the situation in Figure 13.1 in which the correlation between the IQ and attainment test is +0.6 the predicted EQ from an IQ of 85 would be 91; and one would expect an EQ of 106 from an IQ of 110. It is also the case, statistically, that as many people will 'overfunction' as 'underfunction' (Yule, *et al.* 1974). With such a complicated concept, therefore, it is clearly important that any IQ/EQ comparisons are mediated by both *statistical* and *educational* considerations.

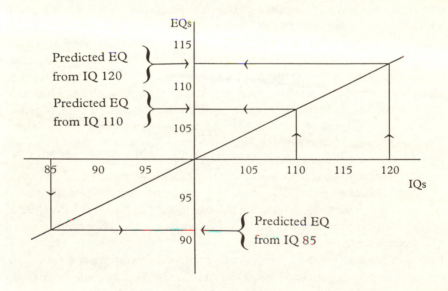

Figure 13.1 The regression of EQ on IQ where $r_{EQ.IQ} = .6$

One way of coping with this problem might be to use regression data to predict *expected* levels of attainment and then to compare these with *actual* attainment, as suggested by Yule *et al.* (1982) There is a problem, however, in using formulae obtained from *group* data to inform decisions about *individual* cases; and the 'unthinking' application of such formulae can result in the failure to identify some lower IQ children (especially upper juniors) (Moseley 1975) who on common- sense grounds require some help. Such children can creep into the 'satisfactory' zone on the basis of reading the first couple of lines or so on a word recognition test! 'Satisfactory' in this context might mean, for example, achieving a score which places the pupil just above the equivalent of a two-year retardation cut-off point in relation to predicted reading age. On this basis a nine-year-old child with IQ of 85 and predicted EQ of 91 (reading age 8 years 3 months) would be considered 'satisfactory' if scoring just above a reading age of 6 years 3 months. Most teachers and psychologists would probably agree that such a judgement fits rather uncomfortably with a common-sense view of the situation and Moseley (1975) suggests that one possible way of counteracting such anomalies would be to use different cut-off points for different IQ levels.

Even if a relatively satisfactory method of measuring underfunctioning is found, however, there are still logistical difficulties to be faced. To obtain an assessment of a pupil using an individual intelligence test requires the services of an educational psychologist and any screening approach for dyslexia would be immensely time consuming for the overworked and understaffed School Psychological Services. So we are driven to ask: can we find other methods of identifying dyslexic children within a school-based context? A tentative affirmative can be offered to this question and some interesting possibilities for developing curriculum-based assessments in the framework of the National Curriculum are discussed later on in this chapter.

Another problem with the traditional approach concerns the fact that identification procedures tend to concentrate on the able child. Thus able children showing the typical 'dyslexic' profiles on the WISC or BAS, together with depressed attainment scores, would tend to be given the label 'dyslexic'. On the other hand, less able children showing similar sub-test profiles *but whose IQ scores are too low for the discrepancy between IQ and attainment to be readily apparent* would often 'miss out' on the label. When one considers that the *curricular requirements* in relation to written language and its associated sub-skills are essentially similar for the two types of child the difference in attitude and treatment which often follows from the presence or absence of a label does seem distinctly unjust.

There are also other problems inherent in the 'traditional' approach to the identification of dyslexia by psychometric testing. Since the 'global' IQ measure includes information from sub-tests *which have been shown to present specific problems for dyslexics* (for example, items involving coding tasks or recall of digits) it has sometimes been argued that such items should be omitted from the IQ calculations for potential dyslexics. Whilst accepting that the argument has some force, the consequence of such 'partial' testing is to inflate the dyslexic's IQ score artificially and to render comparison with normative data and with the calculation of 'expected attainment scores' null and void. Further, if we base a dyslexic's IQ score on the child's best items then we ought, in fairness, to do the same for the normative sample! The inflation of the 'prospective' dyslexic's IQ score on this practice will also have the effect of *increasing the discrepancy between IQ and attainment and thus increasing the chances of the 'prospective' dyslexic actually being diagnosed as such.* In other words the diagnosis of dyslexia can depend, to some extent, upon the particular test approach adopted. Perhaps the best guideline in this context is to look at the child's all-round performance as carefully as possible (including IQ scores calculated on the basis of different combinations of sub-tests) but then to concentrate on the *profile* of performance rather than allowing any IQ score *on its own* to categorise a child's learning potential or become the main arbiter of educational decision making. As Thomson (1982) observes in reviewing the arguments: 'An IQ *figure* is not particularly important, but what is of relevance is the particular range of learning potential the child has, and its relationship to other abilities' (p.475).

Traditional testing also tends to ignore 'situational' factors. Commonly, the pupil will be taken to an office to be interviewed by the educational psychologist and standardised items from an individual intelligence test will be administered together with a word recognition test and perhaps other attainment/diagnostic tests. The procedure and the task demands tend to be divorced from the *actual* curricular demands which the pupil faces every day. It is as if the testing takes place in an enclosed capsule and despite any attempts to assess the classroom and home environments separately, the danger is that all too frequently the 'assessment' and recommendations do not match the 'pupil-in-school-problem'. A greater element of teacher-based assessment would, therefore, be helpful in procedures designed to identify the dyslexic pupil's problems. Again there are hopeful signs, as we shall see later, that the National Curriculum assessment procedures may help in this respect.

A final difficulty with the traditional approach relates to the 'normative' context in which most assessments have been carried out. Children achieving a level of progress in written language which is appropriate for their *age group* often tend to be considered to be progressing satisfactorily in school *irrespective of their individual cognitive capabilities*. Articulate middle-class parents who 'know' that their children are functioning in some areas at levels well above their chronological age-group will sometimes harass the school into taking action or refer their children on their own initiative for assessment by the educational psychologist. This is the classic 'middle-class' scenario: the children of the vociferous middle-class parents receive the label 'dyslexic' whilst the children of less articulate and educationally less sophisticated parents are left as 'lazy little sods'. More emphasis, therefore, needs to be placed on 'ipsative' or 'self- referencing' profiles to identify areas of written language requiring specific help in children who are achieving a 'chronologically satisfactory' level of performance. Without appropriate help such children are likely to enter on the downward spiral of poorer performance on tasks relating to written language, greater frustration in schoolwork, lower levels of measured IQ (since the tests at higher age levels tend to be more language-dependent) and, paradoxically, *less likelihood of being identified as dyslexic because the discrepancy between IQ score and attainment is less pronounced!* In the context of this traditional approach to identifying dyslexia, therefore, children with such specific learning difficulties have often been abandoned as 'failures' because the nature of their problem has not been identified at a sufficiently early stage.

Curriculum-based assessments: a way forward?

The traditional approach to assessment has, therefore, many limitations and it has failed, in particular, to match up with sufficient care the developmental nature of the disorder with the changing curricular demands on the pupil. It has also tended to concentrate on the identification of a few individual pupils with a view to arranging special educational provision for example, by periodic withdrawal from mainstream classes for special remedial work or by full-time placement in a special unit. Following the 1981 Education Act (HMSO 1981) the emphasis has changed (at least theoretically) from one of locational separation to a policy of integrating children with special needs within the mainstream setting wherever possible. Assessment techniques should, therefore, aim at identifying pupil needs and informing strategies for meeting those needs *within a mainstream context*. The 1988 Education Reform Act (HMSO 1988) has further stressed the legal requirement for pupils to have access to a broadly balanced curriculum (to include the National Curriculum) and for the implementation of curriculum-based assessment by classroom teachers. In this context, therefore, it makes sense to look at the possibilities of using the Standard Assessment Tasks (related to National Curricula criteria and given at ages 7, 11, 14 and 16) as a basis for screening pupils for dyslexic-type problems. Such an approach might also have the effect of increasing the chances of dyslexic pupils being identified and remedial action taken at an earlier stage and their problems and progress being monitored within the framework of the mainstream classroom.

Given that the dyslexic's problems are exhibited predominantly in written language tasks the way forward with respect to assessment may be to look at the five designated attainment targets in the National Curriculum English assessments. These are speaking and listening; reading; writing; presentation; and handwriting. It is reasonable to predict that dyslexic children will exhibit discrepant levels of development and that their performance in the written aspects of English will be poorer than their performance in speaking and listening.[7] There are, of course, obvious problems with National Curriculum assessments particularly in relation to their reliability and validity. There is as yet no published data from the National Curriculum Council concerning inter-rater reliability although speaking and listening was not included in the 1991 SATs for seven-year-olds presumably because it was considered to be an unreliable measure at this age. With respect to validity, SoA (Statements of Attainment) have been criticised because they have not been demonstrated

---

7   For a discussion of the merits of using a measure of 'listening comprehension' rather than IQ in
    discrepancy definitions of dyslexia see Stanovich (1991)

empirically to match children's *actual* attainments or to correspond closely to the sequence in which children learn (Jones *et al.* 1989). This obviously presents a problem if such assessment procedures are to be used to guide pedagogy. A recent report from the British Psychological Society to the Committee on Educational Science and Arts also doubts whether National Curriculum assessments would 'yield information of any greater utility than that hitherto available from a pupil's classwork' (BPS 1991 p.469). Nevertheless, such assessments are the only *nationwide* assessment procedures available to us, linked as they are to the legislated delivery of the National Curriculum. We would argue, therefore, that an exploration of their potential contribution to the assessment and monitoring of dyslexic pupils is of considerable importance.

Such an investigation is, in fact, being carried out as part of a three year DES-funded research project based at Harris City Technology College in Croydon and co-ordinated by research staff from the Special Needs Department at Canterbury, Christ Church College, Kent. A group of Year 7 (11–12-year-old) dyslexic pupils were assessed using classroom administered national curriculum English assessments and the results from this sample compared with those of their mainstream peer group. Preliminary findings are encouraging and indicate that National Curriculum classroom-based assessment could serve to differentiate dyslexic pupils from their non-dyslexic peers.

Conclusions

We have argued that the concept of dyslexia has taken root within an educational context which has generally endorsed separatist provision for children with special needs and has developed appropriate measurement techniques for identifying children who fall outside the 'normal' range of expected attainment. The techniques developed to serve this model have included psychometric testing, the use of measured IQ as a predictive indicator of expected levels of attainment, and the identification of specific cognitive deficits by the use of norm-referenced criteria. The legacy of this approach has been the tendency for the identification of dyslexic pupils and provision for their teaching to be left to the 'experts'. Mainstream teachers have felt unqualified to deal with the specific learning difficulties they have observed and 'special needs' identification procedures tend to have concentrated resources on pupils of above average ability. Those dyslexic pupils who have been performing in the normal range but well below parental expectations have been recognised only reluctantly by schools whose yardsticks for assessing pupil potential tend to remain firmly within their school-based expectations. Children of less than high average ability who are failing have tended to be excluded altogether from consideration because of the folklore that has arisen that to be dyslexic a pupil must be 'of at least average intelligence'.

In the traditional setting, therefore, dyslexics have been identified within a norm-referenced psychometric framework and taught primarily through a remedial system in which pupils are withdrawn from their regular classrooms and provided with remedial teaching on a periodic or more permanent basis. Research work has, therefore, focused for the most part on informing strategies for 'specialist' teaching whereas research aiming to develop assessment and teaching techniques for dyslexics *within the mainstream setting* has been much less in evidence. Following the 1981 and 1988 Education Acts, however, the position has changed radically. The emphasis is now upon the concepts of *pupil needs* and *access to the National Curriculum*. Indeed, there is a legal requirement (with a very few 'opt out' clauses) for pupils to be given access to the National Curriculum; and all teachers are required to keep individual records of children's National Curriculum attainments. The dyslexic child will not necessarily be dependent upon vociferous parental demands, well above average ability or residence within the boundaries of a particular LEA, in order to obtain an assessment of oral and written language. It is now a legislative requirement. The move to National Curriculum-based assessments administered by classroom teachers and utilising ipsative rather than normative referencing, offers us an opportunity to define dyslexia in a *functional, curriculum-related* sense and to develop teaching strategies informed by these assessments. Whilst acknowledging the contribution which specialist teaching has made to the education of dyslexic pupils, the challenge now is to determine the extent to which provision for such children can be delivered in an *integrated* setting. Preliminary findings from the Harris Dyslexia Research Project which has adopted such an approach are encouraging.

The emphasis on mainstreaming also prescribes the need to develop whole-school policies for the teaching of written language across the curriculum. Such policies should aim to facilitate access for dyslexic pupils to each area of the National Curriculum. At present the 'failure' of dyslexic children is too often, in effect, *created* by the undifferentiated curricular and examination demands which are placed upon them. Some schools and examination boards are making allowances for the dyslexic's problems in certain curricular areas. We need, however, to go much further in our approach to differentiated curriculum delivery in order to ensure that dyslexic pupils are helped to access all parts of the curriculum and to develop their written language skills *within the mainstream setting*. In this context the whole-school approach affords a central concept around which the wealth of expert knowledge provided by educational psychologists, information technologists, support teachers and researchers could be usefully focused; and given the adoption of such an approach the education system which has created failure for the dyslexic child will be fundamentally changed. Instead of creating failure, the system will serve to meet the pupils' needs and facilitate access to the curriculum – even for the 'lazy little sods'!

References

BPS (1991) Reading Standards: Evidence to the Select Committee on Educational Science and Arts. *The Psychologist*, Vol. 14, 10 p.469.

Bryant, P. and Bradley, L. (1985) *Children's Reading Problems*. Oxford: Blackwell.

Clark, M.M. (1979) *Reading Difficulties in Schools*, 2nd edition. London: Heinemann.

Congdon, P.J. (1989) *Dyslexia. A Pattern of Strengths and Weaknesses: A study of 160 clinical cases*. Solihull: Gifted Children's Information Centre.

Critchley, M. (1964) *Developmental Dyslexia*. London: Heinemann.

DES (1972) *Children with Specific Reading Difficulties*. London: HMSO.

DES (1978) *Special Educational Needs (Report of the Committee of Enquiry into the Education of Handicapped Children and Young People)* (Warnock Report). London: HMSO.

DES (1992) *The Parent's Charter*. London: DES.

Elliott, C.D., Murray, D.J. and Pearson, L.S. (1983) *British Ability Scales – Revised*. Slough: NFER-Nelson.

Gulliford, R. (1971) *Special Educational Needs*. London: RKP.

HMSO, (1981) *Education Act*. London: HMSO.

HMSO, (1988) *Education Reform Act*. London: HMSO.

Jones, G., Cato, V., Hargreaves, M. and Wetton, C. (1989) *Touchstones. Cross-curricular Group Assessments*. Windsor: NFER-Nelson.

Lewis, D.G. (1967) *Statistical Methods in Education*. London: Hodder & Stoughton.

Miles, T.R. (1983) *The Bangor Dyslexia Test*. Wisbech: Learning Development Aids.

Morris, J.M. (1966) *Standards and Progress in Reading*. Slough: NFER.

Moseley, D. (1975) *Special Provision for Reading: when will they ever learn?*. Windsor: NFER-Nelson.

Newton M.J. and Thomson, M.E. (1976) *The Aston Index: A screening procedure for written language difficulties*. Wisbech. Learning Development Aids.

Newton, M. (1970) A neuro-psychological investigation into dyslexia. In Franklin, A.W. and Naidoo, S. (eds.), *Assessment and Teaching of Dyslexic Children*. London: ICAA.

Presland, J. (1991) Explaining away dyslexia. *Educational Psychology in Practice*, Vol. 6, 4 pp.215–21.

Pumfrey, P. and Reason, R. (1991) *Specific Learning Difficulties (Dyslexia): Challenges and Responses*. Slough: NFER-Nelson.

Satterly, D. (1981) *Assessment in Schools*. Oxford: Blackwell.

Snowling, M. (1987) *Dyslexia: A cognitive developmental perspective*. Oxford: Blackwell.

Stanovich, K.E. (1991) The theoretical and practical consequences of discrepancy definitions of dyslexia. In Snowling, M. and Thomson, M. (eds.), *Dyslexia: Integrating Theory and Practice*. London and Jersey: Whurr Publishers.

Thomson, M. (1982) The assessment of children with special reading difficulties (dyslexia) using the British Ability Scales. *British Journal of Psychology*, Vol. 73 pp.461–78.

Thomson, M. (1990) *Developmental Dyslexia: Its nature, assessment and remediation.* 3rd edition. London: Whurr Publishers.

Tyler, S. and Elliott, C.D. (1988) Cognitive profiles of groups of poor readers and dyslexic children on the British Ability Scales. *British Journal of Psychology*, Vol. 79 pp.493–508.

Vernon, P. (1969) *Intelligence and Cultural Environment.* London: Methuen.

Wechsler, D. (1976) *Wechsler Intelligence Scale for Children (R).* New York: The Psychological Corporation.

Yule, W., Lansdown, R. and Urbanowicz, M-A. (1982) Predicting educational attainment from WISC-R in a primary school sample. *British Journal of Clinical Psychology*, Vol. 21.

Yule, W., Rutter, M., Berger, M. and Thompson, J. (1974) Over- and under-achievement in reading: Distribution in the general population. *British Journal of Educational Psychology*, Vol. 44 pp.1–12.

List of Contributors

Dr Ved P. Varma
is a former teacher and educational psychologist. His previous many books include *How and Why Children Hate*, and as co-editor with Barbara Tizard *Vulnerability and Resilience in Human Development*

Dr James Hemming
is a consultant educationalist

Philip Barker
is Professor, Department of Psychiatry and Paediatrics, University of Calgary Alberta Children's Hospital

Dr Kedar Nath Dwivedi
is Consultant Child, Adolescent and Family Psychiatrist, Northampton Health Authority.

Dr Herbert Etkin
is Consultant Psychiatrist, Colwood Adolescent Unit, Haywards Heath, West Sussex

Joan Freeman, PhD
is President, European Council for High Ability

Gerry German
is Principal Education Officer, Commission for Racial Equality, and Honorary Treasurer, Working Group Against Racism in Children's Resources

Dr Robin Higgins MB, Bch (Cambridge), DPM, BMMS
is a former consultant child and family psychiatrist

Dr Clive Hollin
is Senior Lecturer in Psychology, University of Birmingham and Research Psychologist, Glenthorne Youth Treatment Centre

Michael J.A. Howe PhD
is Professor of Psychology, University of Exeter

Carl Parsons PhD
is Principal Lecturer of Teacher Education and Director of Education Unit, Christ Church College, Canterbury, Kent

Dr Robert Povey MA, PhD C.Psychol, FBPsS
is an educational psychologist, formerly Principal Lecturer in Education at
Christ Church College, Canterbury

Colin Rogers PhD
is Lecturer in Education, Department of Educational Research, Lancaster
University

Janet Tod LCST, BSc, MPhil, C.Psychol
is an educational psychologist and is Senior Lecturer in Special Needs at
Christ Church College, Canterbury

Subject Index

Name Index